EDUCATION, EQUITY AND TRANSFORM

EDUCATION, EQUITY AND TRANSFORMATION

Edited by

CRAIN SOUDIEN

and

PETER KALLAWAY,

with **MIGNONNE BREIER**

Reprinted from
International Review of Education, Vol. 45, Nos. 5–6, 1999.

KLUWER ACADEMIC PUBLISHERS
DORDRECHT / BOSTON / LONDON

Published in cooperation with
UNESCO INSTITUTE FOR EDUCATION • HAMBURG

A C.I.P. Catalogue record for this book is available from the Library of Congress.

ISBN 0-7923-6157-1 (Kluwer)
ISBN 92-820-1100-3 (UIE)

Published by Kluwer Academic Publishers,
P.O. Box 17, 3300 AA Dordrecht, The Netherlands

Sold and distributed in North, Central and South America
by Kluwer Academic Publishers,
101 Philip Drive, Norwell, MA 02061, U.S.A.

In all other countries, sold and distributed
by Kluwer Academic Publishers,
P.O. Box 322, 3300 AH Dordrecht, The Netherlands

In cooperation with the UNESCO Institute for Education

The UNESCO Institute for Education, Hamburg, is a legally independent entity. While the programmes for the Institute are established along the lines laid down by the General Conference
of UNESCO, the publications of the Institute are issued under its sole responsibility; UNESCO
is not responsible for their contents.
The point of view, selection of facts, and opinions expressed are those of the authors and do
not necessarily coincide with official positions of the UNESCO Institute for Education, Hamburg.
The designations employed and the presentation of the material in this publication do not imply
the expression of any opinion whatsoever on the part of the UNESCO Secretariat concerning
the legal status of any country or territory, or its authorities, or concerning the delimitation of
the frontiers of any country or territory.

Printed on acid-free paper

Printed in the Netherlands

TABLE OF CONT~

PAUL BÉLANGER: AN APPRECIATION

This issue of the *International Review of Education* is the last to appear during Paul Bélanger's tenure as Director of the UNESCO Institute for Education (UIE) and Chair of the Editorial Board of the journal. Born in Montréal, Canada, in 1939, Paul Bélanger studied for his BA and MA degrees at the Universities of Ottawa and Montréal. He received a post-graduate diploma in adult education from the University of Manchester, England, and a PhD in sociology from the Sorbonne, Paris. He was Director of the Canadian Institute for Adult Education (1972–1984), President of the Commission for Evaluation of Colleges in French-Speaking Canada (1984–1987), Director of the Institute for Applied Research on Work, Montréal (1987–1989), and Director of UIE, Hamburg (1989–1999).

Dr Bélanger is returning to Canada to take up a professorship in the Faculty of Education at the Université du Québec à Montréal (UQAM), where he will create a research centre on lifelong learning.

The Editorial Board, the Editorial Office and the Publishers of *IRE* wish to pay tribute to Dr Bélanger for the dedication, energy and vision that he brought to his role in the journal over the decade of his tenure, and to convey their warmest wishes to him for the future.

EDITORIAL INTRODUCTION

The papers for this special issue were selected from a pool of nearly 700 presentations which were made at the 10th Congress of the World Council of Comparative Education Societies (WCCES), which was held in Cape Town, South Africa, from 12 to 17 July 1998. The congress was hosted by the Southern African Comparative and History of Education Society (SACHES) and held on the campuses of the University of the Western Cape and the University of Cape Town. The papers were selected by the convenors of the conference's standing commissions, which provided a significant focus for the conference proceedings. These commissions were on the following themes:

- Teachers and teacher education
- Curriculum
- Higher education
- Lifelong learning
- Language, literacy and basic education
- Gender and education
- Policy
- Theory and theory shifts
- Basic education in Africa
- Peace and Justice
- Dependency
- European Education
- Policy Research in Africa
- Culture, Indigenous Knowledge and Learning

The papers presented, as the discussion below makes clear, ranged widely in subject matter and theoretical perspective and addressed issues of concern both to individual countries and to regions of the world. While some of the papers use comparison as an approach, it remains a matter of concern that the comparative perspective is so little in evidence. It is hoped that the comparative research approach will be more in evidence in the future.

This is all the more desirable as important new positions are being developed in the field of comparative education. These positions reflect the pressures, strains, and even fractures, which have begun to manifest themselves in the wider context of the social sciences and must, in the course of time, begin to raise important questions in the field of comparative education. Not least amongst these pressures are the works of scholars reflecting the decon-

 International Review of Education – Internationale Zeitschrift für Erziehungswissenschaft – Revue Internationale de l'Education 45(5/6): 377–383, 1999.
© 1999 *Kluwer Academic Publishers. Printed in the Netherlands.*

structionist trend in the social sciences. These movements seek to extend our investigations around notions of epistemology and their relationship to social and cultural centredness in processes of knowledge production. A question that remains open is the very practice of comparison itself and how comparativists might respond to accusations that the practice of comparison is (consciously or unconsciously) rooted in one or other dominant and epistemologically hegemonic universe.

In what follows brief comment is offered on the papers which were selected for this volume.

Buenfil, Preston and *Tikley*, among others, ask fundamental questions about the nature of comparative education and the challenges for researches in the present context. They argue that there is lack of historical contextualization in policy debates and critique, linked to a neglect of the epistemological/ideological contexts in which such debates take place, which does much to weaken the critique of policy at the present time and limits the impact of research. As Buenfil points out, the implications of that neglect for future policy development are worrying, and these arguments seem to have particular relevance to the Third World, where there are few resources for critical policy research. A lack of emphasis on the relationship between poverty and education and the withdrawal of the state as a major provider in the field of education in many parts of the world raise ethical and human rights questions that need much more attention than they are currently given. There is also not enough attention to the seismic shifts in education that have resulted from the growth of international policy hegemony regarding issues of quality assurance, assessment, qualifications frameworks, and from the replacement of professional approaches to education by a variety of management strategies.

What are the implications for democracy and equity of the shift away from the social democratic vision of education that was characteristic of the 1960s & 1970s? What are the long-term implications of the flight of high quality teachers, lecturers and researchers from the field of education in many parts of the world in the context of the changes outlined? What are the significant trends in the teaching profession and in teacher education globally in the context of the changes outlined? A great deal more is to be expected on these issues from the foremost body of international researchers in the field of comparative education. Buenfil points out in relation to the curriculum for the training of educational researchers that "no sophisticated analysis is needed to realise that epistemology disappeared from the landscape altogether" since the 1980s. She continues to note that in many institutions that prepare educators and researchers "reflections upon how we produce knowledge have been erased from the basic preparation of a qualified producer of knowledge on education". This implies that we face a challenge to either acknowledge or ignore the implications of these changes within the context of the ethical issues involved. If we choose to ignore these issues it implies that decisions about educational policy are naturalised, i.e., presented as the natural result of a course of action, without making the actor/policy-maker or researcher responsible for the course of action pursued. This conceals the political nature of a particular course of action and denies that other courses of action are possible. It also makes it unnecessary for the policy-maker to justify the course of action taken – since it is, by implication, the only possible course open. If that mode is allowed to be dominant in the policy world, the role of critical debate is eliminated.

In the context of teacher preparation such developments might have very specific implications that will be widely recognised by those in the field. In his contribution *Mazibuku* notes that student teachers in Swaziland consider attempts to engage with theoretical implications of their work to be tedious in the extreme and a fundamental waste of time in a crowded curriculum where they are trying to master techniques for survival in the classroom. This phenomenon, recognisable to anyone who has ever been involved in the teaching of comparative education, dovetails only too well at the present time with a conservative agenda that regards an examination of the curriculum and the pedagogy of the school as, at worst, subversive, and, at best, a waste of time. Unless there is a commitment by teachers and researchers to engage with these difficult tasks in a context that is fundamentally hostile to critical research we all face the danger of betraying a sacred educational trust. Many of the contributions to this collection take up these themes in their own contexts.

The articles reflect a panorama of educational policy issues that are unique and appropriate to the times. The ambiguous notions of choice and decentralization in relationship to educational policy are taken up with clarity and precision by *Plank* and *Sykes* in the context of the Illinois schools system, but also reflect the intense policy contestation over these issues in the global context. They seek to locate these common sense explanations of policy within a neo-liberal/ conservative/free market approach to educational change that seeks to move educational decision-making out of the public realm into the private realm. They indicate the problematic shift that occurs as a result of these processes leading, almost unnoticed, to a fundamental change in the very nature of the educational policy. Although the approach highlights important issues like cost, efficiency, quality, effectiveness and diversity, they argue that it fails to grasp the all important nettle of the relationships between educational change and equity in society.

Still on the issue of policy, but this time in the context of reporting on the development of a "reflective mapping strategy" for the education of girls in Zambia, *Mitchell* and her team outline strategies for supporting the practices of those working in the field – government agencies, non-governmental organisations, donor organisations, teacher educators, experienced and beginning teachers, parents and communities – and the girls themselves. The participatory approach is intended to stimulate engagement of all partners in the development and monitoring of policy to avoid the pitfalls of a top-down approach. The mode of policy development and reporting has specific importance for this sensitive area of educational intervention.

Staying with the issue of gender and education, *Sutherland*, the chair of the Gender and Education Commission, gives an overview of a variety of initiatives relating to gender equity and education and calls for further comparative work to understand why certain educational contexts lead to the relative disadvantage of girls or boys. *Mannathoko* takes up the challenge of Sutherland's paper in the context of Eastern and Southern Africa and explores the nature of the relationships between women's oppression and notions of difference, oppression, inequality and development. She is concerned to locate the origins of gender equity in the specific context of African culture and to link global theoretical discourses on the topic to the local indigenous practices in the context of the struggle against colonialism and partiarchy.

As indicated above, Buenfil takes up the issue of the challenge facing comparative education in relation to the curriculum for educational researchers. How are such researchers to be trained in the face of contemporary ideological shifts that amount to the "withdrawal of theory" from educational practice and policy debates where the cult of efficiency rules in the practice of educational research and policy development? She poses the question of how a future generation of policy analysts will be trained in this world devoid of epistemological debate. *De Alba* poses a set of difficult problems relating to the question of "Curriculum and Culture Contact" in a context where the very norms and essences of western thought (perhaps modern thought) have been fundamentally challenged. In the context of "the death of the subject" how are we to engage in a debate about the nature of the curriculum? In that context she suggests that it is essential to relate curriculum debate to identity and social/cultural location in order to seek notions of authenticity and positionality. Such moves, she suggests, will provide a means to the establishment of new modes of knowledge to work with.

Nekhwevah, writing in the context of a debate about culture and indigenous knowledge in the new democratic states of Namibia and South Africa, is also concerned to question the relationship between dominant modes of curriculum development, the colonial heritage and education in the new democratic order. He wishes to challenge the globalizing norms that inform policy in the post-apartheid era and wishes to reassert the claims of the emancipatory rhetoric related to the African heritage and the liberation struggle in the face of the dominant globalizing rhetoric of policy developments like the National Qualifications Framework and Outcomes-Based Education.

In relation to the field of higher education, *Subotsky* asks pertinent questions about the role of universities in servicing the needs of social and economic development. In the South African context there is currently an acute crisis in this sector where state policy and funding is increasingly framed in terms of the demands of the widely accepted global norms of the entrepreneurial university. Such policies are framed in terms that favoured formerly privileged white universities. The challenge he puts to us is that community-education partnerships need to be formulated that will strengthen the position of formerly disadvantaged institutions which serve the poor and those who were disadvantaged in the apartheid era. He poses the challenge of shaping a policy more in keeping with the demands of the Reconstruction and Development Programme in South Africa, but raises a variety of points that apply equally well to higher education policy in other Third World contexts.

In the context of the Commission on Language and Literacy, *Si Moussa* and *Tupin* examine education on the islands of Mauritius and Réunion, neighbouring islands with geographical and cultural similarities but markedly different educational policies. Si Moussa and Tupin compare these policies and assess their impact in relation to the democratisation of education.

The development of continuing education and lifelong learning (LLL) is clearly one of the most significant tasks for educational planning for the next millennium, especially in relation to educational provision for the poor. Whether catering for the needs of "recurrent education", self-directed learning or training for work in a global labour market, the sector features prominently in contemporary educational planning in most countries. *Weber* and *Wittpoth* show how the very similar educational histories of Germany and Switzerland have given rise to rather different approaches to the problem in keeping with their particular cultural and political traditions. In particular they examine how each country has dealt with issues of public and private provision. *Walters* is concerned to explore the "emancipatory potential" of lifelong learning strategies in the context of affirmative action in higher education in Southern Africa. Although she is keen to expand the scope of the initiative in terms of its potential for personal empowerment and personal development, she is wary to defend lifelong learning against the strong claims of the market in defining its goals and curriculum. *Preston*, though acknowledging the truth of "the positivist narrative of lifelong learning" for many, is much less sanguine about the outcome of such courses when they are targeted at the long-term unemployed or the marginalised poor. While it is of course true that various forms of LLL have helped many to increase their life chances and promote social mobility in the manner promised by traditional adult learning practices, she notes that lifelong learning has increasingly become an "artifact of the market". While it presents itself in terms of "an attractive vocabulary associated with personal development and empowerment," she is concerned to demonstrate that this often masks other economic and social purposes associated with the global labour market and the state's divestment of responsibility for the marginalised. Commercially packaged courses are marketed for "consumers" (the unemployed or disadvantaged) who wish to "buy" commodified learning opportunities that promise immediate gains in terms of work opportunities or financial gain. The outcomes are seldom positive. In short, LLL has very different implications and possibilities for the included and the excluded.

The Teacher Education Commission is represented by *Mazibuku*'s paper which attempts to understand the experiences of beginning secondary school teachers in Swaziland. Although the paper emphasises the variety of experiences of these students – in relation to the schools, supervisors, staff, curriculum and pedagogy, classroom management and discipline, and the actual personal experience of each of the students – it focuses on the very real personal journey taken by the student teachers and reminds us that the need to motivate these young people lies at the heart of the enterprise of education.

To conclude, the excellent paper by *Tikley* invites a consideration of the relevance of recent developments in postcolonial theory for expanding our understanding of the nature and origins, and the strengths and weaknesses, of comparative education research. By viewing the enterprise of comparative education through the lens of race, culture, language and curriculum, he argues for a less Eurocentric understanding of the relationship between globalisation and education. He thereby raises important issues about the nature and history of comparative education as a field of intellectual endeavour and its relation to the development of policy over time.

The lack of contextualisation was pointed out as a key feature of much contemporary policy work. This issue can, in part, be linked to the lack of institutional attention to colleagues in the Third World and their ability to attend conferences of this kind at this critical time in the history of educational policy. An increase in such participation would strengthen the whole community of educational scholars and widen the spectrum of debate, as we experienced in Cape Town. This would seem to point to the need for a systematic initiative on the part of the comparative education community in general and the WCCES in particular to enable such scholars and policy-makers to attend these conferences and thus enable them to participate in joint research initiatives. The experience of Cape Town has to be built on to ensure that African scholarship (and indeed the scholarship of other marginal areas of the world) is fully encompassed within the mainstream of the work of structures such as the World Council. Attempts have to be made to ensure that each conference reflects the presence of Africa, Asia and Latin America more fully. This requires that the organisers and hosts of all educational conferences should be required to explore funding mechanisms to make such participation possible. Attention needs to be paid to these issues if Comparative Education is to flourish as a truly global enterprise.

CRAIN SOUDIEN and PETER KALLAWAY

The guest editors

Crain Soudien teaches at the School of Education, University of Cape Town, where he is an Associate Professor. He has written extensively in the area of race, class and gender in education, educational policy and public history. Previously a schoolteacher, he remains heavily involved in community activities and is the chairperson of a pioneering project called Primary Open-Learning Pathways. He holds a PhD from the State University of New York at Buffalo.

Contact address: Assoc. Prof. Crain Soudien, School of Education, University of Cape Town, Private Bag, Rondebosch, Cape 7701, South Africa.

Peter Kallaway studied at Rhodes University, the University of Cape Town and London University, and has taught at the University of the Witwatersrand and the University of Cape Town. He is currently Professor of Education at the University of the Western Cape. His research areas include the historical, policy and sociological aspects of education and development in Africa, as well as history education in schools. He has published the following books: *Apartheid and Education: The Education of Black South Africans* (Ravan Press, 1984) and *Education after Apartheid*, with G. Kruss, A. Fataar and G. Donn (UCT Press, 1997).

Contact address: Prof. Peter Kallaway, University of the Western Cape, Private Bag X17, Bellville 7535, South Africa. E-mail: pkallawa@uwc.ac.za.

Mignonne Breier is a senior researcher and former acting director in the Education Policy Unit at the University of the Western Cape, South Africa. She has participated in and co-ordinated several major research projects in the field of higher and adult education. She holds an MPhil from the University of Cape Town and is currently working on a doctorate on the recognition of prior learning. Before joining the University of the Western Cape in 1994 she was a lecturer at the University of Cape Town. She has also worked as a journalist.

Contact address: Mignonne Breier, Senior Researcher, Education Policy Unit, University of the Western Cape, Private Bag X17, Bellville 7535, South Africa.

HOW CHOICE CHANGES THE EDUCATION SYSTEM: A MICHIGAN CASE STUDY

DAVID N. PLANK and GARY SYKES

Abstract – In countries around the world policy makers propose that parents should exercise more control over the choice of schools that their children attend. This paper considers the ways in which the introduction of new opportunities for school choice changes the education system. It argues that choice affects the education system as a whole by introducing new actors into the system, by changing the terms of relationships among existing actors, and by creating new pressures within the system that require new responses. The nature, magnitude, and consequences of these effects cannot be predicted in advance, as they depend on a number of factors including the social and economic context. The empirical basis for this paper derives from a case study of the implementation of choice policies in the state of Michigan in the US, but the conceptual issues raised have important implications for the study of school choice wherever such policies are adopted.

Zusammenfassung – In vielen Ländern der Welt wird von Politikern vorgeschlagen, daß Eltern einen starken Einfluß auf die Wahl der Schule, die ihre Kinder besuchen, ausüben sollten. Dieser Artikel untersucht, in welcher Weise die Einführung neuer Möglichkeiten für die Wahl der Schule das Bildungssystem verändert. Es legt dar, daß die Auswahl das Bildungssystem als Ganzes berührt, indem neue Akteure im System aufgenommen werden, durch Veränderungen der Beziehungen zwischen bereits vorhandenen Akteuren sowie durch die Entstehung von neuem Druck, der neue Antworten erfordert. Die Art, Ausmaß und die Konsequenzen dieser Auswirkungen sind nicht vorhersagbar, da sie von einigen Faktoren abhängig sind, einschließlich dem sozialen und wirtschaftlichen Zusammenhang. Die empirische Grundlage dieses Artikels resultiert aus einer Fallstudie über die Realisierung einer Auswahlpolitik im Staat Michigan in den USA, jedoch haben die bezüglich des Konzepts erhobenen Fragen eine große Bedeutung für die Studie der Schulwahl an Orten, wo eine solche Politik angewendet wird.

Résumé – Dans de nombreux pays, les responsables de politiques préconisent que les parents décident davantage de l'école fréquentée par leurs enfants. Cet article analyse comment la mise en place de nouvelles possibilités de choisir une école modifie le système éducatif. L'auteur avance que ce choix influe sur le sytème éducatif dans son ensemble en introduisant de nouveaux acteurs dans le système, en transformant les relations entre les acteurs existants, et en créant de nouvelles pressions qui exigent de nouvelles réactions. La nature, l'ampleur et les répercussions de cette influence ne peuvent être anticipées car elles dépendent de plusieurs facteurs, dont le contexte socio-économique. La base empirique de cet article se fonde sur une étude de cas menée dans l'Etat américain du Michigan sur la mise en oeuvre de politiques en faveur du choix scolaire. Mais les questions conceptuelles soulevées sont importantes pour étudier le choix scolaire, sans distinction du lieu où ces politiques sont adoptées.

International Review of Education – Internationale Zeitschrift für Erziehungswissenschaft – Revue Internationale de l'Education 45(5/6): 385–416, 1999.
© 1999 *Kluwer Academic Publishers. Printed in the Netherlands.*

Resumen – En muchos países del mundo, los políticos proponen que los padres deberían ejercer un mayor control sobre la elección de los colegios a los que acuden sus hijos. Este trabajo se ocupa de cómo la introducción de nuevas oportunidades de elección del instituto de enseñanza cambia el sistema educativo. Argumenta que la elección afecta al sistema de la educación en su conjunto, introduciendo en el mismo nuevos protagonistas, cambiando los modos de relación entre los protagonistas existentes y creando nuevas presiones que exigen nuevas respuestas. No se pueden predecir la naturaleza, magnitud ni las consecuencias de estos efectos, ya que dependen de un número de factores, incluyendo el contexto social y económico. La base empírica de este trabajo deriva de un caso de estudio sobre la implementación de políticas de elección en el estado de Michigan, EE.UU., pero los puntos conceptuales planteados tienen consecuencias importantes para el estudio de la elección escolar dondequiera que se adopten estas políticas.

Резюме - Во многих странах мира люди, принимающие политические решения, предлагают предоставить родителем более широкое право выбора по отношению школы, в которой учатся их дети. В этом труде рассматриваются варианты того, как внедрение новых возможностей по выбору школы меняет систему образования. Утверждается, что фактор выбора действует на всю систему обучения путем ввода новых "игроков", меняя условия отношений между уже существующими игроками и, создавая новые рычаги давления, которые требуют новых ответов. Характер, размеры и последствия этих результатов заранее непредсказуемы, поскольку они зависят от целого ряда факторов, в том числе и от социального и экономического контекста. Эмпирическая основа этого труда основана на исследовании одного конкретно взятого случая внедрения политик свободного выбора в штате Мичиган в США, однако поднятые концептуальные вопросы имеют важное влияние на исследование выбора школ, где бы такая политика ни проводилась.

The decentralization trend in education

In countries around the world the power of the central state over the educational system has diminished in the past two decades. In educational systems where control was formerly exercised by a powerful national Ministry of Education, including France and China, administrative authority has been devolved to regional or local governments, and often beyond to the school level (DeLany and Paine 1991; Fowler 1997). In less centralized systems, including Brazil and the UK, in which authority was already lodged at subnational levels of government, an increased degree of control has shifted to communities and schools (Plank 1996; Glatter, Woods, and Bagley 1997). Issues related to administrative decentralization dominate the educational policy agenda in these and other countries, and in virtually all countries the advocates of further decentralization are winning the policy debate.

The worldwide trend toward administrative decentralization can be explained in a variety of ways. Those who support these trends have a variety of different motives, and the relative weight of these motives in the determination of policy choices varies substantially across countries. In South Africa and Brazil, for example, the move to decentralize administrative authority is associated with powerful pressures to increase democratic accountability in previously authoritarian political systems (Plank 1996; Pampallis 1998). These moves may also be associated with an obligation or at least a willingness to acknowledge and respect ethnic or regional differences in parents' and communities' expectations for the educational system, including for example variation in preferences with respect to the language of instruction. They may also originate in the desire of central governments to shift intractable political and policy problems to other spheres of government or, as in the case of the US, out of the public sector altogether. (Plank and Boyd 1994).

In other countries including New Zealand and China administrative decentralization is in significant part attributable to efforts to increase efficiency and reduce public expenditure in the educational system (see also an analysis of the introduction of choice into Sweden in Daun and Slenning 1998). Different governments have sought to accomplish this by fostering competition among service providers, by privatizing previously public services, or by mobilizing additional resources from communities and households. In some instances, notably including the UK and the US, these efforts are accompanied by explicit ambitions to limit the power and capacity of the state and the "education establishment" by generating competitive, "market" pressures on public sector institutions (Chubb and Moe 1990). In other instances, in contrast, as Teresa Tatto has recently argued with respect to Mexico, administrative decentralization may reflect a strategy to *strengthen* the central state at the expense of rival centers of power including state or local governments and teachers' unions (Tatto, in press). In other countries, including many in Africa, the move to decentralize authority and responsibility in the educational system originates in the incapacity of the central state to provide educational services of acceptable quality to all who demand them (Mwiria 1990; World Bank 1997).

Many of these decentralizing moves include expanded opportunities for parents to make choices about the schools their children attend. In the US and the UK the array of public sector alternatives has been significantly increased through the establishment of grant-maintained and charter schools, and through the removal of previous obstacles to mobility of individual scholars between regular public schools (Glatter, Woods, and Bagley 1997; Peterson and Hassel 1998; Whitty, Power, and Halpin 1998; Whitty 1997). Similar changes have taken place in South Africa, as the end of apartheid has opened up opportunities for children to attend schools previously reserved for members of other "racial" groups (Pampallis 1998). In Australia and Chile the array of choices available to parents has been expanded to include private and religious schools in addition to schools provided by the state (Angus and Cuttance 1998; Carnoy 1998). In China, Tanzania, and other formerly socialist countries the public sector monopoly on educational provision has been broken, and the array of choices open to parents has come to include private schools for the first time (DeLany and Paine 1991; Samoff 1987). Expanding the set of enrollment choices available to parents is sometimes an explicit goal of government policy, as in the UK or the US, and sometimes an artifact of other policy changes, as in South Korea (Lee 1998).

In this paper we present some preliminary observations on how the introduction of new opportunities for parents to choose the schools their children attend affects the educational system, based on our ongoing study of the consequences of expanded choice in a mid-sized metropolitan area in Michigan. Our research seeks answers to two related questions. First, how do established actors including public and private school systems respond to the introduction of new competitors (e.g., charter schools) into the educational system? Second, how do established school systems respond to new "rules of the game" that place them in direct competition with one another for students and funds? In this paper we present some preliminary work from that project, in which we seek to identify the key actors in the educational system, and to characterize the ways in which their relationships have changed with the advent of choice. Our basic argument is that the expansion of opportunities for parental and student choice affects the character of the educational system as a whole, by changing the terms of the relationships among key actors in the system, by introducing new actors into the system, and by creating new pressures that require new responses. The nature, magnitude, and consequences of these effects cannot be predicted in advance, however, as they are highly contingent on a number of variables including the policy regime governing choice and the social and economic context in which choice policies are implemented.

Our empirical work involves the collection and analysis of three kinds of data. First, we are compiling information on the flow of students and the associated flow of dollars among the providers of educational services. In this part of our analysis we seek to identify those who gain and lose under the present choice regime, and to identify the factors that determine which students move and which educational organizations seek to take advantage of their increased opportunities for mobility. Second, we are collecting information on the strategies that different actors have adopted in their efforts to maximize their gains or perhaps minimize their losses under the choice regime. We have conducted interviews with school district superintendents, local union presidents, and charter school principals, and surveyed school board members from the 16 districts in the metropolitan area. Our goal is to understand how the expansion of parents' opportunities to choose has affected their organizations, and to learn how they are responding to the new threats and opportunities that choice poses for them. Third, through surveys of principals and teachers we seek to learn whether choice is bringing about change at the instructional core of the educational enterprise, in schools and classrooms, and what forms such changes might take.

It is essential to acknowledge at the outset that our theoretical approach to these questions aspires to generalization, but our empirical focus is resolutely parochial. Our original case study is thoroughly idiosyncratic. We have recently extended our empirical work to include two additional metropolitan areas in Michigan, but our findings about how choice has affected the educational system in our original research site cannot be generalized to other metropolitan areas in Michigan, much less to other states or other countries. At the same time, careful analysis of this case may be helpful by providing a way to characterize the complexity of educational systems more generally, by illustrating how relationships among actors within the system may be altered through policy change, and by showing how the responses of one set of actors may affect others within the system. In the sections that follow we briefly characterize previous policy research on choice; describe the policy background in Michigan; set forth some caveats and conceptual distinctions; present preliminary findings; and conclude with some summary observations.

Previous research

The policy debate over educational choice revolves around three sets of issues. The first of these concerns the enrollment decisions of individual students and households. The fundamental question in this line of research was posed in the title of a recent book: *Who chooses? Who loses?* (Fuller and Elmore 1996). The central concern is the effect of various choice plans on social stratification within and across communities. In the US the scholarly debate on these issues is deeply rooted in a long line of inquiry and argument about equity in the educational system, which in recent decades has focused on the issue of equal opportunity and school desegregation. Similar questions about the effects of expanded choice have arisen in South Africa and other countries (Pampallis 1998).

The second set of issues concerns the consequences of expanded choice for schools and classrooms. The central question here is whether choice and the implicit or explicit competitive pressures that it introduces bring about significant changes in governance, curriculum, pedagogy, and ultimately student achievement in affected schools, including both those that are actively participating in the choice system (e.g., charter schools) and "ordinary" public schools that now face new competitors. This line of inquiry builds on a long tradition of research on educational reform, curricular and pedagogical innovation, and school improvement.

The third set of issues concerns the consequences of choice for the public school system as a whole. At this level the central question is whether and how increased competition and expanded opportunities for choice affect the structure and operation of existing schools and school districts, and whether the introduction of choice represents a necessary spur to improvement or a fundamental threat to the democratic tradition of the common school.

Empirical research on the consequences of expanded choice has looked almost exclusively at the first two issues. There is an extensive literature on the determinants of the choices made by individual households, and on the unequal and inequitable distribution of information and opportunity in many choice systems (Rasell and Rothstein 1993; Fuller and Elmore 1996). There is now a growing literature on the school-level effects of choice, which has developed directly out of an earlier literature on the differences between private/parochial schools and public schools (Bryk, Lee, and Holland 1993; Coleman, Hoffer, and Kilgore 1982). At present, for example, much scholarly attention has been focused on charter schools and the ways in which they differ from "ordinary" public schools (Nathan 1996; RPP 1998; Sarason 1998; Wells 1998).

To date, however, the debate over the system-level effects of expanded choice has been driven largely by theory and ideology rather than empirical research. Advocates of choice and charter schools generally take a benign view of the consequences of policy change, either dismissing the possibility of harm or celebrating the evolutionary benefits of killing off the fat and lazy. They commonly argue that the exigencies of competition will make public school systems more efficient, more productive, and more responsive to the demands of students, parents, and communities (Chubb and Moe 1990; Peterson and Hassel 1998). Critics of choice generally take a dimmer view, focusing on the risks inherent in tampering with apparently successful institutions and mindful of the unanticipated consequences of massive social and institutional changes. They argue that the diversion of funds, students, and attention from existing public schools will make the problems they face even more difficult, and may lead over time to the dismantling of a relatively successful, socially and politically crucial, but nevertheless fragile public institution (Cookson 1994; Henig 1994).

Policy background

The most important recent shift in Michigan's educational policy regime was not the introduction of charter schools or inter-district choice, but the adoption of a radically new school finance system. Voters approved a new tax regime (known as Proposal A) in 1994. The primary goal of the tax reformers was to reduce property taxes, which were higher in Michigan than in almost any other state (Vergari 1995; Addonizio, Boulus, and Kearney 1995). Proposal A accomplished this goal by shifting the principal source of school funding from the local property tax to the state sales tax, which was increased by 50 per cent to make up for lost property tax revenue. Some other taxes were also increased, with the new revenues dedicated to support of the public schools. At the same time, local school districts were prohibited from levying local taxes to supplement their state appropriations, except under some very restrictive conditions.

Beyond the reduction of local property taxes, Proposal A had three main consequences for Michigan's education system. First, it shifted the primary responsibility for funding schools from local school districts to the state. Under the previous finance system the state accounted for approximately one-third of educational revenues; since the approval of Proposal A the state has provided approximately 80 per cent. As a result, decisions about the funding available for local schools are now made in the Legislature rather than in local tax referenda. This shift has greatly increased the power of state government in educational policy debates, and correspondingly diminished the power of local school boards and teachers' unions. Moreover, with the level of educational appropriations determined through political bargaining in the Legislature, the prospect of large real increases in educational funding for *any* school district has diminished substantially, and the local option to provide supplementary operating funds has been foreclosed.[1]

Second, state funds are now distributed to school districts according to a funding formula which is essentially driven by the number of pupils enrolled in district schools. The absolute level of the per pupil allocation also depends on the level of local expenditures under the previous system, in order to "hold harmless" those districts that raised the most revenue under the previous funding system. Local school districts thus continue to vary significantly in the level of their per pupil spending, but the rate of increase in spending is effectively the same for all districts. Under these circumstances, the only way to increase district revenues is to enroll additional students. (By the same token, in districts where enrollments decline, revenues decline commensurately.) Attracting and keeping students has consequently acquired the political and financial importance previously accorded to the passage of local property tax increases.

The third main consequence of Proposal A is that the effective "ownership" of educational revenues has been shifted from school districts to individual students. Under the previous finance system the revenues available to local school districts depended on local property wealth and the property tax rate that voters in the district were willing to pay. The revenues that districts collected "belonged" to the district, and varied independently of the number of students who actually enrolled in public schools. For example, if a household within the district chose to send its children to private or parochial schools they nevertheless continued to pay property taxes to support the public schools, despite the fact that they chose not to take advantage of the services that the district provided. Under the new finance system, in contrast, the basic accounting unit is the student rather than the district. When a household chooses to enroll their children in private or parochial schools the local district now loses the revenue associated with those children. In principle, therefore, state education subsidies under Proposal A are fully portable; when a student moves from one school or district to another their state subsidy can now move with them.

Since 1994 the Legislature has approved two additional policy changes that have greatly increased the policy significance of these changes in the system of school finance. The first of these established charter schools in Michigan; the second allowed students to transfer between schools and school districts, but within Intermediate School District (ISD) boundaries that are roughly contiguous with counties. These two innovations made the theoretical portability of state subsidies a reality, by giving students the means to shift their subsidies from their local school district to alternative suppliers of educational services. The provision of public funds for charter schools allows the entry of new competitors into the public school system; opening up student choice of schools in other districts allows established actors to compete with one another for students and revenues. Together these two changes pose radically new challenges for local school districts, by obliging them to compete for students and revenues in ways that they have not previously done.

In summary, Proposal A created a quasi-market in Michigan's educational system, which makes the state the single best case of a "voucher-ready" school finance system in the US. Public educational subsidies are assigned to children, and are therefore fully portable. At present these subsidies can be assigned to the student's district of residence, to another school district, or to a charter school. The unfolding policy debate in Michigan revolves around the relatively simple question of which suppliers of educational services should be eligible to receive public subsidies. In Michigan, expanding the array of acceptable suppliers will require a constitutional amendment, because public subsidies to private and religious schools are explicitly forbidden by the Michigan Constitution. Supporters of vouchers are now working to have a popular vote on such an amendment in November 2000. The press to expand the number of suppliers eligible to receive public subsidies to include private and religious schools is therefore virtually certain to intensify in the very near future.

Conceptual issues

In the research that is underway, we are interested in how the introduction of policies that expand parental choice of schools comes to affect the present system of schooling. We ask this question in a number of ways. For example, how does the system of schooling respond to the introduction of choice? Or, what are the consequences of choice policies for the educational system? These questions all presuppose certain matters. One is the state or status of the "system" prior to the introduction of choice. Another is the way in which – the concepts and language with which – we characterize the entity under investigation. Note that to this point we have smuggled into our description the word "system," without saying precisely what we mean by this term. Other terms frequently used to characterize education as an organized aspect of modern life are monopoly, market, institution, ecology, network, community, culture, and perhaps "mold," as in the contemporary US interest in "break the mold" schools. Each of these terms draws attention to some features of education, not others; each creates a distinctive metaphorical halo around formal education.

Yet another matter concerns the dynamics of change that we presuppose. Choice policies typically presume some theory of action through which the expansion of parental choices will come to have broad effects on education. Parental choice may be advocated as a good in itself, a basic value that ought not to be denied to any family, or restricted to certain privileged families, regardless of the social consequences. But policy discourse typically features claims of various kinds about what will ensue when family choice of schooling is expanded. So we have an interest in process accounts or theories of action that formalize assumptions about the effects of choice and about how such effects obtain.

From this brief account of our research interest, a number of elements may be distinguished that together create the implicit framework for our studies. These elements include (1) *an outline of the historical background to the existing state of affairs* (i.e. the nature of the schooling enterprise prior to the introduction of the new choice policies); (2) the location of the work *within an entity variously characterized* (e.g., the concepts and metaphors selected for analysis); (3) *the characterization of the context into which an intervention is introduced* (e.g., the new choice policies); (4) *a statement of the ways in the intervention produces changes in the pre-existing state of affairs*; (5) *a detailed specification and description of the processes followed.* Finally, we might add a normative concern (6) which seeks to arrive at *a judgment about the overall desirability of the changes together with predictions and recommendations for future policy and practice.* The full study that we are embarked upon eventually will address these six elements.

Before proceeding further, however, several observations immediately stand out. For one, this framework should not be conceived as the replacement of one discrete state by another, crudely characterized as pre- vs. post-choice. American education has long featured a wide range of formal and informal choices that extend from deciding where to purchase a home and whether to educate children at home, in private schools, or in public schools, to choices over individual teachers, special programs, and alternative schools within the public sector. To understand the effects of choice on education requires first an understanding of how choice has operated within American education together with the distinctive approaches currently introduced or under consideration. We envision, then, an historical continuum rather than a radical break with the past.

A second observation concerns the nature of the model to be used. The model must include a conception of boundaries as well as of internally differentiated elements, the nature of interaction among these elements, the arenas within which they interact, the rules which constrain these interactions, and finally exogenous influences that simultaneously shape the effects of choice. As our description of current Michigan choice policy has indicated, state statute established a regional agency, set within the state's counties, as the boundary for inter-district transfer of students. This rule then effectively but not entirely creates the boundary for the local ecology of choice. It does not entirely do so because students may cross county or Intermediate School District lines to attend charter schools. The full set of boundary conditions then will include some mix of legal or statutory limits with behavioral responses and preferences, for example, parents' willingness to transport children to schools at some distance from home. The rules set parameters for behavior that are also influenced by social, cultural, and economic considerations and calculations.

A third observation concerns causal inferences. An implication of the framework is that the intervention under study is the primary if not sole causal agent in producing whatever changes our inquiries uncover. But this research will be unable to pin down such unambiguous causal connections. What we termed "exogenous factors" may exercise significant influence in addition to or in interaction with the specific choice policies under investigation. For example, in the urban school district that forms the hub of the metro area we are studying, the city mayor in conjunction with the school district superintendent and the president of the nearby state university joined in announcing the formation of a blue ribbon task force to examine the status of the city's public schools and to make recommendations for reform. Some of our informants described this Commission as a direct response to the challenge posed by choice to the district. Yet other events contributed as well, including the rumored relocation of a major plant, upon which much of the city's economy depended, to another city. Reassuring the business community about the future viability of the public schools, evidently under threat by the new choice policies, appeared as a central motive in establishing the task force.

Finally, we are mindful of our perspective in time and place as a basis upon which to offer descriptions and to make predictions. If choice policies are to work fundamental changes in public education, this can only occur over an extended period. Yet we initiated a series of studies in 1997 of policies dating from 1994. Our admittedly foreshortened perspective on events and trends may be suspect on several grounds. Early developments may not predict what occurs later in a time series or evolutionary sequence. Policy as prime mover for good or ill may itself be modified in the course of implementation, in ways that policy analysts do not anticipate. And, deep or lasting effects may lag over long spans of time. As futurists are by now well aware, extrapolations from current, short-term trends frequently suffer discontinuities in time series data, the emergence of unanticipated policy developments, and lagged effects.

Likewise, our work on choice is situated within a single state among the United States. Many varieties of choice are unfolding rapidly across the country, and the details make a difference. To take one example, Michigan charter schools operate independently of school districts. They are chartered largely by universities, and they compete directly with districts for both dollars and students. Teachers in Michigan's charter schools by and large are not members of union-sponsored collective bargaining units; the terms and conditions of their employment are set by the individual charter schools. In California, in contrast, which includes the second greatest number of charter schools nationwide, districts are the primary chartering agent, and most teachers are members of the collective bargaining unit. These differences, we suspect, have profound consequences for such matters as school autonomy, teacher recruitment to charter schools, and for their collective influence within them.[2] The congressionally mandated national study of charter schools currently underway eventually will provide systematic cross-state comparisons of charter statutes and their effects, but at present no such comparative profiles are available. The reader should be aware then that we are not asserting that as Michigan goes, so goes the nation. Rather, we are starkly aware of dramatic differences across states and localities in choice policies and their effects.

With these caveats in mind, we offer some initial thoughts on a conceptual approach to the effects of choice upon public education in the state of Michigan. As with the foregoing, these are remarks about a conceptual framework, rather than constituting the framework itself, but this reflects the preliminary state of our studies. Our remarks take up certain formal elements of our study including the impact, agents, rules, and change dynamics associated with choice policy.

Impact

The first element in our conceptual approach focuses on categories or kinds of impact that choice has on public education. We begin with a number of commonplace effects that include the following.

Student flows
One category of impact simply concerns the movement of students among the schools in the local ecology under investigation. Absolute numbers and percentages, together with changes over time constitute one important outcome of parental choice of schooling. We note as well that the flow of students among schools not only may alter distributions of students along lines of race and class, but also categories such as special needs, non- or limited-English speaking, and others. One kind of impact, then, concerns the question of who goes to school with whom, which has been a vital social policy question in the US. We have discovered another outcome associated with student flows, which we have termed "turbulence." Choice appears to increase the movement of students in and out of schools, which adds to the already considerable turbulence in urban schools. In the metropolitan area that we are studying, for example, a substantial number of students left the regular public schools for charter schools, only to return to the public schools later,

presumably because of disappointment with the charter offerings. Student movement among alternatives, then, is an unanticipated outcome of increased choice that creates a variety of difficulties for schools, including disruptions in already-formed classes and the loss of revenue after the official "student count" day in the Fall of each year.

Dollar flows

Funds follow the student, so there are budgetary consequences associated with the new choice policies. The impact here concerns the overall dollar impact on school districts due to choice, together with the budgetary decisions around either additional or lost revenue. To interpret these figures, however, requires an understanding of how exogenous factors are simultaneously influencing the budget. For example, urban schools routinely lose students to private and parochial schools at the middle school and secondary school levels. If families that intended to send their students to private schools at certain grade levels now make use of charter schools or interdistrict transfers, the net loss of revenue to urban districts is unaffected. Considerations such as these make it difficult to interpret the financial impact of choice on urban districts.

Innovation

Another broad category of impact concerns evidence of innovation on the part of public school districts in response to choice. We use this term broadly to indicate any responses in programs or organizational routines to competitive pressures exerted by choice. Of importance here is a detailed understanding of both the extent of innovation and the kinds of innovation that emerge in response to choice pressures (Mintrom 1997). Eventually we may want to categorize kinds of innovation that we uncover, then interpret our categories in terms of general conclusions. We have some speculations along these lines in our preliminary findings.

Purposes

An important but amorphous category of impact concerns how choice influences the fundamental purposes established for public education. The purposes of education in a society may be categorized in a variety of ways, and we have not settled on a final set of distinctions, but we can indicate generally what is at stake. In the US, schooling has been justified as both a public and a private good. As a public good, education is considered the cornerstone of the democratic state, the vehicle through which future citizens are prepared to exercise their democratic rights and responsibilities. In a multi-cultural nation made up of immigrants from many lands, education also performs a vital social role in creating a common culture. In a vibrant capitalist economy, education plays a critical role in preparing a workforce, and in responding to shifting imperatives for educated workers. And in an unequal society, education serves, in principle at least, the goals of equity and social justice. At the same time, education is pursued for private goals of individual mobility and opportunity (Labaree 1997). We can ask, then, about the effects of choice upon the range of purposes that have been established via custom, tradition, law, and culture. At the same time, however, we acknowledge the difficulty of establishing empirically the effects of choice on educational purposes. Purposes serve as the rhetorical touchstones in debates about choice, and so constitute primary concerns, even as they are difficult to measure over time.

Agents

Within the local arena that constitutes the site for our study, we have begun to catalogue the full set of agents that are implicated by the new choice policies. One unexpected result has been the discovery of new agents that are affected by, or make use of, choice in ways the policy did not anticipate. In our original formulation, we conceived the primary agents to be school districts operating within an ISD or county, in this case a metropolitan area. We expected to observe new forms of strategic interaction – competition and cooperation – in response to the choice policies. But the full set of agents who are involved is much greater. In addition to public school districts (and within them, individual schools, which may operate somewhat independently from district offices), we also have discovered other agents occupying this arena. They include the following.

Private and parochial schools

Such schools face a new set of choices and consequences. For example, small, struggling private schools may convert to charter status and receive public funding in return for giving up their overtly religious cast. Some church-affiliated schools in the state have taken this path, as a means of enhancing their enrollments. Also, the new choice laws have drawn students out of private and parochial schools charging tuition into charter schools, where parents do not have to pay. Interviews with parochial school administrators reveal that they are not worried about the loss of students, but rather are interested in strengthening the religious mission of their schools, and in recruiting students who explicitly seek a religious experience.

Home schooling

Yet another segment of the school population are students who receive their education at home. Here too, reports indicate that some proportion of charter school students have come from the home school population, but the exact numbers are difficult to determine. While Michigan's total charter school student enrollment approaches 20,000, we have received estimates of the state's home school population ranging from 10,000 to 100,000. Charter schools today are attracting attention, but the home school population at present appears to be considerably larger, even as it remains invisible (and undocumented). This is a case of one segment of the education market that has gone largely unnoticed. And, it is a case of a pre-existing choice option that evidently appeals to a small but significant (and apparently growing) fraction of families. Of interest is the impact that the new choice policies may have on this market segment, but estimates are difficult to obtain, because many home school families deliberately seek to avoid entanglements with the state, and so resist efforts to identify them or collect information about their children.

Institutions of higher education

In Michigan, universities make up the majority of chartering agents, and their behavior is a potentially significant aspect of the new choice dynamics. Additionally, however, we have discovered that community colleges and universities also are becoming active in cooperative ventures with school districts around vocational and technical education. The typical pattern involves student and revenue sharing arrangements, permitted by state code, where senior secondary students attend high schools for a portion of their day, to complete academic education, then attend local colleges or universities for technical training of various kinds. In one case in our sample, the local community college indicated it might set up an independent charter school unless the local district agreed to a cooperative endeavor of this kind, which eventually emerged. The charter law created a new means for the community college to exert leverage on the district. The case reveals how choice policies may create new forms of interaction among agents in the local educational arena.

Corporate and business firms

In a number of cases around the state, the private sector has become involved in schooling in new ways. Three such forms have appeared. One is the corporate-founded or affiliated charter school aimed at preparing students for careers in the sponsor industry or field. The Ford Motor Company, for example, has established such a school in the Detroit area. Another is the for-profit educational firm that establishes new schools or that manages existing schools. As indicated, the Edison Project now operates a number of regular public and charter schools in Michigan. And a third form is the for-profit management company that provides capital, technical assistance, and other services to charter schools, many of which are struggling with start-up problems. Several of the charter schools in our study either are managed by corporate entities or are franchised versions of corporate-developed school models.

The entry of private and for-profit enterprises into the public schools represents a fascinating new development in American education, whose consequences have scarcely begun to be reckoned. They represent another strand of choice policy in the US, referred to as contracting. Advocates for contracting argue that schools and districts can operate more efficiently if they contract services to outside firms on a competitive basis. Such practice has long been the norm around such functions as transportation and food services in the schools, but the principle might be applied to a much broader range of functions. To a greater degree than in the past, private interests now are exerting influence over public education, often in contexts where the profit motive comes into play. Understanding the impact of private interests in public education is a vitally important question opened up by choice policy.

Rules

Within neo-institutional theory, rules are treated as a critical element in organizational environments. As rules change, organizations adapt. Conversely, organizations are not passive agents, but actively seek to shape the rules that regulate their existence and behavior (Powell and Dimaggio 1991). We conceive the new policies in Michigan, including Proposal A, charter schools, interdistrict transfers, and several others (e.g., PA 112, which prohibits teachers' unions from striking), as significant alterations in the rule regime influencing the local educational arena. Our approach regards the metropolitan area that serves as our primary research site as a multi-lateral bargaining arena among a set of agents. We are interested in how the new "rules of the game" influence the dynamics and the outcomes of bargaining among the agents occupying the arena, including the new entrants.

This formulation calls for us to develop a typology or characterization of the rules that define strategic interactions, and perhaps of the "meta-rules" (i.e., rules for how to use the rules) that govern the responses and moves of agents in the bargaining arena (Angus 1998). This analytic task we have not yet undertaken, but we can point to one important kind of rule, associated with the establishment of boundaries. We argue that choice policy creates or channels opportunities by redrawing boundaries. For example, economic boundaries prevent poor families from sending their children to parochial schools. In most countries around the world, public assistance for private schooling has been established, but such provision is explicitly forbidden in Michigan. Boundaries perform two social functions. They channel access and opportunity, and they create the bases for inclusion and exclusion. Choice policies, we hypothesize, introduce explicit boundaries and result in implicit, often unanticipated boundaries around the question of who goes to school with whom.

Several examples illustrate the importance of boundaries in modeling the arena for choice. Most obviously, the state statute authorizing interdistrict transfers created the ISD as the boundary line. Students can transfer to other district's schools, but only within their resident ISD. A foreign observer might find this boundary condition somewhat odd, because the best alternative schools for families living on the ISD boundary may be across the line. To understand this restriction, then, brings into account the political construction of choice in order to simultaneously expand individual opportunity or access while preserving the residential basis for exclusion, typically along lines of race and class.

Another example includes provision for special needs children. Although the charter school law does not allow the exclusion of children with handicaps, new charter schools may simply be unequipped to provide for such children. They do not possess the facilities nor the specially trained staff. Consequently, an informal boundary condition may restrict access to charter schools on the part of families with handicapped children.

Change dynamics

Finally, our analysis requires a process account of how choice exerts influence and produces effects on schooling. While the exit, voice, and loyalty dynamics proposed by Albert Hirschman (1970) offer a framework for understanding the behavior of individual consumers of education, we are interested in concepts that help explain the behavior of agents interacting in the policy arena of choice. The theory of choice posits that competitive pressures within the newly created quasi-market of schooling will stimulate developments and responses (Lowery 1998). Neo-institutional theory, however, would predict much slower response to rules changes and much greater stability in organizational routines and structures. Normative and cognitive pillars of institutions are likely to change very slowly even in the face of changes in policy (Meyer and Rowan 1977; Plank 1987; Scott 1995).

These remarks indicate several issues to pursue. One concerns predictions about the patterns of competition and cooperation that are likely to unfold among the set of agents in the local arena under study. Another concerns the likely time frame within which change dynamics may play out, and the non-economic forces that may constrain purely rational behavior (in economists' terms) on the part of actors in the arena. At this point in our inquiry we have not settled on one or another of these theoretical leads to explain our data, while recognizing that forces for both change and constancy are present in the mix.

Some preliminary findings

We have not yet begun systematic analysis of our data, but can offer a number of preliminary observations, based on the interviews with superintendents and other elite informants plus some examination of student movement across districts and to charter schools. In what follows, we identify five findings by these key words: *flows, community, competition, ethos, and innovation.*

Flows

First, of the 11 districts in the ISD that serves as the primary site for our study, the city district has encountered the most significant loss of students and dollars. In fact, of all the school districts in the state, this mid-sized city has felt the greatest impact of choice. Of the two policies, however, the charter school policy has had the larger influence. In the city, five new charter schools have emerged, and these schools have recruited approximately 1785 students from the public system, who take with them $5962 per student. The surrounding suburban, small town, and partially rural districts have felt few effects of the new choice policies and have lost few students either to charter schools or to interdistrict transfers. None of the other districts in the ISD yet has a charter school within its boundaries; these other districts have consequently lost few students to these new schools.

The private school and home school populations also appear to have been affected by the new choice policies. We do not have exact figures in these cases, particularly for home school families, but it appears that a sizable fraction of families have taken advantage of the charter school provision in particular, because they now have publicly funded options that provide a closer fit with their values and that do not require private tuition or other home schooling costs. Of 49,145 students in the public school system in the ISD, 3.6 per cent attend charter schools and 1.08 per cent used the school of choice option in 1997–98. Compared to the state of Michigan average (1.32 percentage of students attend charter schools and 0.68 per cent of students use the choice of school option), the number of students responding to choice in this ISD is greater than the state average.

Of the two new policies, then, charter schools have had the greatest impact on the public schools overall. The districts have made sparing use of the inter-district transfer provisions, either by opting out and refusing to accept transfer students or by setting limits on the numbers and the grade levels where they will accept transfers. One suburban district, contiguous to the city district is the exception. That district has suffered substantial enrollment declines over the last few years, due to a variety of factors, and has aggressively recruited transfer students, mostly drawn from the city district,[3] to help replace its declining enrollments. This district has accepted approximately 222 students under the inter-district transfer policy.

This overall pattern of student and dollar flows suggests two questions: what factors influence parental choices? And, what factors have shaped district responses? Nationally and internationally the first question has received considerable attention in choice research, and we will not pursue this question here. The second question, however, is significant for our inquiry. Note first that districts cannot prevent students from leaving to attend charter schools or to attend schools in other districts that are available. But districts do have control over whether they will accept transfer students, and districts can collude in shaping interdistrict transfer responses. The state rules, then, create a unique set of opportunities for new combinations of both competition and cooperation among districts.

In our interviews, the superintendents have been candid, if guarded, in identifying the factors that influence district responses to the new transfer rules. Fiscal concerns are evidently important. Districts must calculate whether they are at or near capacity in their schools or have substantial unused capacity.

If they are at capacity then they have no incentive to accept large numbers of transfers, for this will result in overcrowding and pressures to expand schools or to build new ones. The superintendents realize that going to the voters with bond issues for new schools that may be populated by students and families who have not paid for them (i.e., because these families live outside the district and so are unaffected by local tax levies) is a potentially volatile issue. However, if district enrollments are declining markedly, yielding excess places, then districts may be more inclined to open up, as in the single case in our sample.

Calculations about future population growth also play a role. In the single district that has recruited substantial numbers of students under the new transfer policy, there is virtually no land left for new homes, businesses, or other developments. The district cannot participate with businesses, real estate developers, and others in systematic expansion to attract new families with school-age children. In many of the other districts, however, growth is planned and the schools will benefit from an influx of new students as a result. In such districts, projections to capacity do not require recruitment of new students, and the districts can afford to be relatively selective in opting for transfer students.

Calculations of this sort are commonplace in American education, and form the staple of traditional strategic planning. But other factors, discussed in more veiled terms, also come into play. Race, class, and ethnicity achieve a renewed role in district concerns. A district may open for transfers and set parameters around the numbers and grade levels, but may not exclude any students who apply. The district must use a lottery system to choose students if they are oversubscribed. The small town and suburban districts surrounding the city are largely white, mixing upscale professional-managerial families with working class and farming communities. The perception, and to some extent the reality of the appeal of interdistrict transfers is the opportunity for inner city, poor, and minority families to gain access to well-provisioned, well regarded suburban schools. Yet these relatively affluent communities often were established or were settled originally as white, middle to working class enclaves, and they clearly seek to preserve their complexion. Consequently, these districts in the persons of their school boards and superintendents are extremely cautious about admitting students from outside district boundaries, whose price of admission may be a home worth $100,00 or more.

In our interviews, this factor is often couched in educational concerns. Superintendents speak of admitting students at transitional grade levels, such as kindergarten or grades 6–7, in order to socialize students to the educational ethos of the district. And, they speak of "hard to educate" students who may not enjoy the social capital provided by most of the district's resident families. They argue, in effect, that district educators may not be well equipped to educate such students, so the district must be cautious in the numbers admitted, lest such students disrupt educational routines that are well adapted to community expectations, norms, and sentiments. This genuine educational concern, however, simply reinforces the powerful tendency in American society to preserve social and racial segregation of public schools. When school boundaries are set by place of residence, this cultural fact of life may be submerged. The inter-district transfer policy, however, re-opens the debate about who should go to school with whom – about the Common School ideal itself – and the American ambivalence, perhaps the American dilemma in Myrdal's (1944) phrase, resurfaces.

Surveys of Michigan citizens reveal that charter schools and other choice options are popular in general, but particularly so among minority groups. Nationwide, charter schools have attracted minority students in disproportionately high numbers, with Michigan leading the way. Of the five charter schools in the city under study, two are Afro-centric academies that appeal almost exclusively to African-American families. These facts all indicate that the new exit options from regular public schools have greatest appeal among disaffected minority families who have lost faith in neighborhood public schools, especially in the inner city. Within Michigan, then, and we suspect within the nation at large, one powerful constituency for choice are minority families who now prefer exit over voice in determining their children's education. Charter schools in Michigan supply this option to a much greater extent than does the interdistrict transfer policy, which largely preserves the ability of communities to exclude those who do not "fit in."

Community

A related finding concerns how the rules established by the new choice policies create options for the formation of communities. One significant effect of choice policy on public education concerns the bases upon which school communities are formed, and how the new choice policies affect the dynamics of community formation. In tension have been two kinds of freedom, both of which are implicated in the new policies. One classic freedom, connected with the market, is *freedom of individual choice*. As the name implies, choice policy is justified or legitimated in terms of this freedom. But also implicated in the new policies is the *freedom of association*, linked to the polis. These two freedoms co-exist in tension, because associational freedom is potentially exclusionary, thereby limiting some individuals' freedom of choice. The new rules of school choice must adjudicate among these freedoms, and the policies in Michigan do so in particular ways.

Charter schools create new options for individuals and so expand market-based freedom of individual choice. As publicly funded entities, charter schools may not exclude students; they must accept those who apply, using lottery methods in cases of over-subscription. However, the rules governing charter schools limit but do not preclude the formation of particularistic communities that appeal to niche segments of the population. Charter school communities may not be formed on overtly religious grounds, but may be constructed on almost any other ground, subject to the constraint that some chartering agent will in fact grant a charter. So charter schools in Michigan now have been organized around Afro-centric education, Armenian education, Native American education, and other ethnic identifications, as well as around particular educational philosophies such as the Montessori method. Charter school law, then, does double duty, first by expanding options for individual choice, then by supplying the basis for associational freedom, insofar as many charter schools establish appeals to like-minded families who wish to congregate with others of similar persuasion. The law fits within American traditions of voluntary affiliation because charter schools do not – and cannot – overtly exclude families, but they can create particular communities of value that attract some families but not others (for an analysis of this trend, see McDonough 1998).

In contrast, the inter-district transfer policy has been politically constructed to favor exclusion and the right to associate with similar or like-minded individuals. Districts may not prevent the departure of families, but they may restrict entry. Furthermore, districts may cooperate in setting common rules for transfer, thus restricting individual access to the participating districts. While individual districts may have incentives to open up and so to enhance enrollments and revenue base, social, cultural, and political factors constrain such competitive moves (for more on this, see below). Political decision-making at several levels reflects the exclusionary tendencies in public education. First, the law itself restricted transfers to moves within county or ISD boundaries, which clearly reflected the desire to limit choice options within the Detroit metropolitan area, which is heavily segregated by race. Second, the law permits districts to opt in or out of choice and to determine how much choice to allow. The districts in our study for the most part have made limited use of the transfer policy, and have provided very limited access to favored schools in affluent, suburban districts.

In part, the rationale for restricted choice reflects the old, but now overturned basis for school finance in Michigan. A school finance system based on local property taxes creates a sense of ownership in the local community for the schools. Communities may be willing to accept higher taxes to educate their own children, but would be loath to bear additional tax burdens to educate children from outside the taxpaying community. Hence, another cherished American value comes into play in these calculations about community: You get what you pay for, but you have to pay for what you get. Under the new system inaugurated by Proposal A, districts have a double motive for restricted transfers: they wish to preserve the social and racial complexion of the community, and they want to appeal to taxpayers' sense of fairness about financing schools, even though local taxes no longer constitute the funding base.

Do these considerations about the impact of choice on community formation indicate any clear conclusions? At this point, we cannot say with certainty, but we can offer some speculations. The new choice policies in Michigan appear to open the way for the formation of particularistic communities of value within public sector schooling, that give scope to the twin freedoms of voluntary association and individual choice. These policies, then, may over time undercut the ideal of the Common School in America in favor of citizen preferences for communities that are more specialized. At the same time, however, the new rules clearly favor the freedom of association over unrestricted freedom of individual choice, by preserving the social bases for exclusion that historically have been nested within the tradition of local control and the neighborhood school, yielding de facto segregation by class and race. The new choice policies, then, will create new options for many families, but will not much upset the traditional bases of privilege within the system, the ability of social and economic elites to create exclusive enclaves of schooling.

Competition

Another tentative conclusion concerns the effects of competition on the public schools. Choice advocates typically refer to the virtues of market-based competition as a stimulus for improvements in public education. In addition to asserting the right of families to exercise choice as well as voice, they claim that the spur of competition introduced into the state's largest public monopoly will stimulate greater responsiveness on the part of unwieldy bureaucracies and will create positive dynamics around promising innovations. For example, if technology has great potential for revolutionizing learning, particularly under conditions where schools and homes may be networked and linked to the worldwide web (while evidence indicates that schools are slow to adopt new technologies), then the competition from charter schools and other publicly funded alternatives may well force the pace of innovation and change. In fact, one of the new corporate models of schooling in the US, known as the Edison project, promises a computer for every child to use at home, that will be linked to the school. So-called Edison schools can be implemented directly within public school districts, but they also may be established as independent, public charter schools, as occurred in the city district we are studying.

Has choice introduced significant competitive pressures into the public schools, forcing them to adopt popular programs and innovations pioneered by the charter schools? On the basis of our preliminary evidence, this appears to be the case only in very limited terms and only in a handful of locales. We speculate on several reasons for this finding. Most importantly, charter schools have not yet achieved significant market penetration. There are relatively few such schools in the state, serving a tiny fraction of the school-age population. The analogy one of our respondents used is telling on this point. He compared the charter schools to the rise of foreign-import automobiles into the US. When German and Japanese-made cars constituted a tiny fraction of the total market, US auto manufacturers had little reason to worry – or to respond. But as the foreign market share continued to climb in the 1970s, the revenue losses to American car companies became substantial. The first response was more aggressive marketing and advertising. It was only when the foreign market share approached one fifth to one quarter of domestic sales that the industry recognized they had a fundamental problem with quality that required dramatic changes in the entire enterprise. Eventually, the industry rose to the challenge and began producing better quality automobiles at competitive prices. Charter schools have not reached the tipping point at which the public schools would have to engage in new practices on a large scale.

A second factor concerns the targets of opportunity that charter schools appear to be exploiting. Many of these schools appeal to what might be termed "niche markets," that are highly specialized. Examples of market niches are ethnic-identity schools, religiously-affiliated schools that have converted to charter status while retaining elements of their former ethos; basic skills academies; vocational or technical education alternatives; schools serving troubled adolescents; and others. While some charter schools seek to compete in the mainstream, many have positioned themselves to appeal to special populations and communities. Such schools would not be expected to exert general, competitive pressures on public schools whose mission is to serve all families within their geographic boundary. Consequently, regular public schools would not regard programs or practices in niche market schools as having much applicability outside the singular context of the particular school.

A third reason for the limited response to competition is the uniform hostility directed at charter schools by public school educators. Our interviews with superintendents reflect an interesting ambivalence on this point. On one hand, the superintendents to a person regard charter schools as a destabilizing threat to public school ideals. Yet many also acknowledge some merit to the argument that greater competitive pressure would exert a salutary influence on public schools that have evolved a combination of rapid, superficial reforms with few fundamental changes. In a society as thoroughly capitalist as the US, it would be surprising if prominent figures completely rejected the discipline of the market, yet the American approval of competition as a basic cultural value has not translated into positive reactions to charter schools. As we discuss below under "ethos," public school administrators have sought to block and suppress charter schools rather than learning from them. This is a perfectly understandable initial response to the threat of competition, and it may change over time, but it still appears as the dominant response at the moment.

While these factors together explain the muted response of public schools to competition from charter schools, there is one telling exception. The five charter schools in our sample city district have attracted a sizable fraction of students, largely poor and minority, which has cost the district considerable loss of revenue. There, we do see a number of responses emerging to the competitive challenge of charter schools. Among these responses so far, the most prominent are (1) the allocation of funds (nearly one quarter of a million dollars) in the district budget to marketing and advertising (bill boards around the city, advertising spots on local radio stations, and other outlets now proclaim the "world class" virtues of the district's schools); (2) the introduction of all-day kindergarten into the district in direct response to this option in several of the charter schools; (3) the formation of the blue ribbon task force, mentioned above, which resulted in a range of recommendations including volunteer tutoring programs and others; (4) the creation of a new, student-sharing collaboration with the local community college for vocational-occupational training during the secondary school years; (5) the development of a "community school" in one of the elementary buildings in partnership with the local university; (6) a district-wide effort to align the curriculum to the state's standards, presumably as part of an effort to elevate student achievement scores on the state-mandated tests administered in grades 4, 8, and 11; (7) a contract for better truancy management with an independent institute devoted to serving troubled youth; and (8) a new middle school honors program that appeals to academically motivated students at those grade levels.

These developments suggest several observations. At present in Michigan, most districts appear insulated from competitive pressures introduced by the new choice policies. The exception may be urban districts where discontent among minority and other communities with the schools is relatively high. There, families are likely to avail themselves of new, policy-driven options, threatening urban districts with the loss of students and revenue. Critics of urban education may regard such pressure as long overdue, arguing that public schools will have no choice but to improve (Peterson and Hassel 1998); others, however, see such developments as further weakening public schools, rendering them *less* able to meet the needs of poor, minority communities (Kozol 1991). This clearly is a pivotal policy issue related to the impact of choice on public education, but we cannot yet offer any definitive conclusions.

If one issue concerns where choice is likely to exert impact, another concerns the kinds of responses that districts are likely to make. In the list above, we see an interesting range of responses. We make several observations about these reforms in the section on "innovation" below.

Ethos

Another element that appears to play a role in muting the response of districts to the new choice policies is associated with what we might term the administrative ethos – the shared beliefs, norms, and values held by American school administrators and school board members, as a function of their socialization, career paths, task requirements, reference group pressures, and related factors. The choice policies create opportunities for new forms of strategic interaction that blend competition with cooperative endeavors, yet relatively little activity of this sort has yet emerged. In our interviews, we detected several aspects of this ethos that appear to influence reactions to charter schools and choice. First, it appears that professional solidarity is maintained via social networks linking administrators. Any who break ranks by advocating for charter schools or proposing to establish them, or who aggressively recruit students from other districts will face social sanctions from their peers, ostracism, and potential loss of career mobility to other positions. Administrators exert peer pressure on one another to preserve the status quo and to maintain professional solidarity around defense of the public school system as currently constituted. The ethic constantly invoked in the interviews is cooperation. American schools preach the gospel of cooperation at all levels. Cooperative learning infuses myriad classrooms; teacher collegiality is regarded as a hallmark of positive school culture; parent-teacher cooperation along with school-community collaboration are first principles of effective schools. Within a professional culture suffused with the ethic of cooperation, a sudden turn to competition, to raiding nearby districts for students, is unlikely. The few exceptions that we uncovered tend to prove the rule, for the administrators who have broken ranks become high profile cases, cautionary tales for how not to behave.

Other normative elements also enter. Suburban superintendents express equity-related concerns for urban schools, and frown on any moves that would further weaken such schools. These concerns seem genuine to us, but it is important to recognize that they simultaneously reinforce the interests of suburban districts in maintaining class and racial separation of schooling and avoiding responsibility for addressing the needs of "hard to educate" students. Within the city district, the superintendent claimed allegiance to the long-standing court order to desegregate the schools, but noted a generational split within the African-American community. Older community leaders, whose formative experiences came from within the Civil Rights movement of the sixties, and the Brown-influenced decision to pursue racial integration through the schools, are ambivalent about choice policies that increase racial segregation of schools. Younger African-Americans, however, simply want good schools for their children; many now believe that all-Black schools may be the better alternative. Urban school administrators of a certain age have spent a good part of their careers working on school desegregation and integration within communities that are multi-cultural and multi-racial. Choice policy, however, creates new opportunities for segregated schools, not as imposed by white elites, but as chosen – and constructed – by ethnic and minority families. The administrative ethos appears to favor integration (at least within district boundaries) and a concern for equity that the new choice policies may threaten.

Less clear in our data is the emergence of new cooperative ventures as a competitive response to choice. For example, district consortia might join in creating specialized schools which draw across district boundaries, making sure that all the participating districts have one or more such schools so no district's enrollments are affected adversely. Arrangements of this sort have long been present in relation to specialized vocational and technical training at the secondary level, and some new developments along these lines have emerged via ISD-sponsored ventures. However, with respect to the core academic subjects of the K-12 schools, few new ventures have appeared. High transaction costs (and transportation costs) may explain the relative absence of such new arrangements, but the tradition of local control and the preference of communities for their own, neighborhood schools also helps explain the reluctance of administrators to exploit the new rules. As several superintendents pointed out, many communities in America enjoy athletic rivalries among local high schools that cathect fierce loyalties, that go back many years, and that provide community esprit. Creating new mixes of students in public schools, especially at the secondary level, disrupts these loyalties and rivalries, provoking strong opposition from local communities. Cultural factors such as these play a powerful, informal role in constraining joint ventures.

Finally, while the premise of our research is that changes in the policy environment of school districts will provoke adaptive responses evident in new forms of strategic interaction, our interviews uncovered an alternative interpretation made by administrators, that might be captured by the phrase, "this too shall pass." Rather than assuming that choice is here to stay and will exert ever-greater pressure on public schools, many administrators appear to assume that the new choice policies will be overturned in due time, and that the system eventually will "snap back into shape." Such a stance is also part of the administrative ethos in a democratically controlled school system that historically has been susceptible to ever-changing priorities and policies. Administrators learn early that one response to new rules and regulations is to hunker down, to ignore, deflect, and modify new mandates and programs in the interest of stability, to respond selectively to those policy initiatives that support the local, dominant coalition, while resisting other incursions from the policy environment. Consequently, rather than regarding the new school finance law and the accompanying choice policies as the dawn of a new era in state policy, administrators might decide to resist the changes, to wait for the next turn of the electoral cycle that will yield the next round of policy. Sentiments along these lines appeared frequently in the interviews.

The administrative ethos, then, functions as a constraining influence in responding to the imperative for change. Choice represents another in a long line of policy pressures that administrators have discretion in responding to. They will consult one another in calculating what response to make, how serious and long-term are the envisioned reforms, and how much they must do. Most of the administrators we interviewed have adopted a "wait and see" attitude, rather than launching major initiatives to take advantage of the new rules. This, however, may change over time.

Innovation

Another tenet of faith in the market is that choice will stimulate innovation on the supply side, as it responds to consumer preferences on the demand side. Our study raises questions about the kinds and the extent of innovative activity that emerge in response to choice. Here, a question asked by educational historians is pertinent: what reforms last? The historical record supports several generalizations. One is that reforms which are added onto the system (e.g., kindergarten), rather than seeking to change the system, tend to persist and to become part of "the system" (Cuban 1992a,b; Plank 1987; Tyack and Cuban 1995). Another is that reforms which coalesce powerful constituencies are more likely to last than those which fail to tap organized interests (Kirst and Meister 1985). And a third is that reforms at what organizational theorists refer to as the "technical core" of the enterprise are least likely to endure (Cuban 1993). For schooling, the technical core is composed of curriculum, instruction, and the assessment of learning.

These generalizations refer to past efforts to introduce innovations of various kinds into American public schools. At this early stage in our study, we see similarities with the innovations stimulated by choice. An innovation such as all-day, everyday kindergarten may be added onto the public schools without altering the fundamental operations of any existing schools. So too may districts add new organizational routines around marketing and advertising, without disturbing other routines. Conversely, we see relatively few innovations at the technical core, either in charter schools themselves or in regular public schools in response to competitive pressures supplied by charter schools.

Here we draw a contrast with the agenda of professional elites seeking to reform schools. The professional agenda in the US seeks fundamental changes in such matters as what counts as teaching and learning, the nature of knowledge and knowing, the distribution of knowledge within the school-age population, the structure of schools around such matters as time use, student grouping patterns, adult roles and responsibilities, and other reforms (Elmore, Peterson, and McCarthey 1996). The policy tools utilized by professional elites include new forms of student assessment, new curricular materials and standards, new instructional patterns and practices, intensified professional development for teachers, school restructuring plans of various kinds, and the like. The reforms stimulated by the new choice policies in Michigan appear much less likely to implicate these issues at the technical core of schooling. Instead, we see that many charter schools favor traditional forms of instruction, concentrate on basic skills, and inculcate traditional virtues in children associated with firm discipline and the safety-oriented concerns of parents.

This should not be a surprising result. If family and community preferences are to guide the nature of schooling in a marketplace where new schools must respond to the desires of their clients or consumers, then the conservative educational tendencies of many communities might be expected to emerge. Surveys in the US have uncovered a deep split between public and professional ideals for schooling, and many professionally driven reforms are now encountering a publicly organized backlash (Public Agenda 1994). The market for charter schools, then, may favor the desire for traditional forms of education over professional reforms that many parents neither understand nor trust. Under these cultural circumstances, we would not expect demand-driven choice to produce innovations. Rather, we might expect choice to reaffirm tradition against the incursions of new ideas and practices.

Several exceptions to this general finding are evident, however. Ethnic identity charter schools potentially involve deep changes in the technical core. In at least one of the Afro-centric schools in our study, the faculty is engaged in a thoroughgoing effort to define and to implement explicit principles of Afro-centric education that re-conceive the school's core curriculum and to a lesser extent instructional practice. And, the Edison school design represents a departure on many key dimensions from traditional schools, including the length of the school day and year, time allocations to subject matter, the uses of technology, student grouping practices, and others (Edison Project 1994). Edison also makes use of instructional reforms originating in the R&D community, including the "Success for All" program developed by researchers at the Johns Hopkins University. Charter schools, then, are free to import "professional" reforms but these do not appear dominant.

One other observation about the ecology of innovation is worth noting. The historical record in the US also indicates that elementary and middle schools have been far more open to reform than secondary schools, and this pattern is reflected in the charter school movement as well. Among the population of charter schools, the majority are relatively small schools that include a wide range of grade configurations, mostly at the elementary and middle levels of schooling. Again, this is not surprising. The relative costs and difficulties of starting a new high school are very high. Charter high schools for the most part are specialized around vocational and technical themes, often sponsored by business and corporate interests seeking to build a pool of future employees. The mainstream, comprehensive American high school, which itself was a unique innovation worldwide from the time of its inception, is not likely to face serious challenge from charter schools because of the cost and complexity involved in establishing schools able to offer a comparable array of programs and services. Innovation at this level of schooling is most unlikely to emerge in response to choice.

Whatever its other virtues, then, choice policy, at least as represented in our case, appears more likely to conserve fundamental aspects of schooling than to reform them. Neither the innovations that have appeared in charter schools nor the responses of regular public schools to competitive pressures have yielded fundamental reforms at the technical core of schooling. We hasten to add that this is not a criticism of choice as a policy theme. However, our tentative finding here casts doubt on certain arguments advanced by choice advocates about the power of competition to stimulate technical innovations in schooling. That likelihood appears quite low.

Conclusion

"Choice," as Chubb and Moe (1990) notoriously argued, "is a panacea." It promises solutions to a variety of educational problems, including problems of cost and efficiency, quality and effectiveness, and issues of diversity. It is consequently politically appealing to a wide variety of constituencies, while opposition to expanding choice remains fragmented and incoherent. In our view, therefore, the array of educational choices available to US parents is likely to continue to expand, with vouchers on the not-very-distant horizon in Michigan and other states.

Considered in terms of reform strategy, however, expanding opportunities for choice is a relatively weak intervention, for two main reasons. First, we have uncovered no evidence that providing parents with the opportunity to choose the schools their children attend brings about improvement in the quality of schooling that children receive. Choice enables parents to bring about a closer match between their own preferences about schooling and the values or pedagogical practices of the schools that their children attend, which is in itself a powerful argument in its favor. For now, however, the case that choice and the ensuing competition among schools will increase the efficiency and effectiveness of all schools at best remains open.

Second, "choice" is a profoundly conservative reform strategy in its failure to address the larger issues of social and economic context within which parents in fact make choices. In Michigan, as we have noted, and elsewhere in the US "choice" is primarily an urban reform, with the largest impact on urban school districts. Allowing urban parents to opt out of the failing schools that their children would otherwise be obliged to attend is certainly an advantage to them, as the generally favorable attitudes towards choice of poor and minority parents attest, but it is essential to recognize that the choices that these parents face remain strictly constrained. Desirable educational alternatives remain scarce, and unevenly distributed. Allowing parents to make choices does not in itself affect the array of choices available to them, and the most desirable choices may remain unattainable for reasons of transportation, distance, or exclusion. The continued freedom of schools and school districts to opt in or out of the choice system represents a powerful obstacle to social mobility through the education system.

Insofar as the problems that face poor and minority children originate outside the educational system, however, the effects of choice will be at best palliative. "Choice" promises marginal improvements in the quality of schooling provided to the least advantaged students, but it is virtually certain to leave them in the worst schools, even if these are slightly better than before, and to leave the inequalities that perpetuate their disadvantages intact. As with previous interventions targeted to schools serving poor and minority students, including Head Start and Title I, "choice" may make the worst schools somewhat better than before, but they will nevertheless remain the worst schools.

More generally, the current enthusiasm for educational choice strikes us as an instance of a broader effort to shift the responsibility for addressing deeply-rooted social and economic problems out of the public sphere. This is in part a strategy to reduce the power of the state relative to the power of private actors, both by disparaging the capacity of public institutions to solve public problems and by simultaneously depriving them of the resources that would be required to bring about significant improvement in their performance. It is also a strategy to avoid the obligation to confront the difficult issues associated with poverty and inequality by leaving the "solution" of these problems to the market. Considered in terms of educational policy, choice thus denies (and diminishes) the capacity of the state to address these issues, and promises to resolve them through the operation of the market without the need for sacrifice or structural change in the prevailing opportunity structure.

Acknowledgement

The research reported here was supported in part by a grant from the Spencer Foundation. The views expressed are the responsibility of the authors alone.

Notes

1. One of the interesting features of Proposal A is that capital funds continue to be collected at the local level, which perpetuates inequalities in facilities and access to technology across districts and introduces additional complexity into the strategic decisions that school districts must make with respect to their participation in inter-district choice (see below).
2. We are now exploring these differences with our colleague Amy Stuart Wells, from UCLA, who has written extensively on California charter schools. See her recent study (Wells 1998).
3. It is worth noting that many of the students who moved to the suburban district were residents of the city who previously attended *private* schools. They had already left the public system; interdistrict choice provided them with a low-cost alternative to private schooling rather than an alternative to urban public schools. Interdistrict choice in these cases increases the total number of students in the public school system, to the advantage of the receiving suburban district, but it does not increase the competitive pressure on the urban school district.

References

Addonizio, M. F., Kearney, C. P. and Prince, H. J. 1995. Michigan's High Wire Act. *Journal of Education Finance* (Winter): 235–269.

Angus, M. and Cuttance, P. 1998. The Impact of Public Policy on Diversity of Provision in Australian School Education. Paper presented to the Tenth Biennial Meeting of the World Congress of Comparative Education Societies, Cape Town.

Angus, M. 1998. *The Rules of School Reform*. London: Falmer Press.

Bryk, A. S., Lee, V. E. and Holland, P. B. 1993. *Catholic Schools and the Common Good*. Cambridge, Massachusetts: Harvard University Press.

Carnoy, M. and McEwan, P. 1998. Public Investments or Private Schools? A Reconstruction of Educational Improvements in Chile. Paper presented to the Tenth Biennial Meeting of the World Congress of Comparative Education Societies, Cape Town.

Chubb, J. and Moe, T. 1990. *Politics, Markets, and America's Schools*. Washington, DC: The Brookings Institution.

Coleman, J., Hoffer, T. and Kilgore, S. 1982. *High School Achievement: Public, Catholic, and Private Schools Compared*. New York: Basic Books.

Cookson, P. W. 1994. *School Choice: The Struggle for the Soul of American Education*. New Haven: Yale.

Cuban, L. 1992a. Why Reforms Last: The Case of the Junior High School. *American Educational Research Journal* 29: 227–251.

Cuban, L. 1992b. Why Some Reforms Last: The Case of the Kindergarten. *American Journal of Education* 100: 173–176; 166–194.

Cuban, L. 1993. *How Teachers Taught. Constancy and Change in American Classrooms, 1880–1990*, 2nd Edition. New York: Teachers College Press.

Daun, H. and Slenning, K. 1998. Equity and Introduction of Choice in Education. Case Study Results From Sweden. Paper presented to the tenth biennial meeting of the World Congress of Comparative Education Societies, Cape Town.

DeLany, B. and Paine, L. 1991. Shifting Patterns of Authority in Chinese Schools. *Comparative Education Review* 35 (February): 23–43.

The Edison Project. 1994. *School Design*. New York: Author.

Elmore, R., Peterson, P. and McCarthey, S. 1996. *Restructuring in the Classroom. Teaching, Learning, and School Organization*. San Francisco: Jossey Bass.

Fowler, F. 1997. School Choice Policy in France: Success and Limitations. In: Elchanan Cohn (ed.), *Market Approaches to Education: Vouchers and School Choice*. Oxford: Pergamon.

Fuller, B. and Elmore, R. 1996. *Who Chooses? Who Loses?* New York: Teachers College Press.

Glatter, R., Woods, P.A. and Bagley, C. 1997. *Choice & Diversity in Schooling: Perspectives and Prospects*. London: Routledge.

Henig, J. R. 1994. *Rethinking School Choice: Limits of the Market Metaphor*. Princeton: Princeton.

Hirschman, A. O. 1970. *Exit, Voice, and Loyalty: Responses to Decline in Firms, Organizations, and States*. Cambridge, Massachusetts: Harvard.

Kirst, M. and Meister, G. 1985. Turbulence in American Secondary Education: What Reforms Last? *Curriculum Inquiry* 15: 169–185.

Kozol, J. 1991. *Savage Inequalities: Children in America's Schools*. New York: Crown.

Labaree, D. F. 1997. *How to Succeed in School Without Really Learning: The Credentials Race in American Education*. New Haven, Connecticut: Yale.

Lee, C. J. 1998. The Politics of School Choice Issues in Korean Education. Paper presented to the Tenth Biennial Meeting of the World Congress of Comparative Education Societies, Cape Town.

Lowery, D. 1998. Consumer Sovereignty and Quasi-Market Failure. *Journal of Public Administration Research and Theory* 8: 137–172.

McDonough, K. 1998. Can the Liberal State Support Cultural Identity Schools? *American Journal of Education* 106: 463–499.

Meyer, J. W. and Rowan, B. 1977. Institutionalized Organizations: Formal Structure as Myth and Ceremony. *American Journal of Sociology* 83: 340–363.

Mintrom, M. 1997. Policy Entrepreneurs and the Diffusion of Innovation. *American Journal of Political Science* 41 (Winter): 738–770.

Mwiria, K. 1990. Kenya's Harambee Secondary School Movement: The Contributions of Public Policy. *Comparative Education Review* 34 (August): 350–368.

Myrdal, G. 1944. *An American Dilemma: The Negro Problem and Modern Democracy.* New York: Harper and Brothers.

Nathan, J. 1996. *Charter Schools: Creating Hope and Opportunity for American Education.* San Francisco: Jossey Bass.

Pampallis, J. (1998). The Reform of Schooling in Post-Apartheid South Africa: Issues of Choice, Democracy, and Equity. Paper presented to the Tenth Biennial Meeting of the World Congress of Comparative Education Societies, Cape Town.

Peterson, P. E. and Hassel, B. C. 1998. *Learning from School Choice.* Washington, DC: The Brookings Institution.

Plank, D. N. (1987). Why School Reform Doesn't Change Schools: Political and Organizational Perspectives. In: W. Boyd and C. Kerchner (eds.), *The Politics of Excellence and Choice: The First Annual Politics of Education Yearbook.* Philadelphia: Taylor and Francis.

Plank, D. N. (1996). *The Means of Our Salvation: Public Education in Brazil, 1930–1995.* Boulder: Westview.

Plank, D. N. and Boyd, W. L. 1994. Antipolitics, Education, and Institutional Choice: The Flight from Democracy. *American Educational Research Journal* 31 (Summer): 263–281.

Powell, W. and Dimaggio, P. 1991. *The New Institutionalism in Organizational Analysis.* Chicago: University of Chicago Press.

Public Agenda. 1994. *First Things First: What Americans Expect from the Public Schools.* New York: Author.

Rasell, E. and Rothstein, R. 1993. *School Choice: Examining the Evidence.* Washington, DC: Economic Policy Institute.

RPP International. 1998. *A National Study of Charter Schools: Second Year Report.* Washington, DC: US Department of Education.

Samoff, J. 1987. School Expansion in Tanzania: Private Initiatives and Public Policy. *Comparative Education Review* 31 (August): 333–360.

Sarason, S. B. 1998. *Charter Schools: Another Flawed Educational Reform?* New York: Teachers College.

Scott, W. R. 1995. *Institutions and Organizations.* Thousand Oaks, California: Sage.

416

Tatto, M. T. In press. Education Reform and State Power in Mexico. Accepted for publication by *Comparative Education Review*.

Tiebout, C. 1956. The Pure Theory of Local Expenditure. *Journal of Political Economy* 64: 416–424.

Tyack, D. and Cuban, L. 1995. *Tinkering Toward Utopia*. Cambridge, MA: Harvard University Press.

Vergari, S. (1995). School Finance Reform in the State of Michigan. *Journal of Education Finance* 21 (Fall): 254–270.

Wells, A. S. 1998. *Beyond the Rhetoric of Charter School Reform: A Study of Ten California School Districts*. Los Angeles: Graduate School of Education and Information Sciences, UCLA.

Whitty, G. (1997). Creating Quasi-Markets in Education: A Review of Recent Research on Parental Choice and School Autonomy in Three Countries. *Review of Research in Education* 22 (3–47). Washington: American Educational Research Association.

Whitty, G., Power, S. and Halpin, D. 1998. *Devolution & Choice in Education. The School, the State, and the Market*. Buckingham, UK: Open University Press.

World Bank (1997). *The State in a Changing World*. World Development Report 1997. Washington: IBRD.

The authors

Gary Sykes is Professor in the Departments of Educational Administration and Teacher Education, College of Education, Michigan State University. His primary research interests have focused on policy and practice related to the professionalization of teaching. In conjunction with this theme he helped launch the national Board for Professional Teaching Standards, served on the national staff of the Holmes Group, and has consulted broadly at international, national, and state levels. Currently, he is conducting and managing research on teacher professional development within the federally-funded National Partnership on Excellence and Accountability in Teaching; and working on several studies of school choice in the United States.

Contact address: Prof Gary Sykes, 410 Erickson Hall, Michigan State University, East Lansing, MI 48824-1034. E-mail: garys@msu.edu.

David N. Plank is Professor in the College of Education at Michigan State University, where he specializes in the fields of educational finance and educational policy. He has conducted research and served as a consultant in these areas in Africa, Latin America, and the United States. His most recent book is The Means of Our Salvation: Public Education in Brazil, 1930–1995. His current research focuses on school choice policies in Michigan and the US University of Botswana.

Contact address: Prof David Plank, 419 Erickson Hall, Michigan State Univeristy, East Lansing, MI 48824-1034, E-mail: dnplank@msu.edu.

GIRLS' EDUCATION IN ZAMBIA: EVERYONE'S RESPONSIBILITY – A POLICY FRAMEWORK FOR PARTICIPATORY PROCESS

CLAUDIA MITCHELL, MARILYN BLAESER, BARBARA CHILANGWA and
IRENE M. MAIMBOLWA-SINYANGWE

Abstract – This paper is based on a panel in which the four authors participated at the 10th World Congress of Comparative Education Societies in Cape Town in July 1998. The overall focus of the panel was on how an initiative to promote girls' education in Zambia – involving governments, NGOs, donor organizations, teachers and girls themselves – has influenced policy development to the point where the Zambian Ministry of Educaion now has clear directives on girls' education. The authors analyse some of the important factors that contributed to this outcome.

Zusammenfassung – Dieses Dokument basiert auf einem Podium, an dem die vier Autorinnen während des 10. World Congress of Comparative Education Societies in Kapstadt im Juli 1998 teilnahmen. Der Hauptpunkt dieses Podiums war die Frage, in welcher Weise eine Initiative zur Förderung der Ausbildung von Mädchen in Sambia – unter Beteiligung von Regierungen, Nicht-Regierungsorganisationen, Spender-organisationen, Lehrern sowie der Mädchen selbst – die politische Entwicklung dahingehend beeinflußt hat, daß Bildungsministerium von Sambia nun über klare Richtlinien für die Ausbildung von Mädchen verfügt. Die Autorinnen analysieren einige wichtige Faktoren, die zu diesem Ergebnis beigetragen haben.

Résumé – Cet article émane d'une table ronde à laquelle ont participé les quatre auteures dans le cadre du Xe Congrès mondial des sociétés d'éducation comparative, qui a eu lieu au Cap en juillet 1998. Ce colloque a présenté la démarche d'une initiative en faveur de l'éducation des filles en Zambie – impliquant gouvernements, ONG, organismes de financement, enseignantes ainsi que les élèves elles-mêmes – pour influencer l'élaboration de politiques, au point que le ministère zambien de l'éducation a maintenant émis des directives précises sur l'éducation des filles. Les auteures analysent plusieurs facteurs décisifs qui ont contribué à ce résultat.

Resumen – Este trabajo está basado en un panel del que los cuatro autores partici-paron durante el 10° Congreso Mundial de Sociedades Comparativas de la Educación celebrado en Ciudad del Cabo en julio de 1998. El tema central del panel ha sido la cuestión de cómo una iniciativa destinada a promover la educación de las niñas en Zambia – incluyendo gobiernos, ONGs, organizaciones patrocinadoras, docentes y las niñas mismas – han influenciado el desarrollo de la política hasta el punto de que el Ministro de Educación de Zambia tiene hoy directivas claras sobre la educación de las niñas. Los autores analizan algunos de los factores importantes que han contribuido a este resultado.

Резюме - Эта работа основана на дискуссионной группе, в которой четыре автора приняли участие на 10 Всемирном Конгрессе Сравнительных Образовательных Обществ в Кейптауне, в июле 1998 года. Главным вопросом дискуссионной группы было то, какое

International Review of Education – Internationale Zeitschrift für Erziehungswissenschaft – Revue Internationale de l'Education 45(5/6): 417–430, 1999.
© 1999 *Kluwer Academic Publishers. Printed in the Netherlands.*

влияние на развитие политики, где Министерство образования Замбии сейчас имеет ясные директивы по обучению девочек, имела инициатива по пропаганде обучения девочек, в которой приняло участие правительство, неправительственные организации, спонсоры, учителя и сами девочки. Авторы анализируют несколько важных факторов, которые привели к этим результатам.

> *"This business of womanhood is a heavy burden," she [my mother] said, "How could it not be? Aren't we the ones who bear children? When it is like that you can't just decide today I want to do this, tomorrow I want to do that, the next day I want to be educated! When there are sacrifices to be made, you are the one who has to make them. And these things are not easy; you have to start learning them early, from a very early age. The earlier the better so that it is easy later on. Easy! As if it ever got easy. And these days it is worse, with the poverty of blackness on one side and the weight of womanhood on the other"* (Dangarembga 1988: 16).

We use this excerpt from the beginning of the novel *Nervous Conditions* written by the Zimbabwe novelist Tsitsi Dangarembga as a "starting point" for this essay both for its obvious relevance to girl-child education in sub-Saharan African, but also as a reminder that work on girl-child education and policy development is about "real" girls like Tambu (girls with names), even if *Nervous Conditions* is "only" a novel. At the beginning of the story we meet the main character Tambu reflecting on her girlhood, when, but for the untimely and tragic death of her older brother, Nhamo, she would never have been allowed to attend school beyond the lower primary grades. Set in Zimbabwe at the time of pre-independence but told from Tambu's perspective some years later, the novel might be seen to be a "map" for an awareness of the challenges to girls' education in Africa. Through Tambu's memory, the reader travels back in time to examine the patriarchal structures that keep girls and women positioned in a subservient way. The book is important also because it allows us to see how various actors – male and female (mother, aunt, father, uncle, brother, best friend) and institutions (school and church) collude in their own oppression and the oppression of girls.

The story of how Tambu comes to be educated, is not just about her memories. Inspired by reading this novel, beginning teachers in a Zambian teachers' college reveal that this novel serves as a tool for engaging in some of their own time travel – "reflective mapping" – so that they are able to access their own memories of growing up male and female in a patriarchal society. Like Tambu, they work back through memory, starting with where they are now as students in a teachers' college.

> *I wish I could have been given a chance to be born a boy because by that maybe I would become someone in society. I believe I was born bright but alas time to study or concentrate was not given to me. I had to do all those dirty jobs when my*

boy cousin I stayed with was free to either study or play. This I feel has drawn me back to my present situation. As a wife I have no time to do the work I think I can do because of this and that responsibility. I wish I could change this attitude of men which says that the place of a woman is in the kitchen – with the woman being a source of cheap labour. (Journal excerpt, Stella, Student Teacher, David Livingstone Teachers' College, Zambia)

My mother was the first born of a family of nine. She always told us how she failed to continue her education to go onwards after Standard 6 because her father chose to educate the younger brother because he was a boy and he would be someone in society, whereas my mother just get married. The thing that I hate the most was that Mum told us that her brother was not a bright boy; he was a very slow learner compared to my mother so he did not progress on his own though support was given to him. My mother who was a fast learner was not given that chance to continue. (Journal excerpt, Christopher, student teacher, David Livingstone Teachers' College, Zambia)

I remember one evening my parents were discussing the careers that we would pursue. I've two elder sisters, one was supposed to be a nurse and the second one a teacher. Mum said something I did not get clearly, but my father's response was 'no! unless it was a boy! I was quite young then.' Dad's statement lingered in my mind for years. I worked hard trying to show Dad I could do what boys do. (Journal excerpt, Cristine, student teacher, David Livingstone Teachers' College).

Dangarembga's novel and the journal excerpts remind us that we need to try to hang on to, as much as possible, the whole story, if we are to understand and improve the conditions of girls living in southern Africa. Focusing on the Programme for the Advancement of Girls' Education (PAGE), an initiative of the Ministry of Education of the Government of Zambia, this essay represents our attempt to engage in a type of time travel in which we encapsulate something of the story concerning policy development and girls' education in Zambia. We use the term "reflective mapping" to describe this time travel, evoking both a conceptualization of policy formation (i.e., where does policy come from?), as well as a method for examining policy formation (working back through time).

Programme for the Advancement of Girls' Education and National Policy

As a starting point for our "reflective mapping", we begin with an overview of the Programme for the Advancement of Girls' Education (PAGE). We also identify some of the features of the conditions for girls in Zambia which have come about as a result of PAGE. PAGE is a Zambian Ministry of Education programme which seeks to improve girls' access to school, retention, completion and achievement through improved delivery of education and increased teacher and parental support to girls' learning experiences. The overall goals of PAGE are related to delivering quality basic education to all children, especially girls, and to reducing gender disparities within the educational system. One of the specific goals of PAGE is to engage actively those parties involved in girls' education in policy dialogue with the Ministry in order to influence policy development in the field of girls' education.

The programme started with a situation analysis of girl child education in the country (Kelly 1994). In the design phase, seminars and workshops were used to bring an understanding of the reasons why Zambian girls were not enrolling and participating in school. As much as possible, participatory processes such as VIPP (Visualization in Participatory Planning), focus groups, and other qualitative research methodologies were used to mobilize the emerging partnerships. Interestingly, in spite of the volumes of research carried out in Africa, there was at the time of the development of the project little which was unique to Zambia and which belonged to the community. A research agenda which followed (Mitchell 1994) identified areas for action-oriented research and as a result a number of studies were conducted. The dissemination process was probably the most important event in influencing policy dialogue. Dissemination events were organized at all levels, from the school to a national symposium and involving a variety of media and genres: seminars, workshops, community meetings, television, radio, skits, plays, videos, and campaign leaflets. Discussions about girls' participation in schooling and women's roles in society were becoming common topics at media events and community meetings. From this work and from broad-based stakeholder consultation, the programme was conceptualized. Implementation of the programme was phased in, beginning with a demonstration phase, not just as an experiment, but rather as a strategy for testing out specific interventions with a view to mainstreaming successful ones and for taking the programme to a national scale. Such strategies have included:

- Single sex classrooms for girls in upper primary school.
- FamilyPac (UNICEF 1996a), an initiative to involve parents in helping girls with homework (including ensuring that there is time to do homework).
- Implementation of a gender-across-the curriculum module entitled "The girl friendly school is the child friendly school" with teachers in PAGE pilot schools (UNICEF 1996b),
- Development of a gender-across-the curriculum module with preservice teachers.

The success of the pilot phase of PAGE has attracted donors who have pledged to provide funds for PAGE in four out of nine provinces in Zambia. The Basic Education Sub-Sector Investment Programme (BESSIP) also has amongst its priorities equity interventions, with PAGE having been identified as the programme through which these interventions will be channelled. Similarly, other reforms taking place in the Ministry have incorporated PAGE strategies. For example, the Zambia Teacher Education Reform Programme (ZATERP) has linked up with the gender-across-the curriculum component of PAGE.

What follows is a list of policy initiatives that have have altered the landscape for girls in Zambian schools over several years:

- Re-admission to school of girls expelled due to pregnancy (September 1997).
- The setting aside of 25% of the government student bursaries for female university students, with the remaining 75% to be competed for by male and female applicants (January 1997).
- Selection of an equal number of girls and boys to grades 8 and 10 as opposed to the previous "two girls for every three boys" at secondary level (January 1997).
- Making the wearing of uniforms optional – and thereby reducing some of the school costs (1995).
- Turning "boys-only" secondary schools into co-educational schools.
- Development of a gender module as part of the teacher preparation materials for all beginning teachers.
- Government has increased funding to education. The 1998 budget has allocated 19% of the total public expenditure to education, an increase of 8% over the average expenditure between 1990 and 1996.

One might ask, did the girls' education programme in Zambia emerge because of a policy? Or did the girls' education programme stimulate and influence the Ministry of Education's policy options? While the answer could be quite simply stated as "both," since senior Ministry officials were in the process of developing a new policy framework at the very same time that research studies on girls' education along with pilot studies in schools and teacher education were being carried out, it is worth noting that PAGE got started before the National Policy was completed. While it is beyond the scope of this essay to detail all of the actors, actions and events in the whole process, some key points are worth mentioning:

- Taking into account the need for increased women's participation in development and the slow performance of Zambia's economy in the early 1990s, the World Bank involved a number of Zambian researchers to produce the document *Engendering Sustainable Growth in Zambia: A Gender Strategy for Promoting Economic Effectiveness* (May 1994).
- As part of the preparatory process for the 4th UN World Conference on Women, held at Beijing in 1995, a task force was established to work on Zambia's contribution on gender to the African Statement for the conference. An NGO committee was also established to gather the views of citizens and NGOs to contribute to the Beijing NGO Shadow Report. The culminations of this work carried out by these groups led to a very influential statement by Zambia on the need for increased attention and support to be given to girls' education.
- In 1994–95 Zambia enacted a policy to establish a gender unit in the Cabinet and to appoint gender focal persons at ministerial levels.

During this time, donors and UN agencies were insisting on gender strategies and targets to be part of their bilateral and multilateral projects. Besides engaging in policy dialogue with government partners, donors provided support to projects to run gender and development (GAD) workshops, conduct gender analyses, develop gender-sensitive materials, and train a core group of gender experts. Thus, from various directions there were clear initiatives to spotlight the issue of gender sensitivity in Zambia in the mid 1990s.

The national education policy for Zambia is enshrined in a document entitled *Educating Our Future*, which was developed through a process of consultation and consensus-building between 1993 and 1996. Chapter seven of that document, entitled "Gender in Education", articulates the situation of girls and women with regard to education and training, discusses factors that affect enrolment, retention and performance of girls, and examines the participation of women in the management of the education system. The chapter also states the policy on gender and the strategies that the government will use to operationalize the policy statements.

From practice to policy

In engaging in "reflective mapping" in terms of the influences on policy formation on girls' education, we offer two examples of initiatives which have contributed to policy direction: impetus from NGOs, and pilot work on gender-across-the-curriculum in a teacher education program.

NGOs and girls' education

Well over a decade ago, following the Women's Conference in Nairobi, Kenya in 1985, women in Zambia started to seriously push for change. For example, they called for government attention to the issues of girls' and women's access to education. Enrolments of girls were far less than those of boys at all levels. At the primary level, girls made up only 42 per cent enrolment in 1985. The situation was worse at the higher levels even though women make up 51 per cent of the population. In 1987 women only formed 19 per cent of the graduating students. This proportion remained the same in 1992. The calls for equal participation of girls and boys influenced the decision by the Zambian government to introduce a lower cut-off point for girls to go on to grade eight. This has allowed more girls to go to secondary school than would have otherwise have been the case. NGOs such as the Zambia Association for Research and Development (ZARD) began to identify other practices which they considered discriminatory to girls. For example, there was a practice which permitted schools at the secondary level to have two boys admitted for every one girl. There were also many more secondary schools for boys than girls. The two national technical secondary schools were only open to boys. Although boys-only schools began to admit girls in 1992, it was questionable whether the conditions for learning were favourable for girls.

In 1996 an NGO, the Forum for African Women Educationalists, Zambia Chapter (FAWEZA), was established, which has a specific program that focuses on the education of girls. Some of FAWEZA's objectives include:

- invigorating political commitment to the Education For All (EFA) goals agreed upon at Jomtien in 1990, emphasizing that the two-thirds of eligible children not participating in education were girls;
- stimulating government, NGOs and others donors to increase their investments in education, and in girls' education in particular;
- assisting the development of national skills for the purpose of Strategic Resource Planning (SRP) for the education sector;
- using existing data to design high impact programmes that take into account the special needs of female students and teachers.

FAWEZA has already had an impact on Zambian society through its country-wide advocacy activities which encourage parents, communities and government to support girls' education. One direct influence on policy by FAWEZA took place in 1997 when the Ministry of Education made an announcement that it would no longer expel pregnant girls form a school but would instead allow them to return to school after they had delivered their babies. When the policy announcement was met with opposition from certain sectors of society, FAWEZA came out in full support of the policy as they too had been advocating the readmission of pregnant girls. To drive the point home, FAWEZA produced statistics to show the number of girls who were dropping out of school each year as a result of pregnancy. Since FAWEZA has membership from the school level to the policy level in the Ministry of Education, the implementation of the policy could proceed more smoothly than if the NGO did not exist.

Another NGO which has had direct influence on policy in affecting girls' education in Zambia is the Women and Law in Southern Africa Research Trust (WLSA), an action oriented research organization operating in seven countries in southern Africa (Botswana, Lesotho, Malawi, Mozambique, Swaziland, Zambia and Zimbabwe). Two of WLSA's objectives are to conduct research on gender issues in southern Africa, particularly those related to legal rights, and to provide information on gender and law in order to influence policy and law reform in each country. WLSA influenced the introduction of human rights in the school curriculum both at primary and secondary levels by working with the Curriculum Development Centre of the Ministry of Education, a government branch which FAWEZA has also worked with in terms of introducing life skills and gender into the curriculum.

Mapping backwards: A case study of gender across the curriculum in teacher development

An idea proposed by Shirley Miske and Diane VanBelle-Prouty (1997) of a "Gender-Based Approach to Planning" (GAP), suggests that effective policy planning emerges from a "bottom up" versus "top down" approach to curriculum change. As they observe:

> "A key aspect of the GAP is that policy development and decision-making are grounded in classroom practice. With a more traditional approach to policy development and implementation, efforts begin at the macro-level (national, district, state, and regional) and descend to the micro-level (community, school and classroom). This trickle down approach assumes that central government initiatives lead to changes at the district and school levels (p. 10)."

They describe this as "mapping backward," moving from the classroom to the administrative planning hierarchy. The key concepts underpinning this mapping, as Miske van Belle-Prouty point out, relate to being able to identify the desired changes and concomitant resources (both human and financial), which are capable of raising awareness and understanding of the need for change. This requires the identification of the mechanisms required to implement changes, and being able to recognize and promote the initiatives of those closest to the problem since they have the greatest potential to bring about meaningful change.

An example of this "mapping backwards" can be seen in relation to one of the specific initiatives in teacher education which by 1998 was becoming part of National Policy through ZATERP. That policy was aimed at pre-service teachers at all 11 teachers' college in Zambia who were to receive gender training as part of their overall preparation for teaching. The teachers whose journals we refer to in the first section participated in workshops in 1995 which led to the development of programming and policy around gender and teacher education. Indeed, the purpose of the workshop, appropriately named "curriculum-in-the-making," was to develop and conduct trials for a course on gender studies (Mitchell 1995). The journal data at the beginning of this essay reflect the kind of work that participants engaged in during the project. They became "reflective practitioners" – with both males and females engaging in a process of reflection over gender issues. In addition to reading excerpts from *Nervous Conditions*, they examined their own lives in relation to the question "if I had been born the opposite sex". But even more significantly they began to think about their roles as agents of change and how the lives of their own pupils could be different. In short they were exploring how they as teachers might "teach against the grain" (Cochran-Smith 1991; Simon 1992) by playing a role in bringing about that difference. (Casey 1993; Giroux 1992; Weiler 1988).

The idea of teachers as agents of change infused the pilot project from the very beginning. The course development started not with a group of teacher educators or administrators sitting in an office somewhere developing the course objectives and materials, but with the group made up of student teachers, college lecturers and facilitators all intently engaged in working out the details of a course – engaging "for real" in what Garth Boomer et al. (1983) would call "negotiating the curriculum".

In some ways, the account may sound like some sort of idealized view of teacher training. Students work with their lecturers to develop a course on gender studies and social change. They go through the course. They become sensitized to the plight of girls. They are empowered to act. They go into their practice-teaching placements. They "overturn" the curriculum. They bring about gender equity. In fact, of course, this is not quite what happens. While students (in this case only 20) go through a teacher training program where they come in contact with some new ideas, there are any number of limitations to the above model. Instructors themselves are just coming into contact with the ideas. Access to materials is not easy. Materials that are available are more often than not Western in content. *Nervous Conditions* is an exception. At the same time, some of the material, which is in the form of government reports or donor studies, may be too difficult since the students may have little training in reading through the statistical data for example. They may be highly committed to acting, but they also have many other courses and many other assignments. The may not quite "get" the link between the study of gender and a focus on girl child education since when they visit the schools for their practice teaching placement, there is no guarantee that they will be supported in their work. They may be sensitized but have few strategies for actually implementing the work. Moreover, they may have few strategies for "surviving" the resistance around them, as some of the students who had volunteered to be in the first pilot course pointed out. Taking the course as an extra-curricular activity as they did in the first year that it was offered, they recalled in an interview some months later the taunting criticism they had received. Even the instructors spoke about such barriers, noting that their colleagues sometime said things like "Why are you doing this? What is in it for you?" "Doing gender", students and instructors conclude "is hard work".

All of the above factors represent real barriers to teachers' colleges in southern Africa becoming havens of social change and gender studies. And yet, some two years following the pilot study (which later was replicated and refined in another teachers college), the new curriculum for teacher training in Zambia as it is currently being developed through ZATERP, includes adaptions of units developed in the original workshop: "becoming a reflective practitioner" and "teachers as agents of change".

But this notion of "mapping backwards" also has a great deal to say about how college lecturers might come to see their work. This was highlighted in a workshop at another teachers' college in which one of the lecturers from the original pilot project was discussing the nature of curriculum development. A lecturer asked him: "Didn't you get into trouble for deviating from the course of study?" The response: "We were the ones to start this. We [college lecturers] are so used to waiting until we are sent some sort of curriculum. But this was the opposite. We developed it right in our own college". Implied in his words is a particular ideology that challenges the idea that all change comes from above or that lecturers are only there to reproduce a particular form of knowledge. Indeed, it is this more transformative as opposed to a reproductive ideology that has now become integrated into the reforms taking place in the teachers' colleges. But implied in his words is also an ideology that characterizes college lecturers as agents of change. How can beginning teachers become agents of change if their lecturers are not similarly empowered to act? And how can they see themselves as operating beyond the walls of the school if their lecturers do not similarly participate in extending their work into a broader community?

Maps for moving forward

Throughout this essay we have included the word mapping in several terms: "reflective mapping," where we referred to working back through some of the influences on policy formation around girls' education; and "mapping backwards," where we borrowed the term used by Miske and vanBelle-Prouty (1997) to describe how curriculum reform on gender starts with practice. Maps can be useful for helping us see where we have been. What sometimes seems like random activity – diverse actors, actions and events – when mapped backward as "reflective mapping" – can help to identify key factors or critical incidents. For example, some of the key factors which have contributed to the development of National Policy on girls' education would include the following:

- *Commitments to girls' education made in regional and international fora*
  International conferences and bodies exert pressure on governments and institutions to develop policy. International fora such as the Jomtien EFA conference or Beijing, where countries come together and agree on a set of principles or conventions, are a good example of this phenomenon. Countries respond to these international initiatives by setting new goals for themselves, establishing new or different priorities, and amending current practices.

- *A critical mass of people who are themselves gender sensitive*
  While there is no clear consensus on what "gender sensitivity" means, anecdotal evidence, at least, suggests that people start with themselves and their own personal lives. We recall a workshop in which the four of us participated on qualitative research and "listening to the girl child" where one of the other participants, a male from a senior administrative position, went home and called all of his children together (boys and girls) to find out what they wanted to do in life. As he observed afterwards, it had never occurred to him until after the sessions on listening to children and "making the familiar unfamiliar" (Ely 1991) that his own children might actually be divided along the lines of gender in terms of career interests.

- *The voices of a wide range of stakeholders and partners working on a common agenda*
  Enlisting the support of the school and community, involving them in iden-

tifying the barriers and constraints to girls' education, and to empowering them to seek solutions is critical for sustainability. Involving senior officials, researchers, academics, politicians, traditional leaders, teachers and students, and especially the girls, is warranted if there is to be a lasting influence. As we noted in a previous section, several of the research studies exploring gender and schooling in Zambia conducted in 1994–95, *Listening to the girl-child* (Mwansa 1995), *Learning from the inside* (Maimbolwa-Sinyangwe and Chilangwa 1995), and *Curriculum-in-the making: Gender studies in teacher education* (Mitchell 1995) speak to the significance of all stakeholders having a voice in social change.

- *Communication plays a critical role in policy development*
  To ensure that institutions, stakeholders and local communities will implement the new or revised policy, policy makers must maintain an on-going dialogue about the purpose of the policy. Civil societies must be kept informed about the role of policy in national development. Interestingly, sometimes it is an arm of the government that makes this apparent. In the first half of 1998, for example, NGOs were summoned to appear before committees of parliament to explain how they wished to be supported by members of parliament in their various programs! As Miske and VanBelle-Prouty (1997: 10) observe:

    "A more dynamic and participatory process of policy dialogue and implementation defines policy formation as an ongoing process in which all stakeholders press for a particular vision of policy based on their interpretations of the needs of the education system - particularly those they identify at the school and classroom level . . . Policy initiatives driven by this school and classroom perspective use classroom practice and information from the school environment as the beginning point of decision-making."

In essence, the process of "reflective mapping" offers a reading on "best practices" in policy formation. Too often policy dialogue, frameworks and traditions are developed or controlled by a designated group or team whose task it is to deliver a policy document, a white paper or a set of directives. This body or team may be seen to be distant from the real work; sometimes they are cloistered in their institutions and are difficult to access. Often policy work, quite legitimately, is criticized for missing the mark, being irrelevant, too academic and unrelated to the field, the classrooms, the programmes or institutional practices. Policies can be inappropriate or restrictive and even contradictory rather than facilitative. They can have unintended consequences. They may exist but not be implemented. Having no policy may be better than having a bad policy (Evans 1995). Simply creating policy is not sufficient. As Lewin (1995) observes, the developing world is littered with educational reform proposals that either have not been seriously implemented, or that have been overtaken by events before their effects were apparent.

The PAGE model and its commitment to participatory processes is not unique. Projects all over the world claim to use participatory processes in their work. For PAGE, however, participation started at the very beginning of the programme development. This commitment to participatory process was extended into the implementation phase. The guiding principles of partnership, process, communication, campaigns, co-planning and monitoring were at the centre of the work of PAGE. An iterative model was developed, allowing for adjustments and revisions to take place. Many of the partners who were involved in the research, were also involved in the design and implementation phases. The Zambian experience with girls' education has demonstrated that through partnerships, and by working from the "bottom up", a number of interrelated issues connected with girls' education – access, retention, achievement and quality in education – can be addressed. In this way policy both influences and is influenced by the lives of real girls. The Zambian experience has also demonstrated that girls' education is everyone's responsibility. As with Tambu's life in *Nervous Conditions* – **that** is the whole story!

Acknowledgements

We acknowledge the contributions of UNICEF and the many Zambian scholars, governmental officials, teachers and students, and especially the girls who have participated directly in the development of PAGE and indirectly in the formation of National Policy. In this essay we are particularly grateful to the student teachers and lecturers at David Livingstone Teachers' College whose words we use in the essay. We thank Faith Butler who assisted in the preparation of this manuscript.

References

Boomer, G. et al. eds., 1983. *Negotiating the Curriculum: Learning in the 21st Century*. London: Falmer Press.

Casey, K. 1993. *I Answer with my Life: Life Histories of Women Teachers Working for Social Change*. New York: Routledge.

Cochran-Smith, M. 1991. Learning to Teach Against the Grain. *Harvard Educational Review* 61: 279–310.

Dangarembga, T. 1988. *Nervous Conditions*. London: The Women's Press.

Ely, M. 1991. *Doing Qualitative Research: Circles Within Circles*. London: The Falmer Press.

Evans, J. 1995. Creating a Shared Vision: How Policy Affects Early Childhood Care and Development. In: *The Coordinators' Notebook: An International Resource for Early Childhood Development*. Hardenville, MA: The Consultative Group.

Giroux, H. 1992. *Border Crossings: Cultural Workers and the Politics of Education*. New York: Routledge.

Kelly, M. J. 1994. *Below the Poverty Line in Education: A Situation Analysis of Girl Child Education in Zambia*. Lusaka, Zambia: UNICEF.

Lewin, K. M. 1995. Development of Policy and Science Education in South Africa: Reflections on Post-Fordism and Praxis. *Comparative Education* 31: 201–221.

Maimbolwa-Sinyangwe, I. and Chilangwa, B. 1995. *Learning from Inside the Classroom*. Lusaka, Zambia: UNICEF.

Ministry of Education. 1996, revised 1998. *Educating our Future: National Policy on Education*. Lusaka, Zambia.

Miske, S., and VanBelle-Prouty, D. 1997. *Schools are for Girls Too: Creating an Environment of Validation*. USAID Health and Human Resources Analysis for Africa Project. Technical report No. 41.

Mitchell, C. 1994. *A Research Agenda on the Girl Child*. Lusaka, Zambia: UNICEF.

Mitchell, C. 1995. *Curriculum-in-the-Making: Gender Studies and Social Change in Teacher Education*. Lusaka, Zambia: UNICEF.

Mwansa, D. 1995. *Listening to the Girl Child*. Lusaka, Zambia: UNICEF.

Simon, R. 1992. *Teaching Against the Grain: Texts for a Pedagogy of Possibility*. Toronto: OISE Press.

The Fourth United Nations World Conference on Women. 1995. *The Platform for Action: A Summary*. Beijing, China.

UNICEF. 1996a. *FamilyPac*. Lusaka, Zambia: UNICEF.

UNICEF. 1996b. *The Girl Friendly School is a Child Friendly School*. Lusaka, Zambia: UNICEF

Weiler, K. 1988. *Women Teaching for Change*. Boston: Bergin and Garvey Publishers.

World Bank. 1994. *Engendering Sustainable Growth in Zambia: A Gender Strategy for Promoting Economic Effectiveness*. Report No. 12472-ZA. Washington, DC: World Bank.

The authors

Claudia Mitchell is an Associate Professor in the Faculty of Education, McGill University, Montreal, Canada where she teaches and conducts research in the areas of childhood as a cultural space, literacy, gender issues and girl-child education, and gay and lesbian studies. She is the co-author, with Sandra Weber, of *Reinventing Ourselves as Teachers: Beyond Nostalgia* and *That's Funny, You Don't Look Like a Teacher: Interrogating Images of Identity in Popular Culture*. She is also the Director of the Canada South Africa Education Management Program, a partnership involving the National Department of Education of South Africa, the Canadian International Development Agency (CIDA) and McGill University.

Contact address: 3724 McTavish Duggan House, Montréal, Québec H3A 1Y2, Canada.

Marilyn Blaeser is a Senior Education Specialist at the Policy Branch of the Canadian International Development Agency (CIDA) where her work includes reviewing CIDA's work in the education sector and advising on policy development. Much of Ms Blaeser's work has involved the development of educational programmes and improved educational systems. While employed by UNICEF and UNHCR she worked with Ministries of Education from the developing world (Cote D'Ivoire, Sierra Leone, Pakistan, Nepal, Zambia) in seeking ways of increasing educational access for disenfranchised children, especially girls, school-leavers, and the increasing HIV/AIDS orphan population.

Contact address: Ms Marilyn Blaeser, Canadian International Development Agency (CIDA), 200, Promenade du Portage, Hull, Québec K1A 0G4, Canada.

Barbara Chilangwa is the Deputy Permanent Secretary (Technical Cooperation) at the Ministry of Education in Lusaka, Zambia. Her work entails responsibility for coordination of the Basic Education Sub-sector Investment Programme (BESSIP), Parliamentary liaison, and coordination of the Programme for the Advancement of Girls' Education (PAGE). She has conducted research related to girls' education in Zambia, and the training and utilisation of Teachers in Zambia. She is the chairperson for both the Forum for African Women Educationalists in Zambia (FAWEZA), and the Steering Committee for Female Education in Mathematics and Science (FEMSA). She is also a member ofthe Steering Committee of the Alliance for Community Action for Female Education.

Contact address: Barbara Chilangwa, Deputy Permanent Secretary, Ministry of Education, Technical Cooperation, P.O. Box 50093, Lusaka, Zambia.

Irene M. Maimbolwa-Sinyangwe is the Director of the Forum for African Women Educationalists in Zambia (FAWEZA), an NGO which is responsible for working with other partners on girls' education in Zambia. She teaches in the Gender Studies Unit and the Faculty of Education of the University of Zambia. She has been associated with the Ministry of Education's Programme for the Advancement of Girls' Education (PAGE) from the beginning of the project. Amongst her publications, she has co-authored with Barbara Chilangwa a PAGE study of gender in Zambian classrooms, *Learning from Inside the Classroom.*

Contact address: Irene M. Maimbolwa-Sinyangwe, Gender Studies Unit, School of Humanities and Social Sciences, University of Zambia, P.O. Box 32379, Lusaka, Zambia.

GENDER EQUITY IN SUCCESS AT SCHOOL

MARGARET B. SUTHERLAND

Abstract – Gender equity in education is seen as a logical consequence of recognising education as a basic human right. Concern is now being expressed in various countries about the relative lack of success of boys in school work. Reasons given for this situation are discussed. But in other countries, concern remains about the relative disadvantages of girls in school education. Reasons for this situation also are discussed. From these discussions certain common factors emerge: the importance of the employment situation, the attitudes of teachers, social pressures. It is asserted that there is a need for comparative studies to indicate whether gender equity in education is being achieved, and to investigate what factors may be impeding its success.

Zusammenfassung – Die Gleichberechtigung der Geschlechter in der Bildung wird als logische Konsequenz der Anerkennung der Bildung als Grundrecht der Menschen angesehen. Zur Zeit besteht in einigen Ländern Beunruhigung über den verhältnismäßig geringen schulischen Erfolg von Jungen. Die Gründe für diesen Zustand werden diskutiert. In anderen Ländern dagegen hält die Beunruhigung über die Benachteiligung von Mädchen in der schulischen Ausbildung an. Die Gründe für diesen Zustand werden ebenfalls diskutiert. Aus diesen Diskussionen ergeben sich einige generelle Faktoren: die Bedeutung der Arbeitsmarktlage, das Verhalten der Lehrer, sozialer Druck. Es wird behauptet, daß die Durchführung vergleichender Studien notwendig ist, um festzustellen, ob die Gleichberechtigung in der Bildung erreicht wird und um herauszufinden, welche Faktoren den Erfolg behindern.

Résumé – L'égalité des sexes dans l'éducation est tenue pour une conséquence logique de la reconnaissance de l'éducation aux droits fondamentaux de la personne. Divers pays expriment maintenant leur souci quant au manque relatif de réussite des garçons dans le travail scolaire. L'article analyse les raisons de cette situation. Dans d'autres pays, la préoccupation porte encore sur le désavantage relatif des filles dans l'éducation scolaire, et les causes de ce phénomène sont également étudiées. Il déduit de ces analyses plusieurs facteurs communs: l'importance de la situation de l'emploi, les comportements du corps enseignant et les pressions sociales. L'auteure souligne le besoin d'études comparatives pour établir si l'égalité des sexes est en cours de réalisation dans l'éducation, et détecter les facteurs susceptibles d'entraver sa progression.

Resumen – Se considera que la igualdad de los géneros en la educación es una consecuencia lógica del reconocimiento de la educación como uno de los derechos fundamentales. Ahora, en diversos países se está manifestando la preocupación por la relativa falta de éxito que tienen los varones en su tarea escolar, y se discuten las razones que originaron esa situación. A la vez, en otros países la preocupación sigue centrada en la relativa desventaja que sufren las niñas en la educación escolar, discutiéndose asimismo las razones que la originan. De estas discusiones emergen determinados factores comunes, tales como: la importancia que revisten la situación

 International Review of Education – Internationale Zeitschrift für Erziehungswissenschaft
– Revue Internationale de l'Education 45(5/6): 431–443, 1999.
© 1999 *Kluwer Academic Publishers. Printed in the Netherlands.*

de empleo, las actitudes de los docentes y las presiones sociales. Se impone la necesidad de realizar estudios comparativos a efectos de mostrar si se está alcanzando la igualdad de los géneros en la educación y de investigar cuáles son los factores que podrían estar impidiéndola.

Резюме - Равенство полов в образовании является логическим продолжением признания обучения как фундаментального права человека. Во многих странах в настоящее время высказывается озабоченность по поводу того, что мальчики в школах достигают относительно слабых результатов. Однако в других странах причиной озабоченности являются относительно неблагоприятные условия для девочек в школьном образовании. Также рассматриваются причины этой ситуации. Из этой дискуссии исходит целый ряд общих факторов: важность ситуации трудоустройства, позиция учителей и социальные рычаги. Утверждается, что необходимо проводить сравнительные исследования, чтобы установить, достигается ли равенство полов в образовании, и установить, какие факторы могут этому препятствовать.

Since the right to education is recognised as a basic human right, it seems to follow that females and males should profit equally from education. Yet for centuries there was little concern as to whether both males and females profited equally by education. It was regarded as natural that males should receive more formal schooling than females, and even when school education became compulsory for both gender groups in the majority of countries, it was not, initially, a matter for anxiety that females, over all, achieved less in the way of educational qualifications. Then, in Western countries especially, came the decades in which concern was expressed about girls' relatively disadvantaged situation and efforts were made to get more females through upper secondary education into higher education, and particularly into the study of maths and science. But, more recently still, there has developed a strong body of opinion which regards *boys* as disadvantaged in their school careers: evidence has indicated that girls have been more successful in exams at the end of upper secondary schooling – and in earlier stages of schooling: so progress towards gender equity is said to require efforts to help *boys* to achieve better school results. It would be good to interpret the difference between the former calm acceptance of girls' lower achievement in specific fields and the agitation now shown when boys seem at a disadvantage as proof of a universal advance in gender awareness. But this is perhaps being over optimistic.

What action is in fact required if gender equity in school attainment is to be achieved? To answer this question, we have to look at the situation not only in our own country but in a variety of countries. From the point of view of students of comparative education, it is saddening to find that in so many countries discussion of gender differences is restricted to what is happening within the country's own educational system: generalisations are made about characteristics of males and females without consideration of what is happening in other countries. Yet comparative studies can show which hypotheses about gender differences and their causes may be tenable and which are simply incompatible with facts revealed by an international view.

Disadvantaged boys

In a number of countries, it is currently asserted that it is *boys* who need rescuing from a disadvantaged situation in school. Are boys in fact succeeding less well? For some time there has indeed been evidence of girls' higher achievement in some educational systems. An OECD publication of 1986 showed that in various OECD countries girls were surpassing boys in *general* upper secondary education. In Scotland at that time girls had already been achieving more highly in upper secondary education for some years; more boys than girls were leaving at the end of compulsory education with no school certificate (Sutherland 1988). In England, better School Certificate performance by girls was noted from 1988 and may well have been present earlier (OFSTED/EOC 1996). More recent reports of National Literacy tests in England show a widening gap between the achievements of 11-year-old boys and girls in reading and writing (Pyke 1998). In France since the 1970s more girls than boys have been achieving the baccalauréat. (Cacouault M. and Œuvrard F. 1995). In Germany it is reported that girls obtain better school marks than boys, repeat classes less often, and gain school leaving certificates more successfully (Bundesministerium 1998). Japanese girls have become slightly more likely than boys to proceed to upper secondary education (Kameda 1995). Recent Australian statistics (Page 1996) have shown similar advantages in girls' school successes. In Jamaica, for 20 years now, there has been concern about "the low academic achievement of boys in relation to that of girls" (Evans 1998).

While such differences do raise questions, we must still note that the differences in achievement are not always very great – and vary from subject to subject. It has also been pointed out in England that male candidates are more likely than female candidates to achieve very high scores in A-level exams (OFSTED/EOC 1996). In higher education after school, while women in most of the developed countries enter universities in equal percentages to men (sometimes even in slightly greater percentages than men – though in Japan they tend to go to less prestigious, shorter courses in higher education), in many countries women's superior school performances do not always lead on to better, or even equal, performance at higher levels. For instance, in many countries fewer women than men achieve doctorates (Lie, Malik and Harris

1994). In England there is much debate about the greater frequency of men gaining First Class Honours degrees in the Universities of Oxford and Cambridge (admittedly, men also tend to gain more Thirds).

Reasons adduced for boys' less good performances

Discarding initially the hypothesis that boys simply are inferior (though the hypothesis that girls are inferior is not always so lightly cast aside) let us review reasons which are being currently put forward to explain why boys may perform less satisfactorily in school.

(1) In England it is often suggested that methods of assessing school work have been changed and the new methods give credit to the kind of work in which girls perform better – especially when credit is given for course work rather than one-off exams. But the discrepancy between boys' and girls' success has been found in countries where the examination system has remained unchanged, and even in England it has been found (OFSTED/EOC 1996) that changes leading to greater or lesser amounts of course work did not really affect girls' superiority.

Nevertheless, it is worthwhile to remember that methods of assessment may appeal differently to males and females. For example, there has been evidence to suggest that males perform better than females on multiple-choice tests. In the USA, while males do better on SAT (Scholastic Assessment Test) Maths, women do not later gain lower scores on the differently assessed college maths courses (Valian 1998). Similarly, it has been suggested that women's lower ranking in Oxford and Cambridge Honours results may be affected by examiners' choice of criteria which favour a more "masculine", less cautious style of writing. It is therefore always important to check, as some authorities do, whether the format or type of questions used in an exam are gender-biased.

(2) Much recent discussion in Britain has suggested that the unemployment situation causes male detachment from school work. There are indeed some areas of the country where the prospects for young men are gloomy enough to seem to justify the belief that there is no advantage in working hard at school. This problem of youth unemployment has indeed been recognised throughout Europe. While having better educational qualifications does help employment prospects in some respects, the relationship is clearer for those over the age of 25 (European Commission 1996), and young males at school are unlikely to be impressed by such information. They are more conscious of the fate of those immediately surrounding them. Girls, it has been suggested, at least have the alternative employment prospects given by pregnancy and child care; but for European countries generally, the employment prospects for young women have been rather less good than for young men (European Commission 1996).

Yet, in considering objective information about employment prospects, we have to remember that the situation may well be interpreted differently by the two gender groups, males possibly regarding paid employment as essential to their masculine identity ('man as bread-winner'), while females – though they have in recent decades become much more vocationally-oriented – may still attach rather less weight to having paid employment outside the home. It is also true that in most countries the employment situation varies greatly from one part of the country to another, so the employment prospects cannot be regarded as a factor equally affecting all members of a gender group within a country. And employment prospects differ from one country to another. In Jamaica "males need less education than females to make the same salary" so motivation dependent on employment prospects varies for the two groups (Evans 1998). Social class expectations also vary considerably – as do the employment prospects of young people of different social class backgrounds. (The influence of social class on school attainment has been noted in many countries, even if national differences in defining social classes make international comparisons difficult: in general, evidence indicates an association of higher social class with good attainment in schools (Duru-Bellat 1996).) We have also to recall that in some countries there is, additionally, the important effect of social caste (Ruele 1998).

(3) A popular argument is that boys suffer from an excess of teaching by women, since it is said – women's attitudes to behaviour and learning differ from those of men. This latter premise is questionable, as research at various times has indicated that individuals adopt a variety of teaching styles (Bennett 1976; Galton et al. 1980), so no style can be designated as exclusively masculine or feminine. But it is true that in primary schools in most countries of the Western world women teachers are in a considerable majority (see UNESCO Statistical Yearbooks). Less good performance by boys has often been found to begin at primary school level – 70 per cent of calls recently received by a Literacy Hotline in England showed parents being mainly concerned about boys' progress in literacy (Ghouri 1998): similar differentiation in primary school success has been noted in France (Cacoualt and Œuvrard 1995). While evidence about the relative amount of attention given to boys by both male and female teachers is conflicting, there is no suggestion that boys receive *less* attention than girls. And although it is true that women have made up the majority of teachers in primary schools for very many decades, it is only in comparatively recent times that anxieties about boys' performance have been expressed.

We may also ask whether the qualities of being careful, working neatly, paying attention – the qualities which are said to be alien to boys when this nefarious influence of women teachers is exercised – are not desirable qualities. Surely both gender groups should have the opportunity to cultivate them?

(4) A further explanation of boys' weaker performance, related to the feminisation of the teaching profession, is the absence of "role models". It is asserted that boys need men teachers to provide the models of masculine behaviour and characteristics that may be lacking in their home lives in an

era when, in many countries, divorce is common and women tend to be given custody of children when a marriage comes to an end. It may of course be queried whether the divorced woman always remains without men in her life. But more important is the question of what is meant by "role model". Is this a recurrence of sex stereotypes under a more acceptable name? (A rather worrying interpretation of such an argument was given by a teacher in Finland, who, at an international conference, suggested that possibly men teachers' greater opportunities of promotion in the teaching career should be accepted, since it could encourage more men – as role models – to remain in the profession.)

(5) Other arguments suggest that it is not only a question of adult role models but peer group models. Willingness to work hard in school is said to be seen by boys as feminine, "cissy". Some evidence of such reactions has indeed been found, for instance, in England (Power et al. 1997) and in Jamaica (Evans 1998). Such reactions may admittedly change as pupils become older. It is also not clear whether verbal behaviour corresponds to real behaviour (the policy of pretending not to work, while secretly getting on with it, is well known). It could also be suggested that rejection of work as "cissy" is a cover-up for awareness of weakness or failure?

But there is widely expressed concern about the concept of masculine identity which boys may be forming in different societies. The complexities of integrating the information boys obtain from their surroundings vary from the problem of violence endemic in some societies, violence suffered by boys (Morrell 1998), to boys' attempted comprehension of girls' attitudes (Pattman 1998).

(6) Identity conceptualisation must depend on the culture of the home and the neighbourhood. But again it is probable that such cultural influences will differ in different parts of a country and according to the parents' background. In the UK, findings about the good school performance of children from some ethnic Asiatic families – boys as well as girls – would seem to show the effect of a "work ethic" favoured by the home and not encouraging boys to take life easily at school. Parental values, and attitudes to education, do count.

We have thus a variety of explanations offered for what is seen to be the inferior situation of boys in school achievement in different countries. But we cannot conclude that gender equity calls for remedial action on behalf of boys alone. Looking at other countries we easily find evidence that girls also remain "disadvantaged" in school achievement in some educational systems. We have to consider the causes alleged for this other aspect of gender equity.

Disadvantaged girls

Figures for illiteracy (e.g. UNESCO 1994) show that females in most regions of the world are more likely to be illiterate than males. There are many countries in Asia and Africa where girls' school performance and indeed their participation in school education is clearly inferior to that of boys. It is widely recognised that some educational systems, despite determined efforts by governments, have difficulties, even at the primary phase, in getting equal proportions of girls into school, and in preventing them from dropping out of education prematurely.

A survey of the "Situation of Girls' Education in Anglophone Africa" (Zewide 1994) stated that with a few exceptions (Botswana and Namibia) "women are under-represented in primary, secondary and tertiary levels of education." That survey noted that some research had indicated poorer work by girls in almost all subjects (except English Literature) in O-level exams in Botswana, Zambia, Kenya. Other studies cited, referring to primary level achievement, also seemed to indicate lower achievement by girls generally (though not in Mauritius, where girls' scores were higher than boys'). At the same time, it is to be noted that more recent data from South Africa have indicated girls' level of school participation as higher than that of boys, and their success rates at a comparable level (Morrell 1998). Reports of widespread disadvantage for girls in school education have come also from Frenchspeaking African countries (Lallez 1997).

So, when remedial action is proposed, it should be remembered that in some parts of the world it is not only a question of equity in school achievement but of equity in access to school.

The reasons adduced for girls' lower participation and lower achievement, their repetition of classes, their more frequent drop-outs, show some interesting similarities with those presented in other countries for boys' lower achievements.

Reasons adduced for girls' disadvantages

(1) There is the problem of employment prospects. Lallez (1997) has pointed out the low representation of women in sectors of the economy where they should be expected to play an important part. They are poorly represented at the top levels of management. Recent economic readjustments have worsened the employment situation of women in Benin and Senegal, where disproportionate percentages of women have lost their jobs during this retrenchment. Similarly Tiendrebeogo (1994) noted the "small size of the market for salaried employment in general and for women in particular . . . There is a serious shortage of openings for salaried employment for women. Given such a situation, sending a girl to school can appear to be a waste of time." In these cases, it is not a matter of female pupils themselves finding schoolwork not worth the effort, as boys may do in economically more favoured countries, but a matter of the costs for parents in sending their children to school. Further, since the numbers of women who reach higher education are small, girls' role models of professional women are few: the range of well-paid, highprestige occupations open to women is restricted.

(2) There is the question again of the influence of teachers. Girls at secondary school level may have problems with male teachers' attitudes and behaviours (Gordon 1998). Male teachers have been accused in some cases of lack of sympathy for female pupils. More seriously there are in some regions "the very high rape and sexual harassment rates in school" (Morrell 1998). Adolescent girls, facing hostile or sexually domineering male teachers, may choose a policy of remaining inconspicuous, and apparently unsuccessful, in the school situation (Cabral 1998). The situation is all the more difficult since there are in some African countries insufficient numbers of well-qualified women teachers (Colclough 1994, Walker et al. 1998) .

(3) Social pressures are commonly cited as operating against girls' progress in school. There is the burden of domestic tasks which girls are traditionally expected to cope with – these drain away time and energy needed for study. There is also the over-arching traditional view that domestic work, marriage and child-care are the appropriate life for females. Traditional initiations of girls as they reach adolescence may provide an alternative education (Lengoiboni 1998) which does not reinforce the importance of formal schooling, even if in some cases it offers an important contribution in preparing for adult life (Walker et al. 1998). There may also remain the traditional belief that girls are less intelligent than boys – and girls' failure to progress in school may be taken as justification for this belief.

(4) Allied to parents' traditional expectations for their daughters is the fear that when daughters move away from parental supervision in order to attend school, they will become pregnant (Gordon 1998; Walker et al. 1998). The risk of pregnancy is in fact real: many girls drop out from school, or may be compelled by official regulations, as in Zimbabwe until 1997, and in some other countries, to leave school when they become pregnant, without the possibility of re-entering (Gordon 1998) – even if, occasionally, girls of higher social class may be enabled to surmount this problem (Njau and Wamahiu 1994). (On the other hand, it has been pointed out that in some cases a family might see a teacher as a desirable son-in-law and so be less worried about male teachers' interests in female pupils.)

(5) Peer-group influences have been little studied, so far as the views of other girls are concerned. But some reports have been made of hostile or denigrating attitudes expressed by boys who are fellow-pupils. Here too, violence and sexual harassment may be a problem for girls.

A historical perspective

But before accepting the view that there is a considerable gulf between the situation of girls in "developed" countries and their relatively disadvantaged situation in other countries, it is useful to include a historical perspective. So far as employment is concerned, we find for most Western countries that it is only in comparatively recent times that the range of occupations open to educated women has extended and, more recently still, that their access to the upper levels of any occupation has improved. Role models of successful women executives or even professors still remain relatively scarce.

So far as the teaching profession is concerned, we must also recall that in many Western countries during the first half of the twentieth century there was a marriage bar which meant that women had to give up their teaching posts when they married, and similar bars operated in other occupations, notably the civil service. This inevitably affected the role models available for girls – the stereotype of the spinster woman teacher is still alive, even if long outmoded – though it did not always have the intended results of preserving men's place in the teaching profession (Adams 1990).

As to teachers' attitudes and their effects on pupils, there seems little evidence of sexual harassment of girls by teachers in Western schools in times past, but there are still indications of unhelpful attitudes on the part of male teachers when girls choose to study traditionally male subjects. Girls opting for technical, engineering subjects in school or in further and higher education have reported discouraging or plainly hostile attitudes on the part of some men teachers. And sexual harassment by male pupils has been reported from some schools (Mahony 1985).

As for social pressures, the gender stereotyping of roles in the family is still alive in many Western societies, even if it has been attacked and reduced in recent decades. The continuing provision of education for schoolgirls who become pregnant still causes problems for some educational administrations in some "developed" countries. And the 1923 Board of Education Committee in England and Wales, reporting on the *Differentiation of the Curriculum for Boys and Girls in Secondary Schools*, commented on the danger of girls' energies being exhausted by their home duties to the "detriment" of girls' intellectual development. The domestic duties of the English schoolgirl early in this century may have been rather less exhausting than those of some of her African peers today, but they too were no aid to her advancement in study.

Peer-group attitudes of the past have been less intensively studied. Fictional school stories would certainly suggest that for both girls and boys the designation of "swot" was to be avoided and more recent studies have indicated that for some girls being seen as "brainy" involves social rejection and suggestions of lack of femininity. – Oddly enough, working hard and excelling at sport does not seem to have provoked the same generally adverse reaction in peer groups, even if a few pupil groups may have regarded this with some disdain.

Conclusions

The need for a greater awareness of the need for gender equity issues in education is now widely accepted in different educational systems. The concern is that one gender group or the other may be receiving unfair treatment, though we may opine that – to adapt the Orwellian dictum – both groups suffer from inequity but one is more unequal than the other. The inequity may lie in access to education at different levels or in failure to respond as effectively as the other gender group to what is offered in schools. But from our survey of alleged causes of girls' and boys' disadvantages in schools in different parts of the world, we find that certain common factors emerge. These are

(a) employment prospects related to levels of education
(b) the composition and attitudes of the teaching staff
(c) the attitudes of parents and society
(d) the attitudes of peer groups.

We note also that such factors may exert different influences in different parts of a country: regional differences show varying amounts of school success (Ndimurukundo 1997; Walker et al. 1998). We have further to keep in mind that change is common to educational systems, so that present-day differences may have emerged mainly because one system has evolved in a different historical mode from another or that change was more rapid in one context than another. Or there may be economic or social reasons for the differences. Whatever the cause it is widely recognised that there is a need for governmental effort to introduce greater gender equity in education. Encouragingly, there is already some evidence of this, for example, the analysis of text-books in Kenya (Abagi 1998), community studies in rural areas of Mozambique (Walker et al. 1998), South Africa's Gender Equity Task Team (Morrell 1998): progress has also been made by many projects in Australia, the United States, Canada, as well as by the work of the Equal Opportunities Commission in the United Kingdom. It is commendable too that in many cases such projects are designed for the improvement of the lot of *both* gender groups.

Education authorities should obviously realise not only the implications of the employment situation for adults, old and young, but also its complex interactions with young people's response to schools – though certainly governments and teachers must also keep in mind that education is not simply vocational preparation but has more important intrinsic values.

Most obviously, if gender equity is to be achieved in education, it is essential to have a well-educated teaching force, fair-minded, including women and men equally. Such teachers may ensure the development of unprejudiced attitudes among pupils, eliminating all forms of peer-group harassment. And development of this kind in the schools may gradually lead also to the improvement of attitudes in society generally. Naïve comparisons between the achievements of the two gender groups are probably undesirable, when we consider how many other variables – region of a country, social class, caste, ethnic and home backgrounds – affect the achievement of both boys and girls. Yet in the present stage of development, such gender grouping seems inevitable.

Finally, further comparative studies of similarities and differences will produce better awareness of the situation within each country and in other countries, and so protect politicians, educators, psychologists – and, if possible, parents also – against the influence of extremists of either gender, or of facile generalisations, based on highly publicised but anomalous cases. So gender equity, and other equities, may eventually be achieved.

References

Abagi, O. 1998. Engendering school curricula for social transformation: research, policy and practice from Kenya's experience. Paper presented to the Gender Commission, WCCES Congress, Cape Town.

Adams, C. 1990. Divide and Rule: The Marriage Ban 1918–1945. In: F. M. S.Paterson and J. Fewell, eds., *Girls in Their Prime* (89–108). Edinburgh: Scottish Academic Press.

Bennett, N. 1976. *Teaching Styles and Pupil Progress.* London: Open Books.

Board of Education. 1923. Report of the Consultative Committee on *Differentiation of the Curriculum for Boys and Girls in Secondary Schools.* London: HMSO.

Bundesministerium für Familie, Senioren, Frauen und Jugend. 1998. *Frauen in der Bundesrepublik Deutschland.* Bonn: Bundesministerium.

Cabral, Z. 1998. Issues in girls' education in Mozambique. Paper presented to the Gender Commission, WCCES Congress, Cape Town.

Cacouault, M. and Œuvrard, F. 1995. *Sociologie de l'Education.* Paris: Editions La Découverte.

Colclough, C. 1994. *Under-enrolment and Low Quality in African Primary Schooling: Towards a Gender-sensitive Solution.* Nairobi: FAWE Working Papers Series No. 6.

Duru-Bellat, M. 1996. Family Socialization Processes and Pupils' Academic Success and Adaptation. Paper presented to the Comparative and International Education Society Conference, Williamsburg.

Evans, H. 1998. Gender differences in education in Jamaica. Paper presented to the Gender Commission, WCCES Congress, Cape Town.

European Commission. 1996. *Employment in Europe.* Luxembourg, Directorate – General for Employment, Industrial Relations and Social Affairs.

Galton, M.,Simon, B. and Croll, P. 1980. *Inside the Primary Classroom.* London: Routledge & Kegan Paul.

Ghouri, N. 1998. Boys Focus of Literacy Hotline. London: *The Times Educational Supplement* (8) 20 Feb.

Gordon, R. and Cleghorn, A. 1998. The effects and meaning of Economic Structural Adjustment (ESAP) in the lives and education of girls and women in Zimbabwe. Paper presented to the Gender Commission, WCCES Congress, Cape Town.

Kameda, A. 1995. Sexism and Gender Stereotyping in Schools. In: K. Fujimura-Fanselow, A. Kameda, eds., *Japanese Women* (107–124). New York: The Feminist Press at the City University of New York.

Lallez, R. 1997. *La prise en compte de la diversité filles-garçons par les institutions éducatives de l'Afrique Subsaharienne francophone.* Louvain-la-Neuve: Colloque de l'Association Francophone d'Education Comparée.

Lie, S., Malik, L. and Harris, D. eds. 1994. *The Gender Gap in Higher Education*. London: Kogan Page Ltd.

Mahony, P. 1985. *Schools for the Boys? Coeducation reassessed*. London: Hutchinson.

Morrell, R. 1998. Policy, reality and masculinity in South African education: current reflections. Paper presented to the Gender Commission, WCCES Congress, Cape Town.

Ndimurukundo, N. 1997. Vers une scolarisation totale des filles au Burundi. Draft statement.

Njau,W. and Wamahiu, S. P. 1994. *Ministerial Consultation on School Drop-out and Adolescent Pregnancy*. Nairobi: FAWE, Working Papers Series No. 7.

OECD. 1986. *Girls and Women in Education*. Paris: OECD.

OFSTED (Office for Standards in Education), EOC (Equal Opportunities Commission). 1996. *The Gender Divide: Performance Differences between Boys and Girls at School*. London: HMSO.

Page, C. 1996. The new framework for gender equity in education in Australia. Paper presented to the Gender Commission, WCCES Congress, Sydney.

Pattman, R. 1998. "Boys have a heart but they don't think that much" – investigating how 11-14 year old boys in London identify themselves. Paper presented to the Gender Commission, WCCES Congress, Cape Town.

Power, S., Whitty, G., Edwards, T. and Wigfall, V. 1997. Schoolboys and Schoolwork: Gender Identification and Academic Achievement. *International Journal of Inclusive Education* 2(2), 135–153.

Pyke, N. 1998. Boys will still lag in literacy stakes. London: *The Times Educational Supplement*: 27 Nov 5.

Ruele, M. A. 1998. Gender, ethnicity and equity in Botswana out of class education. A case for Basarwa women. Paper presented to the Gender Commission, WCCES Congress, Cape Town.

Sutherland, M. B. 1988. Research and Change in the Education of Girls and Women in Scotland. In: S. Brown and R. Wake, eds., *Education in Transition* (35–46). Edinburgh: Scottish Council for Research in Education.

Tiendrebeogo, A. 1994. *General Overview of Girls' Education in Africa*. Nairobi: FAWE, Working Paper Series No.10.

UNESCO 1994. *Basic Education, Population and Development: Status and Trends*. Paris: UNESCO.

Valian, V. 1998. *Why So Slow? The Advancement of Women*. USA: Massachusetts Institute of Technology.

Walker, B., Martins, A., Uamusse, D., Sabino, H., Wachave, F. and Nhantumbo, L. 1998. Gender and Basic Education in Mozambique: Community Strategies in the Rural Areas. Paper presented to the Gender Commission, WCCES Congress, Cape Town.

Zewide, G. 1994. *The Situation of Girls' Education in Anglophone Africa*. Nairobi: FAWE, Working Paper Series No. 5.

The author

Margaret B. Sutherland, Emeritus Professor of Education at University of Leeds, UK, is a Fellow of the Scottish Council for Research in Education, an Honorary Member of the Comparative Education Society in Europe, Past President of AFEC (Association Francophone d'Education Comparée). In books and articles she has published extensively on the subject of the education of girls and women, and she has chaired or co-chaired the Gender Commission at various WCCES congresses.

Contact address: Professor Margaret B. Sutherland, 46 The Scores, St. Andrews KY16 9AS, Scotland, UK. E-mail: m.b.sutherland@dundee.ac.uk.

THEORETICAL PERSPECTIVES ON GENDER IN EDUCATION: THE CASE OF EASTERN AND SOUTHERN AFRICA

CHANGU MANNATHOKO

Abstract – In recent years, throughout Eastern and Southern Africa, there has been a proliferation of research on gender in education. It is possible to point to a wide variety of publications, courses and programmes planned and organized by universities, national governments, international organizations, non-governmental organizations and the private sector relating to this field. This article examines the feminist and gender theories underpinning all these endeavors. The theories are assessed for their potential capacity to assist in elucidating the complex relationship between gender and development within the region.

Zusammenfassung – Während der letzten Jahre wurde die Forschung bezüglich geschlechtsspezifischer Fragen auf dem Gebiet der Bildung in Ost- und Südafrika erheblich ausgeweitet. Es ist möglich, auf eine Vielzahl von Publikationen, Kursen und Programmen, die von Universitäten, nationalen Regierungen, internationalen Organisationen, Nicht-Regierungsorganisationen und dem nationalen privaten Sektor für diesen Bereich geplant und durchgeführt wurden, zu verweisen. Dieser Artikel untersucht die feministischen und geschlechtsspezifischen Theorien, die diese Bestrebungen unterstützen. Die Theorien werden bezüglich ihrer potentiellen Möglichkeiten untersucht, bei der Klärung der komplexen Beziehung zwischen den Geschlechtern und der Entwicklung innerhalb der Region behilflich zu sein.

Résumé – Ces dernières années, on assiste en Afrique orientale et australe à une prolifération d'études scientifiques sur les questions d'égalité des sexes dans l'éducation. On peut énumérer une accumulation de publications, de cours et de programmes préparés et réalisés par des universités, des gouvernements nationaux, des organismes internationaux, des organisations non gouvernementales et des entités du secteur privé actives dans ce domaine. Cet article analyse les théories féministe et paritaire sur lesquelles reposent tous ces efforts. Il évalue ces théories par rapport à leur contribution potentielle à clarifier la relation complexe entre égalité des sexes et développement dans cette région du monde.

Resumen – Durante los últimos años, a lo largo de Africa Oriental y del Sur ha tenido lugar una proliferación de la investigación sobre los géneros en la educación. Se puede hacer referencia a una gran variedad de publicaciones, cursos y programas proyectados y organizados por universidades, gobiernos nacionales, organizaciones internacionales, organizaciones no gubernamentales y el sector privado, relacionados con esta temática. Este artículo examina las teorías feministas y de géneros, corroborando todos esos esfuerzos. Estas teorías serán evaluadas en cuanto a su capacidad potencial de contribuir a dilucidar la compleja relación que existe entre el papel de los géneros y el desarrollo en esta región.

International Review of Education – Internationale Zeitschrift für Erziehungswissenschaft – Revue Internationale de l'Education **45**(5/6): 445–460, 1999.
© 1999 *Kluwer Academic Publishers. Printed in the Netherlands.*

Резюме - В последние годы в восточной и южной Африке расширилось изучение фактора пола в процессе образования. В этой области можно указать широкий спектр публикаций, курсов и программ, запланированных и организованных университетами, правительствами разных стран, международными организациями, негосударственными организациями и частным сектором. В статье рассматриваются теория феминизма и теория пола, которые стоят за этими усилиями. Эти теории рассматриваются с точки зрения их потенциальной способности пролить свет на сложные отношения между полами и развитием в регионе.

This aim of this paper is to examine the relationship between gender theories and education in Eastern and Southern Africa. It will begin by discussing why it is important to promote discourse on the different gender paradigms and how the theories and perspectives within these paradigms are connected to education. The paper will then identify three gender perspectives which will be the focus of the paper, namely the notions of *difference*, *inequality* and *oppression*. A selection of education research studies from the region will be used to describe and examine the gender theories or perspectives "generously" by assessing each on its own terms, against its own understanding of knowledge, power, truth, practice, difference, inequality or domination. This will then permit an assessment of the theories (as analytical tools) for their potential capacity to assist in narrating and unravelling the complex relationship between gender, education and development within the region. Lastly, it will be argued that the United Nations Beijing Platform of Action (1995) challenges education researchers to design and implement education strategies that institutionalize gender equitable development (UNO 1995: 1–4). The empowerment perspective is emerging as an indigenous approach aimed at transforming gender relations and analysing of gender injustices prevalent in the gender order and education gender regimes.

The importance of promoting discourse on the different gender paradigms

Throughout Eastern and Southern Africa, feminism and its gender theories are evolving strongly in the analysis of gender relations – within the context of educational research. There is a wide variety of gender in education courses, research studies and programmes planned and organized by universities, national governments, international organizations, non-governmental organizations and the private sector. However, the gender theories underpinning these education development efforts are inadequately analysed. Throughout the region feminist and gender researchers working in the realm of education either consciously or unconsciously use one or several gender theories in our research methodology and writing up of gender research studies. However, there is inadequate discussion of why and how we use these theories. It is essential to interrogate the gender theories underpinning the conceptualization of education and training in all these endeavors. The presupposition of this paper is that the merits and demerits of each theory are being decided on the ground in the everyday experiences of women and men as they interact in the education arena. It is the process of these interactions which decides the relevance, and analytical power of a theory. The varied feminist perspectives applied in the case studies, will be deconstructed to assess the analytical strengths of their frameworks in explaining and describing the problems under investigation. This gender analysis will hopefully assist understanding of the usage of appropriate feminist theories in studies done throughout the region.

Discussions of gender theories in the context of education and training can enable feminists, activists, educators and policy makers to unpack some of the contradictions and tensions that arise as women and men interact. It is these gender concepts and theories that describe and explain why and how education is gendered and how the gendering of education and training leads to gender injustices.

The discourse on application of gender theories to education also demonstrates that feminism has its roots in the African condition (Mannathoko 1992; Meena 1992: 4–5). Women in this continent have always been aware of the prevailing oppressive gender relations that subordinate them. Throughout history, African women have challenged these oppressive gender relations in a variety of ways (Mafela 1993; Mahlase 1997). It is incorrect to view feminism as a western ideology reflecting western culture. Feminism just like other social theories (such as Marxism), has emerged as a result of the complex interrelations between indigenous cultures and external factors such as colonialism and imperialism. The economic might of the North versus the South has to be taken into account in these considerations.

Inequality theories

Theories which focus on inequality explanations describe women's situation in terms of liberal feminism's view of unequal opportunity structures and Marxist explanations of women's position as part of a complex class system of exploitation both in terms of gender and social class (Lengermann and Niebrugge-Brantley 1992). Liberal feminism's explanation of gender inequality begins with the pinpointing of the sexual division of labour and the prevalence of separate private and public spheres of social activity. Women's primary location is seen to be in the private sphere and men's in the public sphere, and the socialization of children is viewed as a preparation for their adult roles and work in the spheres appropriate for their sex (Dorsey et al. 1990; Nyati-Ramahabo 1992). To them the private sphere is composed of an endless round of tedious, senseless, unpaid and undervalued activities linked to child rearing, housework and support of adult men. In contrast, it is in the public sphere that the true rewards of social life are to be found – status, power, money, freedom, self-esteem and personal development.

There is an abundance of education studies within the region which have used liberal feminism to describe and explain the prevalent inequalities in the education system (Gordon 1994; Nyati-Ramahobo 1992; Wamahiu et al. 1996). In 1990 the University of Zimbabwe and the Ford Foundation sponsored a research project on factors affecting academic careers for women at the University of Zimbabwe (Dorsey et al. 1990). The focus of the study was the problem of the under-representation of women on the academic staff of the university. Their study established that there was indeed an under-representation of women in academia. For instance women represented 21 per cent of the academic staff, which was an increase of a mere 4 per cent over a period of ten years (1980–1990).

Women were concentrated in lower academic ranks and were little involved in decision making committees and academic administration. What was worrying was the low academic productivity of women. Academic women published less often than the men. Dorsey et al. use feminist theories of liberal feminism and socialization to explain why academic women at their university are marginalized and powerless. They also propose strategies for change. They use socialization theory to explain that the status of women academics is lower than that of men because of gender stereotypes prevalent in society. They provide examples of masculine and feminist stereotypes which perceive men as dominant and women as subordinate in the public sphere.

Gender inequality is created by a system that restricts women's access to the public sphere by burdening and isolating them with private sphere responsibilities. They view sexism as similar to racism because it is characterized by prejudices and discriminatory practices against women. Further, the ideology of sexism sustains beliefs about the biological differences between men and women that account for their different social fortunes. Sexism is responsible for the social restrictions and confining of females from childhood so that they mature into adulthood as helpless, mindless and dependent beings. The liberals perceive nothing of value in the private sphere, with the exception of its promotion of emotional openness. Its major focus is the denial of equal rights to women, equal rights with a specific focus on equal access to education, health and employment. Discrimination against women is specifically connected to prejudice against them. Prejudice is often linked to sexist attitudes which sustain the situation of subordination of women.

Education studies conducted throughout the region demonstrate that educational stereotyping is contributing to the marginalization of women (Duncan 1989; Motlotle 1989; Mbilinyi et al. 1991). In Botswana, Kenya and Tanzania the above researchers among others have identified gender stereotyping in subjects such as science, social studies, English, and Setswana. For instance pictures in senior secondary science textbooks reinforce the image that natural science careers such as medicine, engineering and geology are for men.

An example of a gender theory of inequality

Kenya: Access of girls to science education & vocational training

"Women have made remarkable contribution to the national economy and socio-cultural life of the society all over the world. However, gender imbalance is still evident in most of the African countries Kenya included. . . . The trend of education since Kenya's independence in 1963 has shown a lot of progress with numbers of learning and training institutions increasing to meet the demands for education. For example, primary school enrolment has increased from 1 million in 1983 to 2.5 millions in 1988 and 5 millions in 1996. . . . Generally decline in school enrolment is still more pronounced among girls (Abagi and Wamahiu 1997). Among those enrolled it is also noted that most girls do not enrole in mathematics, sciences and vocational training. Those who enrole also lag behind boys in boys in their performance" (Tumuti 1997: 5).

Throughout the region liberal feminists in the field of education have contributed immensely to the critique of conventional policy priorities in state education. A case in point in countries such as Botswana is the emphasis they have placed on the provision of day-care centers for children who are not yet of school age. From the 1960s to this day, women's NGOs throughout the region (for example Botswana Council of Women and YWCA) have provided day care centers for young children. This service releases women to find employment outside the home. Liberal feminism should not be underestimated in the Southern Africa region because it was the power of liberal principles such as individualism, equality, modernization, development and democracy that gave women's organizations the strength to fight for the rights of women to have access to education, formal employment, and to provide day care centers for working women (Mannathoko 1992; Bitamazire 1996).

Development in Southern Africa has components within it that are based on liberal feminism. For example, education studies maintain that gender inequalities limit female access and retention in certain education fields (Marope 1992; Juma 1996; Kadzamira 1996). Education for girls and women is thus considered as an investment with probably higher economic returns than that of boys and men. In both Botswana and Lesotho there are more women than men in literacy classes (Government of Botswana 1997). This is a historical trend that can be traced to the colonial era in the region when men from throughout the region went to work in South African mines as migrant laborers. In the South African mines these men were not exposed to literacy education but on returning home were not prepared to attend literacy classes with women because of their gender stereotypes. To them it was embarrassing for them to attend literacy classes with women because it would expose their ignorance to the women and fellow men.

Liberalism is often criticized for its inability to address deep-rooted gender inequities and the interdependencies between gender and other indicators of equity such as ethnicity and social class. The approach has limitations in regard to the analysis of the social structuring of gender inequities.

Contemporary Marxist feminism's standpoint brings together Marxist class analysis and feminist social protest. Yet the result is a muted statement of gender inequality rather than an intensified theory of oppression. Marxist feminists maintain that the quality of each individual's life experiences is a reflection first, of a person's class position and only second, or the person being male or female (Gaidzanwa 1992). Therefore in contemporary capitalist class system, gender relations are buried within the more fundamental structure of the class system. Women are unequal to men not because of gender issues but because of matters linked to social class oppression. The consequences of giving priority to social class and race first and gender last have been detrimental to black women during the liberation struggle in Namibia, South Africa and Zimbabwe. Anecdotal and historical evidence emerging shows that some of the women freedom fighters were sexually harassed and abused by their fellow male freedom fighters and they suffered in silence because the women concurred with the political movements which argued that political liberation first and other issues such as violence against women will be confronted once the countries were liberated (Open University 1992). To dogmatic Marxist feminists gender inequalities will only be destroyed when class divisions are destroyed. The most important aspect of criticism of Marxist feminism is its emphasis on social class division and capitalism in the oppression of women, and its failure to give adequate or equal space to issues of patriarchy.

One shortcoming of inequality theories is the focus on access and equality of opportunity. Findings from research carried out on the education of females in the region suggest that increasing their access to education does not guarantee the improvement of the quality of their lives. It is theories of difference such as institutional socialization and social psychology that indicate that gender-based discriminatory practices in institutions such as the family and the school need to be addressed in order to improve the status of women and girl-children.

The theories of difference

Theories that perceive women's situation as basically different from men's explain that difference in terms of bio-social conditioning, institutional socialization, social-psychological linkages and third-wave feminism (Lengermann and Niebrugge-Brantley 1992). Conservative biological explanations of gender differences, traced the different personality structures of men and women to their different physical bodies, and different cognitive and affective processes (Connell 1987). The fundamental assumption of biological differences theories is that the physiological make-up of human bodies is the foundation of the social relations of gender. These theories maintain that biology determines gender and society reflects what nature determines. Freud traced the beginning of the biological differences to children's discovery of their physiological differences. Though Freud's method paved the way for one of the most radical social analyses of sex and gender, he ultimately believed in biological determinism.

Examples of theories of gender difference which have some impact in the Southern Africa region are those focusing on institutional socialization and social psychology. Institutional socialization theory or sex role theory, just like bio-social differences theories, also emphasizes women's distinctive functions in childbearing and rearing. At the same time this manner of theorizing about gender shifts away from biological assumptions about sex differences. Instead, it emphasizes the different behaviors between men and women as they respond to social expectations. The most fruitful research motivated by role theory investigated how these social expectations are defined in the mass media and in school curricula (Duncan 1989; Motlotle 1989). The main message of research studies within this paradigm is that gender discrimination is a social fact. Studies of the girl-child in Kenya (Wamahiu et al. 1996) demonstrate that discriminatory practices depress the status of woman. Socialization of girl-children and boy-children in the home, school and community at large has a major impact on the children's education. The research informs us that the girl-child has the status of a visitor in her parents' home which she will leave when she gets married. Other researchers report the negative attitudes of male and female teachers to the education of the girl-child and women particularly at secondary school and tertiary levels (Taole 1996; Fuller et al. 1994). Most sex role theory is based on analysis of normative values, instead aiming at the exposure of problems in social interaction. In that light its limitations include:

a) inability to theorize power and social interest;
b) dependence on biological determinism and non social perception of structure;
c) dependence on attitudes and systematic misinterpretation of resistance; and
d) inability to theorize the historical nature of gender.

However, the strengths in sex role theory lie in its productive research on stereotypes of femininity and masculinity – the analysis of sex roles as social constructs, cultural ideals, curriculum contents and media images.

Two examples of studies using the difference paradigm

A study on the Girl-Child in Botswana: educational constraints and prospects (Nyati-Ramahobo 1996: 5)

An in depth comparison of the boy and the girl-child with regard to educational opportunities was conducted at three levels; the household, the community and the school. The study was carried out in one rural area (Mmankgodi village) and one urban centre (Gaborone).

The study established that the socialisation process is one of the major constraints impacting on the girl-child's participation in education. This process starts in the family and continues in the schools and the society at large. In the Setswana culture like many other African cultures, right from birth children are socialised to accept different roles. In this culture a newly born baby boy signifies inheritance and perpetuation of the family lineage. Associated with this is power and identity associated with the father. On the other hand a girl signifies a care-taker in the home from here own both the verbal and non-verbal behaviour of both parents continue to perpetuate this stereotype.

Botswana female youth: perception of sexuality and risk-taking behaviours (Seboni 1997: 15)

Female teenagers' sexuality is embedded in relationships with the significant others. It is an everyday experience that is influenced by micro and macro environmental factors. They experienced both healthy and risky sexual behaviours. Healthy teenage sexuality is experienced through struggle and negotiations with themselves and those around them. The respondents were found to uphold certain values and they expressed several sexual concerns. Their understanding of their sexual self concept is strongly influenced by cultural constructions of womanhood.

Socio-psychoanalytical approaches within this paradigm such as that of Seboni (1997) are used to tease out issues of sexuality. These include asking how the female psyche is conditioned by patriarchal culture and politics to cushion and take care of men (Seboni 1997). It assists researchers to explore individual women's and men's emotions when the status quo is threatened. It goes further to explore taboos round intimate critical discussions of issues directly linked to individual men-women relationships. Mosimakoko-Mosalakgoko (1997) takes this perspective further in her study of Gender Differences and the Self-concept. In her study she notes that there have been numerous studies on gender differences in the performance of boys and girls in Botswana (Juma

1996; Kadzamira 1996; Mosimakolo-Mosalakgoko 1997). However, none of these studies focus on how the individual's "self" is a factor in the performance gap between the girl-child and the boy-child. Her study focused on gender differences in Botswana Junior Secondary School students' perceptions of their self-concept. The study identified significant differences in the way male and female students perceived their self-concept. Male students in urban areas were tolerant as they viewed female students as equally able in the science subjects; in contrast, the male students in the villages had gender stereotypical attitudes towards girls in line with the gender differentiation in society.

Theories of gender oppression

Theories of gender oppression describe women's condition as the result of a direct power relationship between men and women – in which men, effectively implement those interests which reinforce their control, use subjugation and oppression on women. The theories of gender oppression reviewed below are radical feminism and socialist feminism.

Radical feminism perceives all society as oppressive to women, every institution is a vehicle by which men dominate women resulting in gender oppression. They perceive gender oppression as a system of patriarchy, to them patriarchy is the least noticed and yet most important structure of inequality (Measor and Sykes 1992).

The radical feminists are concerned with investigating how patriarchy spreads its web in society. For instance, in schools males dominate females in classrooms which has a negative impact on females' life chances. Therefore males are viewed as a major (not sole) source of the problems that females encounter in schools. Radical feminists also investigate the sexual harassment of females in society. Mahony's research argues that boys concentrate a lot of their time in school on the control of girls (Mahoney 1985). These researchers hold that boys have power to reduce girls' chances of success.

An Example of a study using theories of oppression

South Africa: The careers of women teachers under apartheid (Mahlase 1997: 1, 169)

This study was prompted by a desire to discover what it is like to be a woman teacher working in male-dominated institutions within a racist society. . . . I had observed as a teacher trainer, that attitudes towards women teachers were affected by cultural traditions (i.e. contemporary notions of women's role); and they my lack of political rights as a worker, "confined" to a "Bantustan" system, affected my career planning. There is no study in South Africa which has taken such an "African" female perspective.

This research has shown how class, "race" and gender were interwoven within the South African context. In this context class and gender boundaries were artificially manipulated and imbalanced by racial laws.

The feminist approach I used gave black women a voice and in this way, we now have some insight into how women teachers constructed meaning for themselves in their public and private lives. Notwithstanding the constraints within which the research was conducted, my investigations have, I hope, contributed to an understanding of the experiences of black women in the teaching profession: the ways in which gender and apartheid had framed their perception of their work and their lives, the conditions in which they taught and the structure of their careers.

Radical feminism has brought the issues of sexuality, patriarchy, reproduction, and children's socialization into the forefront of human rights. It has moved the debate away from matters of status, work and public life (Measor and Sikes 1992).

Socialist feminism aims to unite the two most valuable feminist traditions, namely Marxist and radical feminist thought. Capitalist patriarchy and domination are terms used to describe the multi dimensional system of oppression based on patterns of production, class, gender, ethnicity and global situation. There are educational researchers in the region who apply socialist feminism to the study of social inequities in schools.

An example of a study using theories of oppression

Botswana: Politics of gender in teacher education curriculum and pedagogy (Mannathoko 1995: 270)

The concepts of modernity, individualism, gender, power and injustice featured prominently in the social studies lessons I observed across the board, be it a secondary school or primary level college. Time and again during lessons, teachers and lecturers never followed up issues of a gender nature which undergird the knowledge discussed during the lesson. Since the 1980s there has been substantial research and information documented on gender and schooling (Kann 1984; Duncan 1989; Davies 1990; Nyathi-Ramahobo 1992; and Mafela 1993; Fuller, Hua and Synder 1994). Yet, the social studies lectures I observed in the schools and colleges had not incorporated this recent information. The result was that women and girls' lives remained invisible throughout the lessons taught. The discussion on education should have exposed students to knowledge on the gender disparities within education. For example, historical information on how and why at independence (1966), there were more girls than boys in primary schools (Parsons 1984 and Kann 1986). How by 1980, there were more female primary school teachers than male ones (Parsons 1984 and Nyathi-Ramahobo 1992).

More significantly for the students in the all female college, it would certainly have stimulated their reflexivity to discuss and analyse reasons for the large increase in the numbers of females in primary level colleges. Which would require them to discuss the concomitant massive drop in the enrolment of males, leading to the turning of their college into an all female institution in 1973 (refer to the historical background section, chapter 4). Nothing was done to intellectually stimulate students to probe into the reasons for the historically entrenched gender disparities throughout the education system.

Domination describes all forms of social oppression using knowledge of gender and class hierarchies as a foundation to the exploration of all forms of oppression centering on gender, social class, race, age, sexuality and location within the global hierarchy of nations.

The emerging empowerment perspective

What is exciting about the empowerment perspective in the education arena is the capacity of feminist educators to take advantage of pertinent theories of inequality, difference and oppression to develop a conceptual framework that provides for the empowerment of women. The perspective is responsive to the Beijing Platform of Action's (1996) call for action within the arena of education and training. In this paper empowerment is conceptualized as a concept composed of three critical dimensions: *power-within*, *power-with* and *power over*. Power-within focuses on strategies that build the psychological, emotional and intellectual strengths of the disadvantaged girl-child or woman. It aims to provide a conducive cultural milieu for an individual's self-development (Mosimakoko-Mosalakgoko 1997). Power-over describes the legal power of a person in authority and also the authoritarian patriarchal type of power based on male domination.

Power-with encourages cooperation and team work within a marginalized social group aimed at the facilitation of the group empowerment of a marginalized group of females. Mahlase's study of the Careers of Women Teachers Under Apartheid (1995) provides illustrations of power-with among black women teachers working in Apartheid South Africa. The collective coping strategies narrated by teachers in the study were applied both in their schools and communities. These women teachers had a pivotal role to play in the shaping of their local communities. Women teachers were engaged in local women organizations such as Black Housewives League, Ratanang Burial Society and Parents Teachers Associations. These organizations were used to address the needs of poor rural school children and invest in the future education of their children. As Mahlase astutely notes, the indigenous Pedi culture provided the women teachers with strength to cope with wider social issues within their black communities. These research findings are a breath of fresh air because they break away from the deficit view of blacks and women as defenseless, vulnerable and passive reactors to oppression without the capacity for active proactive initiatives that address the oppression. The author effectively and graphically captures, describes and analyses the lives and stories of black women teachers in apartheid South Africa. She has opened a window into an area of research where there is a dearth of information.

The perspective has been further enriched by post-structuralism. Post-structuralist feminism (Kenway 1993; Kenway and Willis et al. 1998) is used especially to investigate women's and girls' powerlessness and silence in classrooms, men's power and domination of interactions in education institutions through speech. Women's voicelessness in education settings such as classrooms and staffrooms is viewed as a confirmation of these sites as arenas that only support those activities that reinforce women's acceptance of patriarchal ideology. Empowerment then would facilitate discourse among women as a collective force and between men and women as unequal stakeholders.

Post-structuralism challenges the everyday lives women have learnt to negotiate. The theory challenges teachers and pupils to interrogate their politics and critique the cultures in their workplaces. It is difficult and at times painful emotional work for both students and teachers. The empowerment perspective can only become transformative if it takes cognizance of the danger posed by patriarchal violence in the everyday existence and livelihood of women.

Concluding remarks

This paper began by conceptualizing feminism in the region. The paper argues that feminism has its roots in the region and dismisses arguments which consider feminism as alien. The research studies carried out in the field of education illustrate that women's oppression has been located in the pre-colonial African society, in the colonial system, in the neo-colonial nature of the Southern Africa nation states, and in the patriarchal ideologies of the now independent Southern African nation states.

The heterogeneity of gender theories in educational research is reflective of the way different individuals have visualized women's oppression, and the diversities in the planning of the research methodologies, conduct of research and implementation of strategies that can liberate women from oppressive gender relations. Feminist research in the region is blending viewpoints from the three paradigms and emerging with an analysis which has the capacity to empower women. All feminist theories have limitations which educational researchers have to be cautious of. For instance, both liberal and radical theories ignore social class disparities within education. Female children from peasant and working class families face a more difficult school life than those children from middle class and ruling class families.

References

Abagi, O., Wamahiu, S. and Owino, W. 1997. *Abridged Research Report on Household Based Factors as Determinants of School Participation of Girls in Kenya.* Nairobi: Academy of Science Publishers.

Bitamazire, G. N. 1996. A Study of Occupational Activity of Female Primary School Leavers in Five Selected Villages in Pigi District. In Educational Research Network in Eastern and Southern Africa (ERNESA), *Educational Research Information for Practitioners* (38–40). Gaborone: ERNESA.

Chilisa, B. 1987. *Who Gets Ahead in Education: A Cross-Sectional Survey of Primary, Secondary and University Students from Mochudi.* Unpublished M.Ed. Dissertation, University of Botswana.

Connell, R. W. 1987. *Gender and Power: Society, the Person and Sexual Politics.* Sydney: Allen and Unwin.

Davies, L. 1990. *Equity and Efficiency School Management in an International Context.* London: Falmer Press.

Davies, L. and Gunawardena, C. 1992. *Women and Men in Educational Management: An International Inquiry.* Paris: International Institute of Educational Planning, UNESCO.

Davison, J. and Kanyuka, M. 1992. Girls' Participation in Basic Education in Southern Malawi. *Comparative Education Review* 36(4): 446–466.

Dorsey, B., Gaidzanwa, R. and Mupawaenda, A. 1990. *Factors Affecting the Careers of Women at the University of Zimbabwe*. Harare: Human resources Research Centre, University of Zimbabwe.

Duncan, L. A. 1989. *Engendering School Learning: Science, Attitudes and Achievement Among Girls and Boys in Botswana*. Stockholm: University of Stockholm.

Fuller, B., Hua, H. and Snyder, C. W. 1994. When Girls Learn More Than Boys: The Influence of Time in School and Pedagogy in Botswana. *Comparative Education Review* 38(3): 347–376.

Gaidzanwa, R. 1992. Bourgeois Theories of Gender and Feminism and their Shortcomings with Reference to Southern African Countries. In: R. Meena, ed., *Gender in Southern Africa: Conceptual and Theoretical Issues*. Harare: SAPES books.

Gaynor, C. 1989. *The Status of Women Teachers in Southern Africa*. Geneva: Joint ILO-UNESCO Publications.

Government of Botswana 1997. *Botswana National Literacy Survey*. Gaborone: Ministry of Education.

Gordon, R. 1994. Education Policy and Gender in Zimbabwe. *Gender and Education* 6(2): 131–139.

Hopkin, A. G. 1997. *Females and Gender Status in Eastern and Southern Africa: A Comparative Critique*. Gaborone: University of Botswana.

Juma, M. N. 1996. Determinants of Female Participation in Primary Education: A Case Study of Kwale and Taita Taveta Districts. In: Educational Research Network in Eastern and Southern Africa (ERNESA), *Educational Research Information for Practitioners* (15–18). Gaborone: ERNESA.

Kadzamira, E. C. 1996. Sex Differences in Performance of Candidates in MSCE Mathematics and Science Subjects 1982–1986. In: Educational Research Network in Eastern and Southern Africa (ERNESA), *Educational Research Information for Practitioners* (23–25). Gaborone: ERNESA.

Kann, U. 1984. Problems of Equity in the Education System: The Provision of Basic Education in Botswana. In: M. Crowder, ed., *Education for Development: Proceedings of a Symposium*. Gaborone: Botswana Society and Macmillan:

Kenway, J. 1993. Non-Traditional Pathways: Are they the Way to the Future? In: J.Blakemore and J. Kenway, eds., *Gender Matters in Educational Administration and Policy: A Feminist Introduction* (81–110). London: Falmer press.

Kenway, J. and Willis, S. with Blackmore, J. and Rennie, L. 1998. *Answering Back: Girls, Boys and feminism in Schools*. London: Routledge.

Kimweri, P. H. and Swai, N. M. P. 1996. The Involvement of Women in Non-Formal Environmental Education Programs: The Case of Hai District Afforestation Project in Kilimanjaro Region Tanzania Mainland. In: Educational Research Network in Eastern and Southern Africa (ERNESA), *Educational Research Information for Practitioners* (30–33). Gaborone: ERNESA.

Lengermann, P. M. and Brantley-Niebrugge, J. 1992. Contemporary Feminist Theory. In: G. Ritzer, ed., *Sociological Theory* (462–463). Singapore: McGraw-Hill.

Mafela, L. 1993. *Competing Gender Ideologies in Education in Bechuanaland Protectorate, c.1880–c. 1945*. Ph.D. Dissertation, Chicago: Northwestern University.

Mahlase, S. M. 1997. *The Careers of Women Teachers Under Apartheid*. Harare: Southern Africa Specialised Studies Series (SAPES).

Mahony, P. 1985. *Schools for the Boys*. London: Hutchinson.

Mannathoko, C. E. 1997. Politics of Gender in Teacher Education Curriculum and Pedagogy. In: P. T. M. Marope and D. W. Chapman, ed., *A Handbook of Research on Education: Teaching and Teacher Education in Botswana* (130–155). Gaborone: Lentswe La Lesedi.

Mannathoko, C. E. 1992. Feminist Theories and the Study of Gender Issues in Southern Africa. In: R. Meena, ed., *Gender in Southern Africa: Conceptual and Theoretical Issues*. Harare: SAPES books.

Marope, M. T. P. 1992. *Determinants of Academic Achievement in Botswana Junior Secondary School*. PhD Dissertation, Chicago, University of Chicago.

Mbilinyi, M., Mbughuni, P., Meena, R. and Olekambaine, P. 1991. Contributions of the Schooling Process and Issues for Gender Transformation. In: Mbilinyi, ed., *Education in Tanzania with a Gender Perspective*. Dar es Salaam: SIDA.

Measor, L. and Sikes, P. J. 1992. *Gender and Schools*. London, Cassell.

Meena, R. 1992 Gender Research/Studies in Southern Africa: An Overview. In: R. Meena, ed., *Gender in Southern Africa: Conceptual and Theoretical Issues*. Harare: SAPES Books.

Mosimakoko-Mosalakgoko, B. T. 1997. *Gender Differences and the Self Concept: Gender Differences in Junior Secondary School Students' Perceptions of their Self-Concept: A Study of the Junior Secondary School Science Students in the Southern Part of Botswana*. A M.Ed Dissertation project, Faculty of Education. Gaborone: University of Botswana.

Motlotle, K. 1989. *Hidden Language in Educational Textbooks; Life Chances of Male and Female Students in Science in Senior Schools*. Paper Presented at the BOLESWA Educational Research Symposium on Educational Research in the SADCC Region: Present and Future, Gaborone, Botswana.

Nyati-Ramahobo, L. 1992. *Girl-Child Study, Part One: State of the Art Review*. Gaborone: UNICEF-FEMNET.

Open University. 1992. *Breaking Out, The Developing World Video Pack*. Milton Keynes: Open University Press.

Parsons, Q. N. 1984. Education and Development in Pre-Colonial Botswana to 1965. In: M. Crowder, ed., *Education for Development: Proceedings of a Symposium* (21–45). Gaborone: Botswana Society and Macmillan.

Schapera, I. 1938. *A History of Tswana Law and Custom*. London, Frank Cass.

Sebakwane, S. 1993. Gender Relations in Lebowa Secondary Schools. *Perspectives in Education* 15(1): 83–100.

Seboni, N. 1997. Botswana Female Youth: Perception of Sexuality and Risk Taking Behaviours. In Mosenodi, *Journal of the Botswana Educational Research Association* 5(1): 15–26.

Tafa, E. M. 1993. Ideology and the JC History Curriculum: Content Analysis of Textbooks in Botswana. *Tonota Journal of Education* 1(1): 46–60.

460

Taole, J. K. 1996. A Comparison of Performance in Mathematics between Boys and Girls in the 1990 Junior Certificate Examination in Botswana. In: Educational Research Network in Eastern and Southern Africa (ERNESA), *Educational Research Information for Practitioners* (30–33). Gaborone: ERNESA.

Tumuti, D. W. 1997. *Viable Alternatives in Science and Vocational Training for Girls*. A paper presented in a sub-regional meeting for English-speaking countries in Scientific, Technical and Vocational Education for Girls in Africa. Harare, Zimbabwe.

United Nations Organisation. 1995. *Platform of Action and the Beijing Declaration.* New York: United Nations Department of Public Information.

Wamahiu, S., Opondo, F. A. and Nyagah, G. 1996. Educational Situation of the Kenyan Girl-Child. In: Educational Research Network in Eastern and Southern Africa (ERNESA), *Educational Research Information for Practitioners* (pp. 30–33). Gaborone: ERNESA.

The author

Changu E. Mannathoko is a senior lecturer at the University of Botswana in the Department of Educational Foundations. She is also the director of a regional course on Gender and Development in Southern Africa.

Contact address: Dr Changu Mannathoko, Educational Foundations, Faculty of Educaton, Private Bag 0022, Gaborone, Botswana. E-mail: Mannath@noka.ub.bw

THE SPECTRE OF THEORY IN CURRICULUM FOR EDUCATIONAL RESEARCHERS: A MEXICAN EXAMPLE

ROSA NIDIA BUENFIL BURGOS

Abstract – Recent educational policies in many parts of the world have tended to underplay the significance of theory in curriculum debates. This article examines examples of this tendency, paying particular attention to a case study of a prestigious education department at a Mexican university where the curriculum over 18 years was systematically drained of theoretical content. The author argues that removing theoretical discussion from the educational field will damage knowledge production in the field and ultimately harm the practice of education.

Zusammenfassung – In vielen Teilen der Welt neigt die neue Bildungspolitik dazu, die Bedeutung der Theorie in Lehrplandebatten unterzubewerten. Dieser Artikel untersucht Beispiele dieser Tendenz, unter besonderer Berücksichtigung einer Fallstudie in einer angesehenen Bildungsabteilung einer mexikanischen Universität, wo dem Lehrplan über einen Zeitraum von 18 Jahren der theoretische Inhalt entzogen wurde. Die Autorin argumentiert, daß das Entfernen der theoretischen Diskussion aus dem Gebiet der Bildung die Wissensbildung auf diesem Gebiet beeinträchtigen und schließlich zu einer Schädigung der Bildungspraxis führen wird.

Résumé – Dans de nombreuses régions du monde, les dernières politiques éducatives ont tendance à limiter l'importance de la théorie dans le débat sur les programmes éducatifs. L'article présente plusieurs exemples de cette tendance, en particulier une étude de cas sur une unité éducative prestigieuse d'une université mexicaine, qui vide systématiquement tout programme de plus de 18 ans de son contenu théorique. L'auteure affirme que la disparition du débat théorique du domaine éducatif nuira à la production du savoir dans ce secteur et portera finalement atteinte à la pratique de l'éducation.

Resumen – En muchas partes del mundo, las políticas de educación más recientes han tendido a subestimar la importancia de la teoría en los debates relacionados con planes de estudio. El presente artículo examina ejemplos de esta tendencia, poniendo especial atención en un caso de estudio relacionado con un prestigioso departamento de educación en una universidad mexicana, donde los planes de estudio han sido vaciados sistemáticamente del contenido teórico durante 18 años. La autora argumenta que la eliminación de la discusión teórica del área de la educación perjudicará la producción del saber y, en definitiva, dañará la práctica de la educación.

Резюме - Недавняя политика образования во многих странах имела тенденцию занижать важность теории в дискуссиях о программе обучения. В статье рассматриваются примеры этой тенденции, уделяя особое внимание исследованию конкретного примера престижного образовательного отдела в одном из университетов Мексики, где в течение более 18 лет из программы систематически изгонялось

462

теоретическое содержание. Автор утверждает, что удаление
теоретической дискуссии из сферы образования нанесет вред
производству знаний в данной области и, в конце концов, повредит
практике образования.

The idea of the spectre is often associated with fear of the unknown. However,
this is not the meaning which is used in this article. Instead, the term spectre
is invoked here as a reminder of that which has been repressed and thus "keeps
coming back" as a phantom or a ghost (Derrida 1996, Zizek 1994). This is
what may be taking place in the educational field with respect to theoretical
debate. It will be argued in this article that suppressing theoretical discussion
in the educational field, especially in the area of curriculum policy for
educational researchers, has political, ethical and epistemological implications
that may damage knowledge production in the field, and will, in the last
instance, damage the field itself.

The purpose of this article is to discuss this process in the perspective of
a discourse political analysis. The article locates the significance of the
Mexican experience of this process from a comparative point of view. It begins
by looking at some examples of educational policies that restrict theoretical
debates; secondly, it seeks to make sense of a particular Mexican case in the
curriculum for educational researchers; this is followed by an explication of
the conceptual tools which are used in the analysis and, finally, the article
draws out some of the implications of the application of these policies for
the field.

Contemporary educational policies

In recent years theoretical issues have been neglected in the field of curriculum
research. They have not been considered to be significant for policy development and have, therefore, been suppressed or given limited attention. From
the point of view of policy makers these moves are understandable. In the real
world of politics, the demands for policy innovation and implementation leave
little time for theoretical reflection. This has been particularly the case in
non-industrialised countries such as Mexico which, in spite of having relatively strong Enlightenment traditions in both the official and the popular consciousness, are far from achieving acceptable rates of literacy[1] and continue
to manifest low standards of living.[2] The question which countries such as
Mexico need to consider is, to what extent the postponement of theoretical
discussions in the field has resolved the problems of oppression and misery,
economic impoverishment, and other social ills; or has even helped to clarify
the role of education with relation to these problems.

In seeking to find answers to these questions, it is salutary to recall some contemporary examples of the tendency to underplay the significance of theoretical work in education. These examples can be traced three decades back and range from international policies for whole geopolitical regions, to domestic plans and recommendations for more localised areas.

1) The first example comes from Latin America. During the seventies schemes had been produced at an international level offering complete educational plans for Latin American countries.[3] The Multinational Project of Educational Technology Transference,[4] for example, was included in the overall developmental strategy sponsored by the Organisation of American States and the Inter-American Development Bank.[5] In the pages of this plan one could find a precise model of schooling structures, contents, teaching methods, expected learning and other practices that allegedly would guarantee results for primary school children. The underlying theory for this plan – Educational Behaviourism – was not available for inspection. Instead, it was assumed that this was the *natural* discourse of the field.

2) The second example is also an international one. It has been apparent for some time now that the international agenda for education has largely been more concerned with the production of sophisticated cost-benefit analyses, planning and taxonomies of objectives (OECD 1971)[6] and has not paid much attention to the question of the type of knowledge being produced, and under what conditions this knowledge is being produced, etcetera. Claims were even made that social theories were not sufficiently developed, were "merely abstract schema . . . [with no claim to universality]" and, therefore, that ". . . outworn ideological schemata and discussions [distant from] the realities of our time must be abandoned in order to concentrate on real problems . . ." (UNESCO 1978: 167).

3) The third example draws from the Mexican experience. From the early eighties onwards, recommendations previously issued by international organisations[7] came to figure strongly at a national level. In Mexico (and other Latin American countries) the central National Council for Science and Technology office for planning and funding research drastically reduced grants for graduate studies in the humanities. In the social sciences, furthermore, it also encouraged the following: positivistic research and graduate curricula oriented to non-theoretical discussions (as the latter were said to be associated with metaphysical speculation); quantitative and statistical information; and the "direct" exploration and solution of "immediate and imperative educational needs."

4) The final example is also Mexican. From the Second National Congress of Educational Research in Mexico, 1992, to the Fourth Congress in 1997, there was an unmistakeable decline of interest in theoretical discussion. Official documentation for the 1992 congress suggested that "theory ought to be postponed for educational graduate curricula".[8] Paradoxically, at this very same congress there was a strong demand in the workshops, panels, individual papers, and even in closing sessions of specific areas, for conceptual debate. Researchers requested theoretical discussion and/or clarification of

issues that had emerged in their field work, as well as conceptual elaboration to inform their analyses, interpretations and intervention in specific educational areas (such as curriculum, didactics, educational agents, specific qualifications etcetera). Confirmation of this decline was again evident in 1995 at the Third Congress where there was a reduction of 60% in the number of papers submitted to the *Commission on Philosophy and Theories of Education*. At the Fourth Congress in 1997, out of 113 selected papers, not a single contribution on Philosophy and Theories of Education was published in the Congress Proceedings.

From these few examples one can see the makings of a tendency that has come to permeate the Mexican system and is indeed evident in most other Latin American countries. (Different examples could probably be drawn from industrialised countries). Granja's work is important in showing the "uses" to which theory has been put and the position theory has acquired in educational research in Mexico in the last two decades (See Granja, J. 1997)[9]. My own interest is around understanding how the suspension of theoretical interrogation begins to constitute a problem when it becomes a characteristic of educational research in the field of curriculum design.[10]

Tracing the agenda for curriculum design for educational researchers at four different times: 1980, 1988, 1994 and 1998

This section is devoted to the examination of an educational department set in an eminent university. The primary task of this department since 1975[11] has been the training of educational researchers. The focus of the case-study is on the withdrawal of theory and theory-related work in the curriculum of the department.

The initial one-year programme which the department developed was orientated towards interdisciplinary research relating to national educational demands. In 1980, this interdisciplinary approach was framed in explicitly theoretical terms: the goal of the department was to attain "theoretical competence to support knowledge production towards educational intervention, diagnosis and evaluation".[12] Its curricular organisation was flexible and was aimed at preparing both general and specialist researchers. Since its establishment, the department has made major adjustments to its formal curriculum on two occasions (in 1980 and 1994). Minor adjustments were also made in 1988 and 1998.

In 1980 the department's curriculuar structure was drastically revised around a two-year programme organised in four semesters. A dual structure was established within the programme:

- One axis articulated the theoretical and methodological tools which were considered to be indispensable for educational research. This axis was constructed around compulsory seminars for all students. This involved, on the

one hand, theoretical debates in sociology, epistemology, political and educational theories, and on the other, the history of the Mexican school system and its impending needs.
• The other axis brought together the strategic activities involved in research, which at the time, were associated, by the lecturers of this department, with the idea of "apprenticeship". This approach was modelled on the artisanal relationship between craftsmen and young apprentices.

While this basic structure, the general orientation and the interdisciplinary basis have remained, subtle shifts concerning the position of theoretical seminars within the whole curricular structure have taken place. What follows is a discussion of the significance of these shifts.

By 1988, a formal process of re-structuring had begun in the department, resulting in the organisation of the two-year programme into six four-month terms (instead of four semesters). The idea of the dual structure was retained but the components within each of the two axes were changed.

• The first change involved the specification of key competencies. Where competence had been constructed broadly as "research competence," in the new arrangement researchers were expected to emerge from the programme with "*empirical* research competence." In addition time and activities devoted to apprenticeship (instead of seminars) were increased.
• The two axes of the curricular structure remained but what had previously been called "theoretical and methodological" was replaced with the notion of a "basic qualification."

A description of this eighteen-year history shows a gradual decrease in the time allocated to theoretical and methodological seminars. A superficial interpretation suggests that curricular spaces for theoretical discussion were reduced. This is illustrated graphically in the table below. In the table I am including all the other curricular units devoted to historical knowledge (such as History of the Medican School System or National educational problems) and to apprenticeship (workshops, tutorials, research seminars and field research), to present the general curriculum panorama. However, I want to emphasise the theoretical issues scheduled, and the position they show in this general structure.

It does not need a sophisticated analysis to show that epistemology has disappeared from the landscape altogether. This development did not take place in an arbitrary way, but was the outcome of prolonged collegial debates where those who held hegemonic positions argued that there was no common epistemological ground on which research training could be built. Instead, they promoted the notion of regional epistemologies and so removed epistemological discussion from the basic curriculum and placed it in optional speciality and thesis seminars. This, in real terms, amounted to leaving the decision of whether epistemology should be read to the judgement of each supervisor. The point is that a course in epistemology was no longer consid-

Table 1. Four moments in eighteen years of a curriculum for educational researchers.

	Semester 1	Semester 2	Semester 3	Semester 4	Axis	%
'80	**S Sc** **E T** **H & SpA** *Research Practice*	**M & E** **I S** *Research Practice*	**M & E** **S S** *Thesis*	**S S** *Research Advance* *Thesis 2*	**Theoretical** 8 *Apprenticeship* 5 Total 13	61

4 month Terms							
	Term 1	Term 2	Term 3	Term 4	Term 5	Term 6	Axis	%
---	---	---	---	---	---	---	---	---
'88	EPP H & SpA * *R Practice* *R-Advance*	**E T** **B C 1** *R-Practice* *R-Advance*	**M & E** **S E** *Thesis 1* *R-Advance*	**E** **M** *Thesis 1* *R-Advance*	B C 2 *Thesis 1* *R-Advance*	B C 3 *Thesis 1* *R-Advice*	*Context* 2 Theoretical **8** *Apprenticeship* 12 Total 22	36
'94	EPP *Workshop*	**L & K** H & SpA *Workshop* *S S 1*	T & E *Workshop* *S S 2* *R-Advance*	L & C C *S S 3* *R-Advance*	*S S 4* *R-Advance*	*RAdvance*	*Context* 2 Theoretical **5** *Apprenticeship* 11 Total 18	27
'84	EPP *Workshop* *S S 1* *Thesis 1*	**T & E** H & SpA *Workshop* *S S 2* *Thesis 2*	L & K L C&E *Workshop* *S S 3* *Thesis 3*	C* *S S 4* *Thesis 4*	*S S 5* *Thesis 5*	*S S 6* *Thesis 6*	*Context* 3 Theoretical **4** *Apprenticeship* 15 Total 22	18

Emphasis: **Bold** for theoretical, *italic* for apprenticeship and underlined for contextual.

Sources: The information is taken from brochures and syllabuses of the example taken.

Key: Where S Sc stands for Social Sciences; I S for interdisciplinary Seminar; M for Methodology; E for Epistemology and M&E for Methodology & Epistemology (as a single seminar); E T for Educational Theories; H & SpA for Historical & Socio-political Analysis; EPP for Educational Problems and Policies: B C for Basic Concepts; S S for Speciality Seminar; L & K for Learning and Knowlege; T & E for Teaching and Education; L & C for Language and Culture; and C for Curriculum.

* Note these seminars which previously involved theoretical issues and according to their abstracts have become contextual.

ered a basic qualification for becoming a researcher working in the area of knowledge production. To put it in other terms, *reflection upon how we produce knowledge was erased from the basic preparation of a qualified producer of knowledge on education* (emphasis in the original). Ironically, theoretical concerns continued to be raised by students and significant numbers of the academic staff and thus like ghosts they returned to haunt and prey on the curriculum.

The gradual withdrawal of theory in this particular instance may be understood as an attempt to enhance practical competence in the learning processes. It may also be understood as part of a complex social process out of which has come the assertion that theory means "not getting one's hand dirty", or worse, of theory not being real but only "office-work".[13]

This process cannot be understood as the mere outcome of the academic atmosphere in the country, and even less as the whim of curricular designers. Interesting and well informed collegial discussions took place before these decisions were taken. These discussions were held in monthly meetings and involved the following: a Piagetian psycholinguistic team; a Weber-Marxian, scholars following Bourdieu and recently Burton Clark's sociology line; a pedagogy trend; a psychoanalytic line; a strong ethnographic team; a group devoted to research on and production of text-books and didactic material, and in the nineties, scholars interested in historical research and discourse analysis. This rich plurality permeated internal policies in all academic activities: research, conferences, publications and, of course, curriculum design.

Overshadowing these discussions, however, were intense "official" pressures. For example, one cannot overlook the pressure exercised by the educational hierarchy in the department – and other authorities within the university – to reduce the time between the completion of the taught-course portion of the programme (two years) and the completion of the thesis. Nor should one underestimate national and regional process which caricatured theoretical interest as a waste of time. It is important to recognise these forces, because, as De Alba (1994) has shown, curricula are political arenas where subject-positions are contested and shaped (Gramsci 1979). These subject positions, in turn, shape the contours of the field.

Some conceptual tools to examine this tendency

This process of the gradual decline of theory in policy debate has been noted for some years now among international educational consultants and policy makers, national official councils and decision makers, specific centres, universities and departments dealing with educational research, and could be interpreted in two ways. First, it could be interpreted as the apotheosis of the "end of theory" movement – a movement that is concerned with efficiency and the construction of a consensual terrain which is characterised by "distortion-free communicative action," where in the last instance, the political possibility of a totally non-exclusionary society and an absolute non-exclusionary education could be achieved. To put it more pessimistically, this movement could be read as the yearning for an education utopia fed by an undigested pragmatism where politics has no place. Alternatively, the decline of theory may be interpreted as the natural result of a closer relationship between educational realities and the knowledge which is necessary to portray it. This, of course, would be the more naive interpretation in so far as it ignores basic and nonetheless important advances in the history of Western knowledge. For example, the debates between rationalism and empiricism which include the contributions of Hegel and Heidegger, not to mention Wittgenstein or more contemporary French Philosophers cannot be ignored. All these different ways of approaching the relationship between reality and knowledge have shown us that there is neither immediacy, nor transparency in the link between reality and representations of reality (Foucault 1972, Rorty 1979, Laclau 1988, Maturana 1990, *inter alia*).

Both interpretations fit very well with an Enlightenment reading of social life,[14] but at the end of the 20th century, too many fissures and cracks have shown that this narrative is somewhat distant from the expectations it has generated. Instead, advances in philosophy, sociology, anthropology and political thinking during the last four decades have both opened up new social questions and provided new intellectual tools to meet the challenge of the present (Lechte 1994).

If we invoke *genealogy* and trace back early educational and pedagogical narratives, we will find that from being highly reflective areas of knowledge, and, in some sense, subsidiaries of Philosophy,[15] at some point[16] speculation became degraded. The field, however, retrieved some legitimacy in the shelter of scientific knowledge, namely, of positivistism. Within this new epistemological framework, education was reduced to schooling, and pedagogy almost lost all rightful ground. According to Popkewitz (1997), "The rise of modern schooling should be considered as [the] joining of pedagogical problems, social science and the state in a revisioning of the governing of the individual". Education came to be the discipline, field and matter[17] of quantitative research, sophisticated definition and measurement. These were supposed to guarantee reliable levels of predictability. Pedagogy, at least in some non-Anglo traditions, came to be the field for prescription of recipes and in even less fortunate cases, a realm for metaphysical speculation. In the struggle between empiricism and rationalism within positivist social sciences, empiricism gained the upper hand.

Three decades ago in the educational field some other perspectives, qualitatively orientated, began to win ground. Firstly, ethno-methodological research; later, critical theories and recently discourse analysis began to emerge in some areas of the field. Bearing in mind that ethnography has been critical of empiricism (Stubbs and Delamont 1976), it is hard to understand why current ethnographic studies in Mexico[18] have tended to overlook the need for conceptualisation. Empiricism has prevailed and, as a result, theoretical debates have again been marginalised in the educational field. How was the pedagogical field both in general and in our particular example, gradually deprived of conceptual inquiry and why did this exclusion take place? The point here is drawn from the example of the department referred to above, where it is clear that the gradual exclusion of theoretical inquiry was neither a natural result of the development of knowledge nor the normal outcome of improved educational policies, but involved political and epistemological struggles which:

- resulted in the exclusion of alternative possibilities.
- had consequences both in epistemological and in political terms.
- have to be accounted for but can also be challenged and reverted.

It is in the context of this that one has to find a language of description and analysis which takes one beyond the simple acceptance of the "reality". This is why, on the one hand, concepts such as overdetermination, spectre, constitutive outside, dislocation and re-constitution; and on the other hand, the critique of the Enlightenment illusion of immediacy and transparency between knowledge and reality, the sign and the referent, may serve as analytical tools for understanding this process.

How can we account for this gradual loss of theoretical interrogation? One possibility is to look for a cause and/or a guilty agent: e.g. international policies or anxiety in the department, national pressure over the length of time it takes students to complete their theses, political processes within the department, or international scientific trends, etcetera. However, if we free ourselves from a hard notion of causality, i.e. "a necessary and sufficient cause", and look for a different horizon of intelligibility, we can find in the category of *overdetermination* (Laplanche and Pontalis 1988, Zizek 1990, Laclau and Mouffe 1985) a logic of understanding that does not trap us either in a fixed logic or in a single cause. Overdetermination refers to the process of condensation (i.e. the fusion of multiple "causes" into one nodal point) and displacement (i.e. the process of circulation of these "causes" throughout multiple signifiers).

Following this line of thinking, it would be useful at this point to try another genealogical approach. As a starting point I consider pedagogy and/or educational theories[19] as a field that has been disturbed both by the very failure of the early Enlightenment project and paradoxically, by the predominance achieved by the positivistic tradition in the social sciences which appeared as the very solution to the loss of legitimacy the field was undergoing. This new horizon in social sciences produces a disruption of the positions previously established in the pedagogical field and a new system of intellectual positions has to be created to re-establish stability. The very moment of disarray of the previous configuration might be called *dislocation* (Laclau 1990). This in turn sets the conditions for a new arrangement that I will call the *re-constitution*. This involves the process of *inclusion* of elements available in the wider field of social sciences and the *exclusion* (Foucault

1979) of others that previously were constitutive of educational thinking. The notion of the *Spectre* thus arises, of that which was present before, or that which may be understood as the 'residue' of something that has been repressed, excluded from a discursive configuration or system (Derrida 1994, Zizek 1996).[20] It is a trace of an act of exclusion and thus should not be confused with a symbolic fiction.[21] If one accepts that exclusion does not involve the annihilation of the excluded entity but only its removal *outside* the system, then the idea of this outside acquires a different status, since what is inside the configuration is such insofar as the outside defines its boundaries. This is, following Staten (1984) and Laclau (1985, 1990), what I will call a "constitutive outside". As one can see, these 'residues' survive the dislocation but assume a different position and function vis-à-vis the newly arranged system. They emerge as reminders of an act of exclusion, as *traces* of the political[22] moment constituting the new configuration as such.

With regard to the critique of immediacy and transparency between knowledge and reality or the sign and its referent, as stated above, one can recall the trajectories of some key traditions in Western thinking such as Structuralism, Phenomenology and Philosophy of Language. Reading through these discourses one can see a marked weakening of these two basic values (cherished especially by Positivism) taking place which is evident, for instance, in the journey that takes one from Saussure to Lacan or Derrida, the transit from Husserl to Heidegger and Derrida or the progress between Wittgenstein's *Tractatus* and his *Philosophical Investigations* (Laclau 1988, Lechte 1994). The point here is that, on the one hand, all relationships between knowledge and reality are discursively mediated (i.e. they depend on the meaningful frame shared by the community). All relationships between reality and knowledge have traces of linguistic and cultural battles, negotiations and agreements imprinted on them throughout history. On the other hand, the relationship between the words we use to re-present reality and the 'referent in the external world' they name, is never isomorphic (i.e. there is no one to one correspondence); in other words, no transparency can be granted to words when referring to objects in the world. Thus, there is an inevitable zone of indeterminacy and ambiguity in language, and *mutatis mutandis* in knowledge (Rorty 1978, 1989, Maturana 1990).

To some extent, the goals anticipated by policies and intellectual trends withdrawing theory from the qualification of future researchers can be associated with that Enlightenment illusion of immediacy and transparency.[23] From this point of view, one can imagine two possibilities: the first is that knowledge about education could be produced in a non-mediated way, i.e. the researcher would be able to have direct contact with reality and the knowledge produced would be able to reproduce this non-mediated reality. The second is that this mediation does not need to be theoretically informed (i.e. it will be commonsensical or reasonable). We know that common sense and the 'reasonable' are culturally constructed and involve ethical and political decisions taken in a frame of symbolically structured perceptions of the 'external world' (i.e. reality). It is important, moreover, that we understand that the political involves processes of inclusion and exclusion which depend not just on reason, but also on passion, prejudices, etcetera. Thus, any attempt to account for knowledge construction outside of a theoretical frame has dire ethical, political and epistemological implications. These are considered below.

Implications of the withdrawal of theory

Political implications

When the withdrawal of theory from educational and pedagogical policy debates is presented as a normal desire for a more efficient form of schooling, one should recognise the presence of at least three types of intertwined operations:

- The discursive dimension, i.e. this is where theory as a signifier is associated with "theory as a waste of time"; "theory as metaphysical speculation"; "theory as an impossible route to reality" etcetera. These associations are never presented as political constructions but as objective-necessary reality.
- The political dimension involved in the policy designed (i.e. any decision concerning a measure or prescription is based on the demarcation of boundaries between what is included and what is excluded (what I identify with the political). Any decision entails a choice of one among a set of possibilities. Other possibilities are never presented. As this movement is not acknowledged, the disjuncture between the included and the excluded and the fixing of boundaries completely erases what was removed and thus conceals and cancels out the political dimension of the gesture[24] and actions which were taken. This erasure is, as Derrida has told us, the naturalising effect involved in the writing of history (which is precisely the type of history we have been discussing here).
- The ethical dimension entailed in the responsibility for this choice is either acknowledged or ignored. Since the act of choosing is obscured and represented as a necessary outcome of a course of action, no responsibility has to be assumed. When a decision is naturalised, i.e. presented as the natural result of a course of action, it tends to appear as universal and necessary, thus concealing its particularity and the fact that in its very construction other possibilities were excluded from the field. This concealment also makes redundant the necessity on the part of the decision-maker to justify his/her decisions.

Epistemological implications

When the withdrawal of theory is presented as a result of the normal course of scientific knowledge moving closer to the portrayal of educational reality, the following may be observed:

- The discursive (cultural, social, linguistic) dimension of knowledge construction is overlooked. Prejudices and personal preferences are given the status of authoritative portraits of reality, since no mediation between knowledge construction and reality is acknowledged.
- Knowledge production in education is isolated from developments in other fields of knowledge. Theoretically informed research in education is unable to account for the presence of ideologies and theories which shape the construction of knowledge.
- The responsibility involved in preparing future educational researchers who will recognise the difference between analytical categories and everyday language is altogether disregarded. Since educational researchers are professionals who will produce knowledge about education, the necessity for some familiarity with epistemological debates cannot easily be overlooked.

Interpreting our case-study: overdetermination and the construction of a new exclusionary system

The withdrawal of theoretical discussions in the case-study presented above, may be seen as an overdetermination of processes, positionalities and tendencies some of which are internal to the department, and others external such as national and international policies and intellectual trends. Thus, at an institutional local level, one can see an overreaction to a previous curricular tendency in the department which had conferred greater weight to theory.[25] At a national level, the emphatic recommendations made by university top-level officers to "decentre theory" in curricula for educational researchers cannot be overlooked. Besides, the pressure to reduce thesis-time, which was exercised by the national scientific and technological council through the dispensing of funds and academic recognition, must also be considered. Moreover, the general utilitarian and managerial tendency imposed by international organisations on national policies can easily be seen in examples such as those presented above.[26] However, the fact that decisions were taken involving the withdrawal of theoretical seminars instead of pursuing other possibilities, cannot be ignored. Other possibilities could have been explored such as examining why students were taking so long to finish their dissertations (perhaps the overwhelming academic standards imposed by the department); organising collegial discussions concerning the different 'uses' of theory and whose responsibility was the fact that 'students got lost in a theoretical stratosphere' (could it be the responsibility of theory?); and exercising alternative ways to bridge the gap between theoretical tools and educational demands.

Thus, the discursive field of this particular curriculum was disturbed by the unexpected and systematic thesis-writing weakness (a failure, a crack showing the incompleteness and precariousness of the ideal curriculum). This dislocation was somehow overcome by means of the construction of a different exclusionary system which tended to expel theories while naturalisisng this exclusion (i.e. constructing it as a necessary outcome of a process and as a necessary means to repair the crack in the curriculum).

A final remark concerns the status and position of theoretical discussions as a constitutive part in the qualification for educational researchers and also in the field as such. Firstly, one has to consider the area of theoretical research in education and/or pedagogy, as a rightful one. Secondly, one has to consider the constitutive theoretical dimension in any kind of educational research for as long as research is understood as knowledge production. Of course educational research does not have to become simply theoretical research but field research should not degenerate to description based on commonsensical information. If there is a distinction between information and research it is that the second involves more than information, it also involves procedures of decision about what is to be informed. Honest and well-intentioned work that is lacking theoretical orientation, misses the point altogether.

I do not expect that curricula will cease to be a political arena in which academic struggles, negotiations and agreements take place. This is the point of discussing my position on this issue. I have tried to argue in this article that once one commits oneself to knowledge production (i.e. research) epistemological discussions cannot be overlooked. Even the epistemological position of rejecting all theoretical consideration (hypothetically sustained by a radical empiricist) should be, at least, posited, explained and accounted for.

The spectre of theory then is a way to interpret how what has been excluded from a field, in this case the field of education and more specifically, the curriculum for educational researchers, as we have seen, did not disappear but became a reminder (souvenir), a remainder (residue) and a constitutive outside threatening what is inside the boundaries of this very field.

Acknowledgements

The author wishes to thank T. Popkewitz for his invitation to the panel where this paper was presented at the Tenth World Congress of Comparative Education and his generous time in reading the first drafts of the paper.

Notes

1. Mexico has been considered to be one of the seven countries with the highest illiteracy rate in the world: 31% of Mexicans are either illiterate or they have not finished primary school.
2. According to CEPAL in Latin America and the Caribbean 40% of the population live in very poor conditions (some 210 million people). Among the illiterate, 80% are unemployed, within the informal economy or housewives, 70% are women and 40% indigenous.
3. Different international organisations have been producing educational programmes for Latin America. See for instance UNESCO (1965) where a managerial view of education was proposed as the view to be held. See also UNESCO-ECLA (1968) prescribing how research in universities had to be done. See also Pan American Union. Dept. of Economic Affairs (c1967)
4. Concerning the general course of Educational Technology in Mexico as a paradigm prevailing in the curriculum during the early seventies, I thank Dr. Alicia de Alba for her advice. Official information about the Organisation of American States concerning education can be consulted in Chaves Reyes, Fernando (1962) *La educación cooperativa en América Latina*, and OAS (1966) *Yearbook of educational, scientific and cultural development in Latin America*. The Inter American Development Bank and its projects for Latin America can be consulted in Davis, Harold Eugene (1950) *Social science trends in Latin America*. Washington: Issued in co-operation with the Inter-American Bibliographical and Library Association, American University Press.
5. See for instance the Chilean journal *Tecnología Educativa* during the 1970s.
6. See for instance UNESCO (1971) *World Survey of Education*, where the importance of planning overruled other aspects of educational issues, research included. The OECD's *Educational Policies for the 1970s Conferences on Policies for Educational Growth* (1971) also recommends educational planning as the centre for articulating educational policies.
7. Consult UNESCO (1981) to understand why albeit educational research was promoted, its orientation was towards making it "scientific" meaning by this, quantitatively sound.
8. This has been literally taken from the speech given in a panel by university top-level officers (see Buenfil B. (coord), De Alba C., García C., Gómez S., Juárez H. y Ortega Z. *Filosofía y Teoría de la Educación: Una Década de Esfuerzo*, II CNIE, in Quintanilla (Coord.) *Teoría, Campo e Historia de la Educación* Consejo Mexicano de Investigación Educativa, México, 1995. See especially the opening interventions to the preparatory Congress *Teoría, Campo e Historia de la Educación* held in Guanajuato, México in Oct 29–30 and Nov 1st 1993 Proceedings.
9. Granja Castro, Josefina (1997) *La teoría como reflexión sobre el conocimiento construido* paper presented at the IV Congreso Nacional de InvestigaciÛn Educativa Simposio "El fantasma de la Teoría" Mérida, Yucatán, México, Octubre 1997.
10. De Alba has done important work concerning the specificity of curriculum designers as "subjects of curricular overdetermination" (in press).
11. The degree it confers is Master of Science (mention in Education) and to get it, students must complete the two year programme, be examined in each one of the seminars, and defend a dissertation which is the product of research.
12. To keep the anonymity of my example the actual sources cannot be properly quoted and I will use the pseudonym ER for the department, Centre X for the centre where the department belongs and MFE for their programme. See ER (1980) Programa MFE México, Centre X, p. 3.

13. I shall not overlook that this association also involved a criticism of a Mexican reading of reproductionist theories in education (Althusser, Bourdieu, *inter alia*) during the seventies. The latter and other sociological approaches to education indeed emphasised only macro levels and gave little attention to microprocesses.
14. See for instance in the XVIII Century, Condorcet's notions in the 8th, 9th and last sections of his *Sketch for a historical picture of the progress of the human mind.*
15. In Western tradition, this can go from the Greeks to almost any philosophical tradition (rationalists, empiricists, romanticists, and find a position given to education and pedagogy). There is a turning point with Enlightenment philosophers who strongly defended the possibility of "elevating" pedagogy into a science. Mainly with the advent of Comtean sociological positivism, one can find the urge to convert pedagogy and/or educational disciplines into a positivistic science.
16. One could say that a turning point is the emergence of Positivism as the leading intellectual trend in the Social Sciences.
17. I am very much against the confusion between a disciplinary knowledge and its subject matter. To some extent the term "education" used for both the discipline and the object/process it deals with, has somehow contributed to this confusion. Elsewhere I have also debated against trends which fuse the pedagogical and the educational subject (Buenfil 1992)
18. This applies obviously not to all ethnographic research, and probably not just in Mexico. Nonetheless, the prevailing view dismisses theory.
19. I do not ignore the controversies opened up by colleagues who mark a distinction among pedagogy, educational sciences and educational theories. In this paper I will not enter this debate and for the specific purpose of my argumentation here I will take them as equivalent. I take them as meaningful constellations dealing more or less systematically with educational matters, i.e. taking educational processes as their study object.
20. For a brief and sharp discussion on the differences between Derrida's and Lacan's concepts of spectre, see also Zizek 1994, Introduction, p. 27 ff. and Endnote 34.
21. Zizek puts it this way: Spectre is not to be confused with symbolic fiction . . . reality is never directly itself, it presents itself only via the incomplete-failed symbolisation, and spectral apparitions emerge in this very gap that forever separates reality from the real . . . the spectre gives body to that which escapes (the symbolically structured) reality (Zizek 1994: 21)
22. I understand the political here not as a topological category referring to a "level of society involving the government and political parties", but to any action referred to as: a) A moment of inclusion/exclusion (Foucault 1979); b) A hegemonic relation involving antagonism and articulation (Laclau 1985) and Hall (1988); c) A decision that is taken by social agents (Schmitt) so as to fix some senses to social relations in an "archipelago of public spaces" (Arditi 1994 and 1995).
23. See for instance Hall, Stuart (1993) from a cultural perspective and Maturana (1990) from a scientific perspective.
24. My gratitude to Silvia Fuentes, M.Sc., who called my attention on this subtle political move involved in the example I have been presenting.
25. Tendency which, according to some department lecturers, was leading the students to pure speculation, "getting lost in a theoretical stratosphere", and never "landing in educational reality". Of course, this way of phrasing it, shows a great deal of presuppositions and preconceptions (one could say prejudices) concerning theoretical work.
26. Once the logic of hard determinism of the general (e.g. international policy) over the particular (e.g. departmental decisions) is brought into question one can see

through this example how educational policies circulate throughout all these different levels, thereby being resignified. Here I have two points to outline: the first, a conceptual consideration, stressing that this circulation or displacement is one side of the process of *overdetermination* mentioned above; the other side is condensation, or the fusion of different meanings in one (See Zizek 1990, Laplanche and Pontalis 1988). The second, is a more academic issue concerning my rejection of the generalised claim (at least amongst Mexican researchers) that policies should not be studied since they are 'far from what really happens in schools and classrooms'. I assume the challenge that further research has to be done in order to display how this circulation takes place, but fine research has already been done and should not be ignored (See Popkewitz 1997).

References

Arditi, Benjamin. 1994. Tracing the Political. *Angelaki* 1(3), Oxford, January 1995, pp. 15–28.

Arditi, Benjamin. 1995. *An Archipelago of Public Space*s. Essex University, working paper.

Buenfil Burgos, Rosa Nidia. 1992. Comentarios. In Puiggrós and Gómez Sollano, *Alternativas Pedagógicas, Sujetos y Prospectiva de la Educación Latinoamericana.* México: UNAM.

Buenfil Burgos, R. N. (coord) (1994), De Alba, C., García, C., Gómez, S. C., Juárez, H. y Ortega, Z. Filosofía y Teoría de la Educación: Una Década de Esfuerzo, II CNIE. In: Quintanilla (Coord.) (1995), *Teoría, Campo e Historia de la Educación.* México: Consejo Mexicano de Investigación Educativa.

Buenfil Burgos, Rosa Nidia. 1995. Education in a Postmodern Horizon: Voices from Latin America. *British Journal of Educational Research.*

CEPAL. 1997. *Séptima conferencia regional sobre la integración de la mujer en el desarrollo económico y social de América Latina y el Caribe.* Chile: CEPAL.

CEPAL-UNESCO. 1992. *Educación y conocimiento: eje de la transformación productiva con equidad.* Chile: CEPAL-UNESCO.

Chaves Reyes, Fernando. 1962. *La educación cooperativa en América Latina.* Washington, DC: OAS.

Condorcet, Jean-Antoine-Nicolas de Caritat, marquis de. 1955. *Sketch for a Historical Picture of the Progress of the Human Mmind.* Trans. June Barraclough. London: Weidenfeld and Nicolson.

Davis, Harold Eugene. 1950. *Social Science Trends in Latin America.* Washington, DC: Issued in co-operation with the Inter-American Bibliographical and Library Association, American University Press.

De Alba, Alicia. 1994. *Curriculum. Mitos y Perspectivas.* México: UNAM.

De Alba, Alicia. In press. *Curriculum, académicos y futuro.* México: CESU/UNAM – Plaza y Valdes.

Derrida, Jacques. 1994. *Specters of Marx: The State of The Debt, The Work of Mourning, And The New International.* Trans. Peggy Kamuf. New York: Routledge.

Foucault, Michel. 1979. *The History of Sexuality, Vol. 1, The Will to Truth.* London: Allen Lane.

Foucault, Michel. 1972. *The Archaeology of Knowledge*. trans. A. M. Sheridan Smith. London: Tavistock Publications.

Foucault, Michel. 1977. *Language, Counter-memory, Practice: Selected Essays and Interviews*. Introd. Donald F. Bouchard; trans. Donald F. Bouchard and Sherry Simon. Ithaca, NY: Cornell University Press.

Gimeno Jose Blat (ed.). 1983. *Education in Latin America and the Caribbean. Trends and Prospects 1970–2000*. United Kingdom, UNESCO.

Gramsci, Antonio. 1992. *Prison Notebooks*. Edit. and introd by Joseph A. Buttigieg. New York: Columbia University Press.

Granja Castro, Josefina. 1997. *La teoría como reflexión sobre el conocimiento construido*. Paper presented at the IV Congreso Nacional de Investigación Educativa, Simposium "El fantasma de la Teoría" Mérida, Yucatán, México, October.

Hall, Stuart. 1988. *The Hard Road to Renewal: Thatcherism and the Crisis of the Left*. London: Verso, 1988.

Hall, Stuart. 1993. Cultural Identity in Question. In: Stuart Hall and T. McGrew (eds.), *Modernity and its Futures*. Cambridge: Polity.

Inter-American Development Bank. Board of Executive Directors. 1970. *Proposal for an Increase in the Resources of the Inter-American Development Bank*. Report of the Board of Executive Directors to the Board of Governors. Washington, DC: Inter-American Development Bank.

Laclau, Ernesto and Mouffe, Chantal. 1985. *Hegemony and Socialist Strategy*. London: Verso.

Laclau, Ernesto. 1988. Politics and the Limits of Modernity. In: A. Ross (ed.), *Universal Abandon?* Minneapolis: University of Minnesota Press.

Laclau, Ernesto. 1990. *New Reflections on the Revolutions of Our Times*. London: Verso.

Laclau, Ernesto. 1994. Why do Empty Signifiers Matter to Politics? In: *The Lesser Evil and the Greater Good. The Theory and Politics of Social Diversity*. London: Oram Press.

Laplanche J. and Pontalis, J. B. 1988. *The Language of Psycho-analysis*. London: Karnac and the Institute of Psycho-Analysis.

Lechte, John. 1994. *Fifty Key Contemporary Thinkers: From Structuralism to Postmodernity*. London: Routledge.

Maturana, Humberto. 1990. *Emociones y Lenguaje en Educación y Política*. Chile: Hachette.

OAS. 1966. *Yearbook of Educational, Scientific and Cultural Development in Latin America*. Washington, DC: OAS.

OECD. 1971. *Educational Policies for the 1970s Conferences on Policies for Educational Growth*. Paris: OECD.

OCDE. 1986. *La naturaleza del desempleo de los jóvenes. Informes de la Organización de Cooperación y Desarrollo Económico*. Madrid: OCDE.

OECD. 1993. *Education at a Glance. Indicators*. Paris: OECD.

Pan American Union. Dept. of Economic Affairs. c1967. *The Alliance for Progress and Latin-American Development Prospects: A Five-year Review 1961–1965*. Baltimore: Published for the Organization of American States by Johns Hopkins Press.

478

Popkewitz, Thomas. 1997. *Re-thinking the Problem of Changes in Educational Systems: A Perspective from Research and Recent Discussion on Poilcies and Curriculum.* Conference at the IV Congreso Nacional de Investigacion Educativa, in Merida, Yucatán, México, October.

Rorty, Richard. 1989. *Contingency, Irony, and Solidarity.* Cambridge: Cambridge University Press.

Rorty, Richard. c1979. *Philosophy and the Mirror of Nature.* Princeton: Princeton University Press.

Schmitt, Carl. 1985. *Political Theology: Four Chapters on the Concept of Sovereignty.* Trans.George Schwab. Cambridge, MA: MIT Press.

Staten, Henry. 1984. *Wittgenstein and Derrida.* Lincoln and London: University of Nebraska Press.

UNESCO. 1965. Lyons (ed.) *Problems and Strategies of Educational Planning.* Belgium: UNESCO and International Institute for Educational Planning.

UNESCO. 1968. *Education, Human Resources and Development in Latin America.* New York: UNESCO-ECLA.

UNESCO. 1971. *World Survey of Education.* Belgium: UNESCO.

UNESCO. 1981. *Curricula and Lifelong Education.* Geneva: UNESCO.

Zizek, Slavoj. 1990. *The Sublime Object of Ideology.* London: Verso.

Zizek, Slavoj. 1994. *Mapping Ideology.* London: Verso.

The author

Rosa Nidia Buenfil Burgos obtained a PhD in Government from Essex University, UK, in 1990. She is Investigador Titular en el Departmento de Investigaciones Educativas, Centro de Investigaciones y Estudios Avanzados (equivalent to Professor at the Department of Educational Research, Center of Research and Advanced Studies), Medico, and Lecturer at the Post-graduate Division, Department of Philosophy, Universidad Nacional Autónoma de México. She has approximately 35 research publications to her name.

    Contact address: Dr Rosa Buenfil Burgos, San Borja, 938 Del Valle, Mexico D.F. cp 03100. E-mail: buenfil@data.net.mx.

CURRICULUM AND SOCIETY: RETHINKING THE LINK

ALICIA DE ALBA

Abstract – This article argues that the link between educational curricula and society as a whole has become critically uncertain. This crisis is linked to a number of factors related to the post-modern world view, including: the disappearance of grand utopian social visions of the kind that used to underpin educational policy; the lack of adequate theoretical tools; and the way in which academics are exposed to a multitude of different cultural contacts. The author argues that this situation calls for a fundamental re-thinking of the link between curriculum and society, based on a more flexible and pluralistic approach.

Zusammenfassung – In diesem Artikel wird dargelegt, daß die Verbindung zwischen Lehrplänen und der Gesellschaft als Ganzes in bedenklicher Weise unsicher geworden ist. Diese Krise wird auf eine Anzahl von mit dem postmodernen Weltbild verbundenen Faktoren zurückgeführt, darunter das Verschwinden der großen utopischen sozialen Visionen, die die Bildungspolitik unterstützten, der Mangel an adäquatem theoretischem Werkzeug und der Tatsache, daß Akademiker unter dem Einfluß einer Vielzahl verschiedener kultureller Zusammenhänge stehen. Der Autor argumentiert, daß dieser Zustand ein grundsätzliches Überdenken der Verbindung zwischen Lehrplan und Gesellschaft erfordert, basierend auf einer flexibleren und pluralistischeren Verfahrensweise.

Résumé – Cet article émet l'avis que la relation entre le programme éducatif et la société dans son ensemble est devenue dangereusement aléatoire. Cette crise est due à divers facteurs liés à la conception du monde postmoderne, comme la disparition de grandes visions sociales utopiques telles qu'elles étaient utilisées pour étayer les politiques éducatives, le manque d'instruments théoriques appropriés, ou le fait que les universitaires sont confrontés à une multitude de normes culturelles différentes. L'auteur soutient que cette situation exige de repenser radicalement la relation entre programme éducatif et société, en partant d'une approche flexible et pluraliste.

Resumen – El artículo sostiene que el nexo existente entre los planes de estudio y la sociedad como un conjunto se ha vuelto críticamente inestable. Esta crisis viene aparejada con un número de factores relacionados con una visión postmoderna, incluyendo la desaparición de grandes visiones sociales utópicas como aquellas que han servido para apuntalar la política educacional, la falta de herramientas teóricas adecuadas y el modo en el que los académicos se ven expuestos a una multitud de diferentes contactos culturales. El autor argumenta que esta situación reclama una reconsideración fundamental del nexo existente entre los planes de estudio y la sociedad, basado sobre un enfoque más flexible y pluralístico.

Резюме - В статье утверждается, что связь между образовательной программой и обществом стала критически неопределенной. Этот кризис связывается с целым рядом факторов, имеющих отношение к

 International Review of Education – Internationale Zeitschrift für Erziehungswissenschaft – Revue Internationale de l'Education **45**(5/6): 479–490, 1999.
© 1999 *Kluwer Academic Publishers. Printed in the Netherlands.*

480

постмодернистскому взгляду на мир, в том числе: исчезновение больших утопических социальных визий, которые в свое время являлись определяющим фактором образовательной политики; недостаток адекватных теоретических инструментов, а также то, как академическое общество подчиняется большому количеству различных культурных норм. Автор утверждает, что эта ситуация требует фундаментального переосмысления связи между программой обучения и обществом, основанной на более гибком и плюралистическом подходе.

> There are different modes of integration, transformation, combination, distortion and appropriation, which make it difficult to delimit movements into classifiable identities. This multiplicity cannot be reduced to a tabular order – fixed and stable – because of differences, on the one hand, between diverse cultural traditions and states, and the opening of spaces among disciplines, on the other.
>
> Michael Peters,
> *Nietzsche, Poststructuralism and Education:*
> *After the Subject?*

In contrast to the situation in the 1960s and 70s, and even parts of the 80s when the school was accorded a particular social role, the link today between curriculum and society has become profoundly uncertain. In the complex and crisis-ridden times we live in, it has become almost impossible to define a role for the curriculum in debates about the shape of the world we wish to inhabit. The making of this link between curriculum and society is rendered all the more difficult because of the absence of what we might call utopian visions.[1] In the past we had access to utopian visions which spawned important social projects, such as socialism, which in turn inspired particular understandings of the role of the school in promoting social change.

The rapid changes that have occurred around the globe after the collapse of the Berlin Wall in 1989, combined with the erosion of the epistemological foundations of Western thought, have placed the educational field and, within it, the curriculum, in an extremely complex situation. This condition can be looked at in a number of ways. Among these, it might be said that:

a) academics have not been able to constitute themselves as subjects (*as agents*) in the context of the process of curricular overdetermination (de Alba 1995a);

b) the complex surface of inscription of education and the curriculum (i.e. the space in which discourse might be inserted), is marked by the presence of split subjects (i.e. subjects who are the products of processes of hybridi-

sation, contestation and negotiation) and is overlaid by the social contours
of a multiplicity of movements, social trends and emergent practices;

c) there is an absence of adequate theoretical tools (until recently these tools
were sufficient for helping us understand educational problems);

d) there has been an increase in cultural contact and this has had a large
impact on both the social and educational spheres.

This article seeks to develop these ways of understanding the relationship
between curriculum and society and begins with the premise that there is a
need to rethink this relationship to enable us to recapture a purposeful, critical
and analytical view of our work in education. In seeking to recapture such a
purposeful, critical and analytic view, it is important to understand the nature
of the crisis in which the field of curriculum finds itself. The field is characterised by a generalised crisis exemplified by the retreat of grand narratives
and the emergence of a multiplicity of competing social trends and movements. Contemporaneous with this crisis, has been an intensification of cultural
contact in a multiform and multidirectional way which has not only contributed to processes of decentring amongst individuals (hence the notion of
split subjects), but has also served to decentre the centre itself.

Surface of inscription:[2] social traits and contours

I have argued elsewhere (de Alba 1991) that the curriculum is a political-
educational project constituted by a synthesis or an articulation of cultural
elements derived from fights, impositions and negotiations amongst different
social subjects. These conflicts and negotiations embrace a range of social-
political projects and portend how society is to be educated.

As mentioned above, one of the most serious developments confronting
us in the area of the curriculum is the retreat of socio-political projects which
involve particular narrations of the curriculum-society relationship and which
help to constitute and sustain the subjects (agents) of the processes of curricular overdetermination. Such subjects play formative roles and sustain
educational projects in relation to these socio-political projects. With the weakening of the grand narrative in education and curriculum, the question that
arises is twofold:

How do we understand and reconstitute the curriculum-society link within
societies that are in crisis and that lack wide and ambitious socio-political
projects? And what is the position of the social and curricular subject in these
societies, given the absence of utopian horizons and projects?

Towards understanding this crisis and the role of subjects within it, it could
be put that through the processes of crisis, what can be observed is the
emergence of social traits and contours which prefigure the articulation of
incipient hegemonic practices. Traits, in this explanation, refer to new or
residual elements from [current and precarious or] previous social configu-

rations, which show themselves in a significant way, in a social space and accomplish two functions. In the first instance, they contribute to the dislocation of the order of things within the crisis situation. In the second, they emerge as traces in the contours of new discursive social configurations. Traits are thus elements which do not have the ability to articulate the past, present and the future, and their importance resides in their ability to erupt (unexpectedly) and to disrupt the textured overlays of meaning which permeate the society. They are, therefore, elements that linger on dangerously in new discursive[3] configurations; but at the same time, because of their very residualness, they might wither altogether (de Alba 1995a). They emerge and are present during the early stages of a social crisis.

Contours are shaped by a set of emerging elements in society in the process of generalised structural crisis. Contours are traits which coalesce and can be identified by their eruptive tendencies. Contours have a greater capacity for articulation than traits and can be observed in advanced moments of the crisis. They are constituted and are present as the articulation of initial and incipient meanings in the making (and genealogy) of a social configuration. They can have, thus, the ability to articulate and constitute themselves as master signifiers.[4] Like traits they can also go in the opposite direction. As new social configurations unfold, they can disappear and be excluded from the social and curricular terrain (de Alba 1995a.)

Seen in this way, social traits and contours are constituted elements on the surface of the inscriptive field of the curriculum. They, in turn, provide the contextual space for the constitution of specific social and curricular subjects. Social traits and contours thus interpellate[5] and provide for the constitution of subjects and, critically, the possibility for the creation of the curriculum-society link. I wish to argue, therefore, that in the contemporary world, it is social traits and contours, as opposed to grand projects, which constitute the surface of inscription of the curriculum. They are inextricably linked with the broad social changes that have impacted on the different spaces and levels of reality which make up our social reality. Amongst the most important, these changes are: environmental crisis, the meteoric advances in science and technology (particularly in information technology), the intensification of cultural contact, geopolitical recomposition, poverty, famine, globalisation[6] and the increasing emphasis of difference.

Subjects of curriculum. After the death of the subject?

The conceptual tools in the field of education and, within that, the field of the curriculum, which were dominant until the 1970s and 80s, have shown themselves to be inadequate in explaining some of the most urgent problems we are facing today. One such problem relates to the withering of a coherent notion of the subject, that is to say the individual self as a conscious source of thought and action.

The notion of a coherent subject – a corner-stone of Western thought – has been seriously eroded. The work of Nietzsche, Heidegger and Wittgenstein, amongst others, has produced new discursive frameworks in which autonomous subjects have all but disappeared in the face of the total-ising discourses of science and progress which have prefigured "the death of the subject". This work has been significantly advanced in post-structuralist thought, with authors like Lacan, Foucault and Derrida. Peters (1997), reflecting on the power of this new theory, suggests that we now cannot continue thinking about the subject in the same way.[7]

The modern subject has been characterised as centred, rational and avant-garde. He/she is a subject centred in a strong, primary identification with rationality as his/her main *motif*. This rationality is embodied in the ideal of a subject able to contribute to the acceleration of structural change and able to shape history. The modern subject is thus the subject of social change operating through and with strong socio-political projects. He/she is the subject of the modern curriculum and has been interpellated for and constituted by the great historical, social and political projects, by the great meta-narratives (Lyotard 1979). However, the modern subject has immense difficulty in realising his or her subjecthood or subjectivity in post-modern societies which are governed by suspicion, uncertainty and scepticism.

Foucault (1972, 1980 and 1982), Lacan (1956–57, 1964, 1987a and 1987b), Derrida (1966 and 1968), Laclau (1990 and 1996), Hall (1996), and Zizek (1990), among others, have reformulated [resettled] the concept of the subject in different ways since its "subject death". They have represented the position of the subject in terms of the subject as lack, the subject as a moment of decision, the subject as reiterative power of discourse (effect of power), and as a subject split by the multiciplicity of discourses surrounding him or her. We thus have a subject that is not pre-determined but rather can be constructed in successive and persistent processes of identification and reidentification.

In the field of education, authors from different around the world have concerned themselves with the question of the subject for the last decade: Peters and Marshall (1997) in Australasia, Giroux (1992) and McLaren (1989, 1995 and 1997) in the United States, Puiggrós (1990, 1992 and 1995), Buenfil (1991 and 1994),Gómez Sollano (1992) and de Alba (1991, 1995a, 1996a and 1997) in Argentina and Mexico, amongst others.

The split subject, the subject that is constituted in the moment of decision, is post-foundational, anti-essentialist, and post-modern. He/she is the subject of the crisis and of the uncertainty of today's world. He/she is the current subject in the process of curricular overdetermination. This subject is interpellated by the social traits and contours emerging from the crisis and is defined by his/her ability to respond to such interpellations.

The question may be asked why it is important to (re)incorporate this split subject into the field of the curriculum (after its supposed 'death') and how it can be done. Reincorporating the split subject is of profound importance because split subjects, in comparison with their singular and 'coherent' antecedents operating in the discursive ether of the grand-narrative, are constituted as subjects with a number of different positions and postures to the world. They do not seek to resolve problems once and for all, and assume their historical and generational responsibility with the awareness that the world they inhabit is one of infinite complexity.

In these new conditions of intelligibility and with these new surfaces of inscription, it is possible to face the crisis, either from a very pessimistic point of view, or to regard it as a terrain of new possibilities. With reference to this discussion, Laclau and Mouffe say:

> There is no room here for disappointment (. . .) Hopelessness in this matter is only proper to those who, to borrow a phrase from J. B. Priestley, have lived for years in a fool's paradise and then abruptly move on to invent a fool's hell for themselves. We are living, on the contrary, in one of the most exhilarating moments of the twentieth century: a moment in which new generations, without the prejudices of the past, without theories presenting themselves as 'absolute truths' of history, are constructing new emancipatory discourses, more human, diversified and democratic. The eschatological and epistemological ambitions are more modest, but the liberating aspirations are wider and deeper. (Laclau and Mouffe 1990: 98)

In seeking to pursue this possibility, it is important that the notion of the subject's positionality is examined as a way of understanding how we might proceed conceptually and politically in the field of the curriculum. Positionality is crucial in the context of the crisis in which we find ourselves. Faced with social traits and contours – instead of grand social projects – what we have in the field are split subjects who live in a world of intense cultural contact which serves as a constant challenge. I want to argue that it is important to confront the issue of positionality and to locate and specify our own positionality in order to construct new modalities of communication with others in a world where cultural contact is increasing each day.

Positionality must be understood as the psychic, cultural, social, geopolitical, economic, etc. space, from which the world is enunciated and through which it is constructed. Discourse positionality is defined by the specificity of the social fabric in which the enunciator belongs. It might, therefore, be understood as an enunciative space (de Alba 1996a: 10).

Curricular overdetermination, cultural contact and traits and contours

We have now seen that the contemporary subject, after the "death of the subject", is constituted and inscribed on the surface of inscription of education by social traits and contours emerging from the dislocated society and is profoundly affected, as a generational subject, by cultural contact.

Even though, in different times in history, there have been moments of intense cultural contact which have given rise to new cultures and nations, it is true to say that the frequency, depth and diversity of cultural interaction is more intense than it has been before. Cultural contact[8] refers to the exchanges of cultural goods and interrelationships among groups, sectors and/or individuals of different cultures. It refers to the transaction of different semiotic codes and the different use of signs (signifiers and signified). As a space in which different discourses interact, its outcomes are new semiotic fields which produce changes in the different subjects inhabiting it. It occurs in several social spaces in a multiplicity of ways interpellated by complex power relationships. Cultural contact is thus relational, unequal, conflictive and productive. It is produced through complex identification processes.[9]

Cultural contact is relational because it is generated, produced and defined in the context of open and precarious relationships. It is constituted and produced within and amongst several articulated meaning systems. That is, it occurs among diverse cultures that have different symbolic economies where symbolic goods and different ways of symbolisation are transacted. The entry of one culture into another and the complex and conflictive encounter which results produce a cultural dislocation that affects the relationality of the meaning systems or cultural systems.

Cultural contact is also conflictive because the subjects involved in it experience structural difficulties in establishing modalities of communication. They are, thus, compelled to construct new arenas of meaning that work as bridges among and between their distinct semiotic codes. While building these arenas, however, they are under pressure to honour and reproduce the constitutive traits of their identity. This struggle is constituted as a relational tension between culture as metonomy and culture as metaphor. One can say it is the expression of different signifiers in their fight to hegemonize the symbolic and cultural space, by trying to reconstitute some signifiers as empty and master signifiers.

From a historical point of view, cultural contact is often unequal because when two or more cultures come into contact they have to negotiate the tension between the desire to dominate and the longing to develop mechanisms which preserve the constitutive traits of their identities. Domination produces its own conditions of possibility in so far as the very conditions of the cultural contact bring with them access to new technology, ideas and practices. A certain productivity emanates from this situation because the relationality, the conflictive characteristics and the unequal relationships which develop during cultural contact permit and accelerate the dislocation of the subjects identities. Multiple interpellations are produced among the subjects, floating signifiers proliferate and through mechanisms of identification new traits and new condensations of meanings are generated. New semiotic and semantic elements permit not only communication among cultures and their subjects but also their transformation and, with long and intense periods of contact, the emergence of new cultures.

The productive character of the process thus refers to its capacity to overdetermine and articulate several discontinuous and uneven moments. It refers to its metaphorical or paradigmatic capacity to take one or several empty signifiers and to make them nodal in so far as they condense and articulate new meanings.

Cultural contact also plays the role of dislocating old certainties as well as producing new and incipient understandings. It changes the language games[10] in which the split subject is constituted and performs. In doing this, it also changes the language games' rules and goes further than any kind of multi-culturalism.

In the current context of crisis, cultural contact is constitutive of new social spaces characterised by traits and contours. Within those spaces are to be found arenas for public discourse from which emanates the curricula. Public spaces are characterised by a) visibility of speech and action (information); b) the possibility of the exchange of ideas, opinions and arguments about information; and c) the possibility of reaching agreements and taking action based on this information and as a result, discussion about this information (see Arditi 1996, and Arendt 1958).

These characteristics – flow and visibility of messages, discussions, agreements and actions – are found in traditional public spaces, what we might call intermittent public spaces, and also virtual public spaces. Traditional public spaces are usually located around issues which are located in specific and known space and time. Intermittent public spaces are located in specific moments and places which appear and disappear and change. And virtual public spaces take place in cyberspace, internet and e-mail, amongst others. This last kind of public space is particularly marked by cultural contact as a result of the necessity of new communicative language forms and the unlimited possibilities of communication and contact.

In the field of the curriculum, the cultural contact serves to disrupt the surface of inscription of the field and presents itself as a challenge to rethink the curriculum and to formulate new proposals. It reveals itself as an experience which is constitutive of the new public spaces in which the curriculum is overdetermined and developed.

Conclusion

In our current crisis-ridden societies it is important to rethink how work in the field of the curriculum might be conducted. While the trajectory of the crisis has been leading towards the disempowerment of the active subject, subjectivity remains possible and might even be pursued. As I have tried to argue in this article, this possibility might be pursued along the following lines:

a) The retrieval and the incorporation of the concept of the subject "after the death of the subject" and the introduction of the notion of position-ality;

b) The recognition of new forms of the curriculum-society link, located in the social traits and contours that emerge from the current processes of crisis; and,

c) the incorporation of cultural contact as a challenge and as a constitutive force within new social spaces.

What an approach such as this makes possible is the recovery of the notion of a social project. Cast in this light, the social project, however, is fundamentally less imperialistic and is underscored by a deep sense of its partiality. It is through this the possibility of establishing the curriculum-society link, from social traits and contours, is enhanced. What this permits is a broad conceptual framework which recognises the possibilities for the emergence of new articulations and the emergence, through cultural contact, of a new and vibrant public sphere, in which many divergent subjects can participate and a new democracy might be forged.

Notes

1. I agree with Laclau (1998) that Neo-Liberalism is in crisis too. In that sense, one cannot consider it a hegemonic social project.
2. I use "surface of inscription" in the Derridean sense. See Derrida 1966 and 1968.
3. Discourse is "a meaningful totality which transcends the distinction between the linguistic and the extra-linguistic. (. . .) the impossibility of a closed totality unties the connection between signifier and signified. In that sense there is a proliferation of 'floating signifiers' in society, and political competition can be seen as attempts by rival political forces to partially fix those signifiers to particular signifying configurations" (Laclau 1993: 435).
4. See Zizek 1990 and Lacan 1987.
5. I am using the notion of interpellation in a Lacanian and Laclaunian way.
6. Globalisation, however, is used mainly in an economic sense. It is used here in the sense of a social contour in the sense that what happens in one part of the world impacts in a multiplicity of ways in other parts of the world too.
7. "I am inclined to paraphrase Ferry and Renault thus: it is impossible to return innocently to the Hegelian or phenomenological subject after Foucault, Derrida, Deleuze and Lyotard (and here these proper names stand as emblems) Peters 1997: 12.
8. About cultural contact, see de Alba and Gutiérrez 1986, González Gaudiano and de Alba 1994 and de Alba 1995.
9. The notion of identification is used mainly from a psychoanalytic view and also from a discourse analaysis view.
10. The notion of language games derives from Wittgenstein 1953.

References

Arditi, B. 1995. *An Archipelago of Public Spaces*. Department of Government, University of Essex, England. 25 pp.

Arendt, Hannah. 1958. *The Human Condition*. Chicago: The University Chicago Press.

488

Buenfil Burgos, Rosa Nidia. 1991. *El debate sobre el sujeto en el discurso marxista: notas críticas sobre el reduccionismo de clase y educación.* México: DIE (Tesis DIE 12).

Buenfil Burgos, Rosa Nidia. 1994. *Cardenismo. Argumentación y antagonismo en educación.* México: DIE-CINVESTAV-IPN/CONACYT.

de Alba, Alicia and Gutiérrez, M. 1986. La pluriculturalidad en la escuela primaria mexicana: un reto hacia la consolidación de la identidad nacional. In: *Educación primaria* (1–101). México: SEP.

de Alba, Alicia. 1991. *Curriculum: crisis, mito y perspectivas.* México: CESU-UNAM.

de Alba, Alicia. 1995a. *Expectativas docentes ante la problemática y los desafíos del curriculum universitario en México.* Madrid: UNED.

de Alba, Alicia. 1995b. Posmodernidad y educación. Implicaciones epistémicas y conceptuales en los discursos educativos. In: *Posmodernidad y educación México* (129–175). Porrúa: CESU-UNAM.

de Alba, Alicia. 1996a. *Sujetos educativos: la tarea de reescribirlos conceptualmente.* Paper presented at International Congress of Education "Education, Crises and Utopias". Buenos Aires, Argentina. 12 pp.

de Alba, Alicia. 1996b. *Crisis y curriculum universitario: Horizontes postmodernos y utópicos.* International Congress of Education "Education, Crises and Utopias". Buenos Aires, Argentina. 19 pp.

de Alba, Alicia. 1997. *Curriculum: crisis y sujetos.* México: CESU-UNAM, 19 pp.

Derrida, Jacques. 1966. Freud y la escena de la escritura. In: *La escritura y la diferencia* (271–317). Barcelona: Anthropos, 1989.

Derrida, Jacques. 1968. La Différence. In: *Márgenes de la Filosofía. Cátedra.*

Foucault, Michel. 1972. *The Archaeology of Knowledge.* London: Tavistock Publications.

Foucault, Michel. 1980. *The History of Sexuality*, Vol. 1. New York: Vintage.

Foucault, Michel. 1982. Afterword: The Subject and Power. In: H. Dreyfus and P. Rabinow (eds) *Michel Foucault: Beyond Structuralism and Hermeneutics.* Chicago: The Harvester Press Ltd.

Giroux, H. 1992. *Border Crossings: Cultural Workers and the Politics of Education.* New York: Routledge.

González Gaudiano, E. and de Alba, Alicia. 1994. Freire – Present and Future Possibilities. In: Peter McLaren and Colin Lankshear (eds) *Politics of Liberation. Paths from Freire* (123–141). London and New York: Routledge.

Hall, S. 1996. Who Needs 'Identity'? In: *Questions of Cultural Identity* (1–36). London: Thousand Oaks/New Delhi: SAGE Publications.

Lacan, Jacques. 1956–1957. *"La relacion de objeto" Seminarios de Lacan 4.* Barcelona: Paidos, 1994.

Lacan, Jacques. 1964. *"Los cuatro principios fundamentales del psicoanálisis" Seminarios de Lacan 11.* Barcelona: Paidós, 1987.

Lacan, Jacques. 1987a. "El estadio del espejo como formador de la función del yo (je) tal y como se nos revela a la experiencia psicoanalítica", "Del sujeto por fin cuestionado" in Escritos 1. México: Siglo XXl.

489

Lacan, Jacques. 1987b. Psicoanálisis y estructura de la personalidad: subversión del sujeto y dialéctica del deseo en el inconsciente freudiano. In *Escritos 2*. Mexico: Ed. Siglo XXI.

Laclau, E. and Mouffe, C. 1990. Post-Marxism without Apologies. In: E. Laclau (ed) *New Reflections on the Revolution of our Time* (97–132). London and New York: Verso.

Laclau, E. 1993. Discourse. In: R. Goodin and P. Pettit (eds) *A Companion to Contemporary Political Philosophy* (431–437). Oxford: Blackwell.

Laclau, E. 1996. *Emancipation(s)*. London and New York, Verso.

Laclau, E. 1998. La ideología neoliberal está perdiendo su capacidad integradora. In: *Excelsior*. México: DF: Sunday 19 April (El búho).

Lyotard, J-F. 1979. *The Postmodern Condition: A Report on Knowledge*. Trans by G. Bennington and B. Massumi. Manchester: Manchester University Press.

McLaren, P. 1989. *Life in Schools*, 3rd edition. New York: Longmans, 1997.

McLaren, P. 1995. *Critical Pedagogy and Predatory Culture*. London and New York, Routledge.

McLaren, P. 1997. *Revolutionary Multiculturalism*. Boulder, CO: Westview Press.

Peters, M. 1997 Nietzsche, Poststructuralism and Education: After the Subject? In: *Educational Philosophy and Theory*, Vol. 29 No. 1, 1997, pp. 1–19.

Puiggrós, A. 1990. *Sujetos, Disciplina y Curriculum*, Second edition. Buenos Aires: Editorial Galerna, 1994.

Puiggrós, A. 1992. Las alternativas pedagógicas y los sujetos. Reflexión crítica sobre el marco teórico de APPEAL. In Puiggrós, Adriana and Marcela Gómez Sollano (coord.) Alternativas Pedagógicas: Sujetos y Prospectiva de la Educación Latinoamericana. México: Facultad de Filosofía y Letras, DGAPA-UNAM. Pp. 68–85.

Puiggrós, A. 1995. *Volver a educar. El desafío de la enseñanza argentina a finales del siglo XX*. Buenos Aires: Ariel.

Puiggrós, A. and Sollano. M. (coord.) (N.D.) *Alternativas Pedagógicas: Sujetos y Prospectiva de la Educación Latinoamericana*. México, Facultad de Filosofía y Letras, DGAPA-UNAM.

Wittgenstein, Ludwig. 1953. Investigaciones Filósoficas. Translation by Alfonso García Suárez and Ulises Moulines. México: Ed. Crítica/Instituto de Investigaciones Filosóficas UNAM, 1988.

Zizek, S. 1990. *The Sublime Object of Ideology*. London: Verso.

The author

Alicia de Alba is Professor at the National Autonomous University of Mexico. She has directed several international projects and has been invited, amongst the most important, by University of Essex, England; University of Buenos Aires, National University of Entre Ríos, University of Cordoba and University of the Centre of Buenos Aires, in Argentina; National Distance University, Autonomous University of Madrid, University of Barcelona, in Spain; National University of Loja, in Ecuador; Queensland University of Technology in Brisbane, Australia; and Miami University in Oxford, Ohio, United States of North America. Amongst her most important books are Theory and Education (1990) Curriculum: crisis, mito y perspectivas (1991), Posmodernidad y educación (1995), and, Curriculum: académicos y futuro (in press).

Contact address: Dr Alicia de Alba, CESU-UNAM, Edificio Bibliográfico 4 piso, Centro Cultural Universitario, C.U. 04510 México. E-mail: dealba@servidor.unam.mx.

NO MATTER HOW LONG THE NIGHT, THE DAY IS SURE TO COME:[1] CULTURE AND EDUCATIONAL TRANSFORMATION IN POST-COLONIAL NAMIBIA AND POST-APARTHEID SOUTH AFRICA

FHULU NEKHWEVHA

Abstract – Following the defeat of Apartheid, the 1990s have witnessed serious attempts by Namibians and South Africans alike to reconstruct their social institutions along democratic lines. While education has not been excluded from these efforts, there is evidence that the new curricula are primarily influenced by western educational models. For example, prescriptions of the International Monetary Fund and the World Bank have been uncritically incorporated into the new educational programme. Consequently the curricula lack an indigenous ingredient, namely the cultural capital of the African masses. It is suggested in this article that the much acclaimed African cultural renaissance in education will only become a reality when educationalists embrace the "pedagogy of hope".

Zusammenfassung – Nach der Abschaffung der Apartheid, wurden während der 90er Jahre von den Einwohnern Namibias und Südafrikas ernsthafte Versuche unternommen, ihre sozialen Einrichtungen gemäß demokratischer Richtlinien wieder aufzubauen. Die Bildung wurde bei diesen Bestrebungen zwar nicht außer acht gelassen, jedoch stellte sich heraus, daß die neuen Lehrpläne sich hauptsächlich an westlichen Bildungsmodellen orientierten. Beispielsweise wurden die Vorschriften des Internationalen Währungsfonds und der Weltbank unverändert in das neue Bildungsprogramm integriert. Folglich mangelt es den neuen Lehrplänen an Inhalten mit einheimischem Charakter, dem kulturellen Kapital der afrikanischen Bevölkerung. Der Artikel stellt fest, daß die vielerseits begrüßte kulturelle Wiedergeburt Afrikas nur realisiert werden kann, wenn die Ausbilder die "Pädagogik der Hoffnung" praktizieren.

Résumé – Après la chute de l'apartheid, les Namibiens et les Sud-Africains ont déployé au cours des années 90 de sérieux efforts pour réorganiser leurs institutions sociales selon des principes démocratiques. Si l'éducation n'a pas été exclue de ces efforts, il est notoire que les programmes éducatifs sont principalement influencés par les modèles pédagogiques occidentaux. Par exemple, les presciptions du Fonds monétaires international et de la Banque mondiale ont été incorporées sans critique dans le nouveqqu programme. Il lui manque par conséquent un élément autochtone, c'est-à-dire le captial culturel des peuples africains. L'article exprime l'avis que la renaissance culturelle africaine tant acclamée ne peut devenir réalité que si les éducateurs adoptent la "pédagogie de l'espoir".

Resumen – Tras la derrota del apartheid, los años noventa han presenciado serios esfuerzos realizados tanto por namibianos como por sudafricanos para reconstruir sus instituciones sociales dentro de delineamientos democráticos. Pese a que la educación no ha quedado excluida de estos esfuerzos, es evidente que los nuevos planes de estudio están influenciados más que nada por modelos de educación occidental. Así por ejemplo, las disposiciones del Fondo Monetario Internacional y del Banco Mundial se han incorporado en el nuevo programa de educación sin

International Review of Education – Internationale Zeitschrift für Erziehungswissenschaft – Revue Internationale de l'Education 45(5/6): 491–506, 1999.
© 1999 *Kluwer Academic Publishers. Printed in the Netherlands.*

492

cuestionarlas. En consecuencia, los planes de estudio carecen de un ingrediente indígena, es decir, del capital cultural de la poblacón africana. Este trabajo sugiere que el tan aclamado renacimiento cultural africano en la educación solamente se hará realidad cuando los responsables de la educación abracen la «pedagogía de la esperanza».

Резюме - После победы над апартедом, в 90-х года были заметны серьезные попытки жителей Намибии и Южной Африки восстановить их социальные институты в соответствии с демократическими стандартами. Несмотря на то, что образование не было исключено из этих попыток, создается впечатление, что новые программы обучения в основном формируются под влиянием западных моделей. Так, в новую программу образования были некритически включены предписания Международного Валютного Фонда и Всемирного Банка. Поэтому программе недостает важного элемента - а именно, культурного наследия африканского населения. В статье указывается, что пресловутое африканское культурное возрождение станет реальностью лишь тогда, когда работники просвещения займутся "педагогикой веры".

Culture as our genesis

> The African philosopher should learn from the traditions, tales, myths and proverbs of his people, so as to draw from them the laws of a true African wisdom complementary to other forms of human wisdom and to bring out the specific categories of African thought . . . the African philosopher . . . [must] divest himself of a possible inferiority complex, which might prevent him from starting from his African being to judge the foreign contribution (in Minogue and Molloy 1974: 228–229).

The above statement emphasizes the importance of culture in education. Culture is both a way of life for a people and a framework within which they make meaning, confront difference and initiate change. Seen in this perspective, culture is a set of beliefs and practices which provide oportunities for human beings to be the agents of their own destinies. Apartheid education in Namibia and South Africa deliberately excluded the culture and language skills of the dominated from the curriculum in order to keep African people in a state of alienation. It is for this reason that scholars such as Hailom Banteyerga believe that:

> Africa today is full of challenges. Education is expected to be an effective tool in coping with these challenges. However, the existing education in Africa is the legacy of colonialism. It has been geared to meet and maintain colonial interests under the cover umbrella phrase "modernizing Africa". What we see today is that the so-called "modern education" is not satisfactorily addressing the problems of Africa to meet the needs and aspirations of the African people. In other words, it

has not done much to boost the material growth and spiritual development of Africa. What is vividly observed is that African wisdom and knowledge is being systematically undermined: African self-concept and pride; African understanding and interpretation of the environment; and all in all the culture and psychological make up of the African. If Africa is to regain its place as the centre of culture and civilization, it needs to re-think and reframe its education in the context of Africa – and its problems and aspirations. (Banteyerga 1994: 1–2)

In attempting to deal with the warning by Banteyerga, the Namibian and South African post-apartheid education transformation programmes will be examined with a view to seeing how change might be effected.

The political context of educational change in post-colonial Namibia and post-apartheid South Africa

The educational transformation in post-colonial Namibia and post-apartheid South Africa should be viewed against the background of the political changes which took place in these two countries. Both countries were beneficiaries and victims of the momentous events which played themselves out in the flowering and subsequent withering of the Cold War. The Namibian and South African liberatory struggles both benefited from the support of the socialist countries. Their liberation forces fought side-by-side in Angola where, with the help of Cuba, they routed the South African army at Cuito Cuanavale. This event, along with the sustained economic boycott by the West of South Africa, served to vitiate the apartheid order in both Namibia and South Africa. At the same time, however, the liberation forces were blunted by the collapse of the Soviet Bloc. These events help us to understand how the antagonists were both forced to the negotiation table, and how Resolution 435 came to be implemented in Namibia and the installation of the Government of National Unity (GNU) came into being in South Africa. Historical circumstances in Namibia and South Africa thus forced the parties in the two countries into an embrace of accommodation and negotiation. The result in each country was thus a *negotiated* settlement.

Students of revolution will argue that a social revolution transforms the whole fabric of society – economic, political, ideological, etc. Change which takes place in the superstructure cannot by definition be characterised as revolution. For this reason, it is important to distinguish between reformative and transformative change. Reformists are for limited or "evolutionary" change. Radical revolutionaries, by contrast, believe in the fundamental and complete remodelling of the social structure (Giddens 1989: 625). In terms of this approach, it cannot be gainsaid that post-colonial Namibian and South African policy have gone the reformative way. As social scientists, it is important that we work with with this distinction and recognise the humanist mask and the radical rhetoric within which the reformative projects in Namibia and South Africa have been launched.

Apartheid education dynamics in South Africa and Namibia – a brief summary

While colonial education in Namibia and South Africa is located in very different historical experiences, both countries became the subjects of apartheid education after 1948. In South Africa the apartheid National Party came into power, while Namibia – then referred to as South West Africa – was colonised by South Africa. The chief architect of Apartheid education and Minister of Native Affairs when the Bantu Education Act was passed in 1953, Dr. H. F. Verwoerd, had this to say with regard to the general aims and objectives of the Act:

> My department's policy is that education should stand with both feet in the reserves and have its roots in the spirit and being of Bantu society . . . the Bantu must be guided to serve his own community in all respects. There is no place for him in the European community above the level of certain forms of labour. Within his own community, however, all doors are open. For that reason it is of no avail for him to receive a training which has as its aim absorption in the European community, where he cannot be absorbed. Until now he has been subjected to a school system which drew him away from his own community and misled him by showing him the green pastures of European society in which he is not allowed to graze. (Verwoerd 1954)

Despite Verwoerd's gestures towards indigenous culture, the society into which he ordered African people was an impoverished and segregated version of the dominant white order. It destroyed the symbiotic bond between socialisation and survival and between education and production, and, in the stressed environment of the urban townships, undermined the values of co-operation and communication. Where traditional education taught young people the values of respect for one's peers and elders, a regard for diligence and trained young people to enter the economy, the kind of education which apartheid laid before African people was that of subservience and subordination. Contrary to conventional wisdom, which has it that formal education in South Africa and Namibia was pioneered by missionaries from Europe (Salia-Bao 1991: 14),[2] it is important to recognise the structured nature of traditional education and the role it played in building community.

According to Julius Nyerere, the former president of Tanzania,

> The fact that pre-colonial Africa did not have "schools" except for short periods of initiation in some tribes – did not mean that children were not educated. They learned by doing . . . Education was thus "informal"; every adult was a teacher to a greater or less degree. But this lack of formality did not mean that there was no education, nor did it affect its importance to society. Indeed, it may have made the education more directly relevant to the society in which the child was growing up. (Nyerere 1967: 49–50)

What may be inferred from Nyerere's statement is that each and every society evolves its own mechanisms of transmitting social skills, norms and values from one generation to another. During this socialisation process education plays a vital role as a means by which culture and behaviour, deemed suitable for a social formation, is transferred to the youth. In South Africa circumcision schools amongst the Xhosa-speaking people, which have survived the cultural invasion strategies of Western colonialism and apartheid domination, attest to the existence of structured education in traditional African society. Similar traditions existed in Namibia. Amukugo explains: "It is a common view that formal education in Africa was introduced by missionaries . . . . The opposite can be argued – that is, that Western education in Namibia and in Africa, was introduced in Societies which had evolved their own distinct educational system(s)." (Amukugo 1993: 32–33)

She carries on to say:

> In this regard, the initiation process, a cultural dimension, constitutes the major formal aspect of traditional African education. Initiation school programmes lasting from a couple of weeks to several months were educational processes by means of which the individual passed from childhood for adulthood. They sought to introduce the young to major components of the culture of their people. As such they were an institution that taught young people some knowledge and skills required by their communities. Through initiation the individuals were initiated into different cults or rituals, and into the rules pertaining to female or male roles. This symbolic act sometimes took place in conjuction with male circumcision. (Amukugo 1993: 37)

If one accepts that these forms of traditional African education provided a foundation for the education of African people, it is not out of place to say that the praxis of German, British, Dutch and Apartheid colonialists in South Africa and Namibia constituted a process of cultural invasion. Cultural invasion, a concept developed by Paulo Freire (1972), is one of the primary characteristics of what Freire calls anti-dialogical action which serves the ends of conquest. Here the invaders destroy the culture of their victims by systematically imposing their own systems of thought, values, and norms at the same time as curbing the invaded people's creativity and self-expression. As a result of this invasion, the invaded people lose their originality. In the process, the invaders assume the position of authors, actors, teachers and choosers while the invaded masses are relegated to being objects, followers of choices made for them. In other words, they remain perpetual children.

For cultural invasion to succeed, the invaded should be convinced of their intrinsic inferiority, as opposed to the superiority of their conquerors. This is followed by the adoption of the latter's dress codes, mannerisms, values and so on. In the Namibian context, the primary aim of cultural imperialism was to establish German monopoly on the ashes of African traditional society (Amukugo 1993: 43). Apartheid colonialism perpertuated this process. Similar strategies were adopted by the Dutch, the British, and the National Party in South Africa. African norms, languages, values, customs and practices were marginalised in the content of education.

Education transformation strategies in Namibia and South Africa

After achieving victory over the Apartheid forces in 1990 and 1994 respectively, Namibia and South Africa initiated similar processes for the development of new education policies. Because of the uniqueness of each country's policy, they will be separately outlined in anticipation of a comparative analysis which is developed below.

"Education For All" in Namibia

After independence in March 1990 the new Namibian government sought to replace the colonial South African schooling system with a new "international" system. After the appointment of several commissions, and the development of proposals, guides and reports, the Ministry of Education and Culture (MEC) adopted a document entitled "Towards Education for All" in 1993 (MEC 1993). The main thrust of this new education policy included the abolition of racial discrimination in education, the establishment of a compulsory education structure from age six to sixteen; the introduction of English as a mediun of instruction from Grade 4 to 12; the creation of one Ministry of Education and Culture for the whole of Namibia; and the introduction of the International General Certificate of Secondary Education (IGCSE) curriculum and syllabi (MEC 1993). In line with this new educational policy, the MEC enlisted the services of the University of Cambridge Local Examination Syndicate (UCLES) (MEC 1995: 1). In view of the scope of the changes and because the policy was cast in a learner-centred frame (Howarth 1995; MEC 1993), the programme was hailed as an educational breakthrough.

The most important reason for the ready acceptance of "Education for All" was its representation in the rhetoric of emancipation. Critically, for example, the policy presented culture as a unifying and nation-building force. The MEC committed itself to the utilisation of all the distinctive and unique elements of the Namibian cultural universe as building blocks of a rich national culture. A necessary condition for the achievement of the goal of cultural unity, in the MEC's perception, was a cross-cultural dialogue whose main purpose was the removal of cultural prejudices amongst the people. In the educational arena the authorities committed themselves to the integration of the diverse heritages of all Namibia's citizens into the school curriculum (MEC 1993: 45–51).

However, this aspect of the Namibian education policy was seriously compromised by the decision to make English the medium of instruction in the Namibian Schools. Vernacular languages were, surprisingly, relegated to media of instruction from Grade 1 to 3. Furthermore, it was left to communities to decide whether they wished to take up this option (MEC 1993: 63–66).

The "Education for All" curriculum was also expected to promote an analytic, imaginative, critical and innovative mind. Equal participation, cooperation, mutual respect and understanding between teachers and learners were to be the cornerstones of the new education system. In the light of the exclusion of the cultural heritages of Namibians from the learning process in the old colonial curriculum, the MEC recommended that the cultural landscape of the learners had to be central in the new curriculum. This suggested that aspects of the Bantu Education curriculum, such as description, memorisation, and punitive discipline were targeted for immediate elimination (MEC 1993: 120–123).

Following these developments, according to the MEC, the new policy sought to move education away from its colonial moorings. The central goal was to promote a spirit of self-reliance and productivity. This could only be done, argued the MEC, through the utilization of the learners' cultural experience for independent and critical thinking. Finally, the MEC expected the learner-centred approach to promote equity and equality in classroom dialogue and participation as well as to encourage democratic values and practices (MEC 1993: 119–120). In sum, the policy contained the characteristics of what one might call a socially and culturally progressive education. However, embedded in the document was an open-mindedness to the "free enterprise" system. Before reflecting on the potential contradictions of this, a brief description of the education transformation of the GNU government in South Africa is needed.

South Africa's outcomes-based education approach

> A new outcomes-based approach to learning . . . facilitate equivalence, articulation, flexibility, progression across different learning institutions and contexts. "Outcomes" provide the foundation for the formal equivalence of certifications. The South African policy experts decided to define outcomes broadly in a non-behaviouristic way, in terms of key generic skills and knowledge, such as the ability to understand a task theoretically, apply skills and knowledge to it and transfer them to another context (42). Outcomes become then, an integral component of learning by complementing curricular content and learning methods. This integration of content, skills and competencies/outcomes in each course/diploma make portability and articulation between different learning contexts and institutions more meaningful and realistic. (De Clercq 1997: 57)

The above statement by Francine de Clercq is offered as guide to understanding what the outcomes-based education approach is all about. The idea of an outcomes-based education (OBE) was first introduced in the White Paper on Education and Training released by the Ministry of Education on March 15, 1995. The relevant section of that document reads:

> 6. In response to such structural changes and economic organisation and technogical development, integrated approaches toward education and training are now a major international trend in curriculum development and the reform of qualification structures.

7. An integrated approach to education and training linked to the development of a new National Qualification Framework (NQF), based on a sytem of credits for learning outcomes achieved will encourage creative work in the design of curricula and recognition of learning attachments whenever education and training are offered. (Ministry of Education, South Africa 1995: 15)

One point is very clear from the above statement – that the primary reason for the adoption of an education and training strategy linked to an Outcomes-based Education approach and a standardised National Qualification Framework (NQF) is the lure and attraction of the international economic and technological order. The implication here is that external, global, market-related influences are prime considerations which a country ignores at its peril. A country's future, the argument goes, is to integrate its polity, economy, and critically, its education system into the standardised structure of the world system. The effect of this is to universalise as common currency the hegemonic knowledge system of the Western world. In pursuit of this, not unexpectedly, local considerations, local knowledges and local understandings of the world were cast aside. Sieborger, who participated in the process which led to the development of both South Africa's new curriculum, Curriculum 2005, and OBE commented that the input of Canadian, Dutch and Scottish advisers to the Department of Education was put in such a way that they were virtually non-negotiable (Sieborger 1997: 4–5). In the same vein, Natheem Hendricks and Joe Samuels reported that members of the standard generating task team (SGTT) could not take issue with the assumed unquestionable status of English as the language to generate standards because they feared the consequences of being marginalised (Hendricks and Samuels 1997: 11–12).

In the Curriculum 2005 (C2005) document (Ministry of Education-SA 1997) unveiled by the Minister of Education, Professor S. Bhengu, in February 1997, OBE's utility was characterised as being not only about increasing the general knowledge of learners but also, and more importantly so, about its ability to develop their skills, critical thinking, attitudes and understanding. In fact the examination is no longer a primary means of achieving these broad outcomes. Instead different assessment strategies were put in place to measure outcomes on an on-going basis (some form of continual assessment). Accompanying these new assessment strategies was the unveiling of a new vocabulary for education. Pupils, for example, were now to be referred to as learners and subjects as learning areas. Each learning area was allocated to a committee composed of representatives of stake-holders and experts whose function was to develop the related learning outcomes and design guidelines for learning programmes for the schools.

The C2005 document identified eight learning areas, viz., Communication, Literacy, and Language Learning; Numeracy and Mathematics; Human and Social Sciences; Natural Sciences; Arts and Culture; Economic and Management Sciences; Life Orientation; and Technology. The reason given for establishing these eight learning areas in this manner was that they provided the appropriate context for the stimulation of generic skills. Koetsier (1997) argues that the new curriculum resembles the "project approach" of education which was in vogue in the sixties in various European countries such as the Netherlands. Moreover, he describes the checklist approach which is used for monitoring critical skills as a carbon copy of the dated curriculum development strategies which were hegemonic in the USA and Europe in the fifties and sixties (Koetsier 1997: 2–7).

The critical cross-field outcomes or essential outcomes directly link OBE with the work of the South African Qualification Authority (SAQA). SAQA has been given the responsibility for the design of outcomes which apply to all the learning areas as part of its mandate to generate a National Qualification Framework (NQF) which is both integrated and conceived of as an important instrument to make possible life-long learning. Skills, in this approach, are portable and transferable. For SAQA, in order to provide uniformity for measuring educational progress across the different regions of the system, it was deemed necessary to have an outcomes-based curriculum. Nevertheless there remained niggling questions marks around inter alia (1) the lack of clarity about specific outcomes, and, (2) the nature of the outcomes themselves. These two questions are linked to the point raised in the introduction about the narrow focus around skill and attitudes outcomes as defined by the market. As critics such as de Clercq (1997) suggest, the outcomes in C2005 appear to be conceived in behaviourist rather than critical terms. Put in this way, the reforms suggest the replacement of one top-down policy by another. More to the point, Koetsier believes that OBE, like the curriculum of the apartheid epoch, reproduces the exclusionary mono-cultural discourse of the West (Koetsier 1997: 2).

The emancipatory rhetoric of "Education for All" and OBE

The position advanced here is that the "critical theory"-derived liberatory rhetoric adopted by both the Namibian "Education for All" and South African OBE serves as a mask for a new period of Western domination in the southern African region. The Namibian "Education for All" discourse, for instance, puts forward the idea that the new education policy is for liberation; that it is problem-posing; and that it is dialogical and a negation of the banking concept of education. All these ideas are subsumed in a learner-centred approach and are presented in the language of critical pedagogy, particularly that of Freire's dialectical humanism. A problem I foresee, however, is that Freire was not explicit about the economic system in which authentic liberation could take place amd left the question open to the people to decide for themselves. It is my considered view that educational and economic liberation are intertwined. In view of this, I would question whether a Freirian-based educational liberation programme can operate within an economic vacuum. Is an emancipatory project which excludes the struggle for land and control over productive forces not empty, meaningless and devoid of content? It would thus seem that the silence and/or vagueness of the MEC on the economic system within which this educational project will operate serves to maintain and perpertuate the dominant capitalist social relations in Namibia. A similar problem can be detected in the South African version of the Outcomes-Based Education.

In Curriculum 2005, differences between the old apartheid education and the OBE approaches are pointed out. On the one hand, apartheid education promoted passive learning, rote-learning, teacher-centredness, and rigid content based syllabi and curricula. On the other, OBE is said to stand for learner-centredness, democratic curricula/programmes, active participation, critical thinking, reasoning, reflection and action. The above distinction is more akin to the Freirian distinction between banking and liberatory education. If indeed OBE is committed to these values and this is not mere rhetoric to satisfy its selection for South Africa, then that makes it progressive. But what about its prescription of specific outcomes? Are these not indicative of a functionalist approach? In addition, Koetsier says the failure of South African education policy makers "to link the curriculum development process to experiences from indigenous eduational movements which in the days of the Anti-apartheid struggle gained recognition" (Kotsier 1997: 14), calls into question the progressiveness of the architects of OBE. These concerns are supported by Peter Dzvimbo who comments:

> The OBE policy represents a bureaucratic curriculum reform which in many way is a design of restructuring. The language of OBE seems very technical, apolitical, cosmetic, and see-through especially in the way it is used in government documents. A good example of this is the way in which OBE has been described as transformative in orientation documents for teachers. These descriptions are a direct copy of a table from an article by Spady and Marshall published in 1991 (6), summarising the concept as it is used in the context of educational change in North America. This reflects the limitations of the restructuring approach to teacher education where it is expected of teachers to learn concepts about teaching defined in terms which are distant from their experience base. The discourse of OBE stays very much a discourse of exclusion because teachers do not own the key concepts. (Dzvimbo 1997: 12)

My intention in making this criticism is not to undermine sincere attempts by South Africans from divergent backgrounds to effect change but to highlight the potential danger of using the international, particularly its "market", as a reference point. Those familiar with development theories will recall that each economic/technological complex has its own values, parameters, norms and logic within which it operates. For the capitalist market, Western values, ideas and way of life are undoubtedly the norm. It could be argued that in seeking to put in place an educational system which is focused on developing in young people the narrow skills to operate efficiently in a competitive market that we could end up with a technically skilled (in terms of the capitalist rationality) but a fundamentality alienated populace in terms of African culture, languages, ideas and values.

The dominant Western influence in the Namibian "Education for All" and South Africa's OBE

In attempting to unravel the nature and form of socialisation and the norms and values promoted in post-independence Namibia and South Africa, we will return to the central policies of both these countries. Article 20 of the Namibian Constitution includes a passage which reads as follows:

> All persons shall have the right to education. Primary education shall be compulsory and the state shall provide reasonable facilities to render effective this right for every resident within Namibia by establishing and maintaining state schools at which primary education will be provided free of charge. (MEC 1993: 3)

These core features of the new Namibian education policy are similar to those adopted in policies of agencies such as UNDP, UNESCO, UNICEF and the World Bank. The major themes of the Jomtien World Conference on "Education for All", were the following: that education is a fundamental right; it is the key to personal and social improvement; and that basic education should therefore be provided to all (World Declaration of Education for All 1990: 2–4). Against this backdrop, the rhetoric within "Education for All" in Namibia, as indeed are the World Conference prouncements, presupposes the acceptance of the neo-liberal ideology which essentially urges that all members of society should receive a basic and free mass education but user-fees should be charged for higher education. Taken together, the above points are a matter of concern – for only the children from better socio-economic backgrounds can afford higher education with the possible result that the class structure will be reproduced.

Another aspect which gives the new Namibian education policy a largely Western character is the wholesale import of the British IGSCE curriculum and the use of University of Cambridge Local Examination Syndicate (ECLES) for the validation of its examinations. Notwithstanding efforts to localise the IGSCE curriculum, problems have arisen which cannot be wished away. These stem from the direct implantation of the British educational structure, its logic, and frameworks. This is discussed in greater length below. Similar trends are noticeable in the South African outcomes-based approach. In the course of the displacement of more radical ideologies, such as people's Education, it might be suggested that neo-liberalism has consolidated its influence in South Africa.

Pam Christie (1997: 111) believes the collapse of a radical approach to education is part of the process of globalisation and the curriculum. In support of this position, and indeed as other key South African scholars such as

502

Nzimande (1997) have warned, I want to suggest that South African fiscal policy has been, to a large extent, influenced by the attitude and ideology of the IMF and the World Bank. For instance, there is ample empirical evidence to suggest that the South African macro-economic and education policies, GEAR and OBE, respectively, have been an outcome of a direct influence by these institutions (Padayachee 1996: 199).

The exclusion of African Culture in "Education for All" and OBE

A marked oversight in both "Education for All" and OBE, is the absence of an understanding of African educational philosophy and culture. High drop-out rates, alienation and unemployment in Africa today are partly caused by an irrelevant Western-based curricula. A curriculum drawing on a traditional African education philosophy could help to counter the strident individualism which is embedded in the current curricula. Towards this, it is important that Africans are taught their own histories. History in both Namibia and South Africa is in danger of disappearing. Disconcerting, for example, is the relegation of Namibian history to a small part of an optional subject within the curriculum (UCLES, IGSCE Report 1993; UCLES, IGCSE History Syllabus 1996).

One of the most challenging developments arising out of the Namibian and South African education systems relate to the adoption of English as the medium of instruction in schools, technikons, colleges and universities. South African educationists Natheem Hendricks and Joe Samuels indicated that standard generation in the new OBE approach is solely in English. For them language expresses culture and cultural values. In their own words:

> By denying or being silent on the rights of people to generate standards in the language of their choice, we are elevating one language and one form of cultural expression at the expense of others, again marginalising those already marginalised. School Governing Bodies should make language an issue and not assume that English is the only language in which standards can be set. (Hendricks and Samuels 1997: 12)

The hegemony of the English language has frequently been justified by its international importance, particularly its use in international, technological and industrial communication. But those who support it forget that its presence in the world today is the result of imperialism and colonialism. A more definitive statement on this matter can be found in Ngugi wa Thiongo's classic work, *Decolonising the Mind* (1986), which reads as follows:

> ... the biggest weapon wielded and actually daily unleashed by imperialism against that collective defiance is the cultural bomb. The effect of a cultural bomb is to annihilate a people's belief in their names, in their language, in their heritage of struggle, in their unity, in their capacities and ultimately in themselves. It makes

them see their past as one wasteland. It makes them want to identity with that which is furthest removed from themselves; for instance, with other people's language rather than their own. . . . Amidst this wasteland which it has created imperialism presents itself as the cure and demands that the dependent sing hymns of praise with the constant refrain: "theft is holy". Indeed this refrain sums up the new creed of the neo-colonial bourgeosie in many "independent" African States. (wa Thiongo 1986: 3)

Indeed it can be argued that no country ever achieved high levels of economic and cultural development where a large number of its citizens were compelled to communicate in their second and/or third languages. Unless Africans hasten to develop their languages for scientific and technological communication these languages might be marginalised forever from the discourse of development in Africa. This of course will have dire consequences for the future of Africa. One important critique of "Education for All" and OBE, therefore, is that they have the potential of excluding the cultural knowledge and experience of the African people and fostering what Freire (1972) called the culture of silence.

Language habits are determiners of social relations through their role in shaping culture. It is also a fact that vernacular education is vital to the cognitive, emotional and socio-cultural development of the individual. There is therefore a need to implement the idea of African languages as central to the education process of an African child. In addition there is a need to indigenise the knowledge base for development.

Conclusion

"Education for All" and OBE are the latest versions of the discourse of modernisation. Against this backdrop, it is important that we African intellectuals move away from our own long "academic sojourn" in the Western imagination and adopt an "insurgency approach" to expose and challenge the new imperialism which is regrouping on our sub-continent. We have to contest the neo-liberal stranglehold on the world and fight to liberate our education, culture and politics from the clutches of Western cultural hegemony. We have to struggle to make African culture and experience the primary constituent of our world view.

African organic intellectuals must leave no stone unturned in searching for African ways and ideas to inform our educational praxis. In the struggle to expose the myth that Western intellectual paradigms are sacrosanct, we must be conscious that the space created by the defeat of apartheid might soon be filled if an African position is not advanced immediately.

504

Notes

1. A proverb from Congo translated to the English language by Anne Hope (1984: 12).
2. The arrival of Jan van Riebeeck in South Africa in 1652 is supposed to mark the beginning of the process of introducing formal education in the country whereas conventional wisdom has it that formal education in Namibia was pioneered by European missionaries in 1888 (see Salia-Bao 1991: 14).

References

Amukugo, M. E. 1993. *Education and Politics in Namibia*. Windhoek: New Namibia Books.

Banteyerga, H. 1994. An Alternative Model in Teacher Education: The Classroom in Focus. A Paper presented at the Pan-African colloqiuim: Educational Innovation in Post-colonial Africa. University of Cape Town, Rondebosch.

Barker, P. H. et al., eds. 1996. *South Africa and the World Economy*. Johannesburg: David Philip.

Christie, P. 1997. Globalisation and the Curriculum: Proposals for the Integration of Education and Training in South Africa. In: P. Kallaway et al., eds., *Education after Apartheid* (111–126) Cape Town: UCT Press.

de Clercq, F. 1995. Policies and Strategies for Implementation: The Unbreakable Partnership: An Evaluation of the New Education and Development Macro Policies. Paper presented at the Kenton Conference. Rhodes University, Grahamstown.

de Clercq, F. 1997. Effective Policies and the Reform Process: An Evaluation of South Africa's New Development and Education Macro Policies. In: P. Kallaway et al., eds., *Education After Apartheid* (142–168). Cape Town: UCT Press.

Dzvimbo, E. P. 1997. Shifting Paradigms in the Discourse Practices of Teacher Education Reform in Southern Africa. Paper presented at the Annual Conference of the Kenton Education Association. Hermanus.

Freire, P. 1972. *Pedagogy of the Oppressed*. Harmondsworth: Penguin.

Giddens, A. 1989. *Sociology*. Oxford: Polity Press.

Hendricks, N. and Samuels, J. 1997. Generating Standards and the National Qualifications Framework: A Critical Reflection, A paper presented at the "Kenton-at-the-Gap" Conference. Hermanus.

Hope, A. 1984. *Training for Transformation: A Handbook for Community Workers*. Book 1. Gweru: Mambo Press.

Howarth, R. 1995. The implementation of the IGSCE curriculum and assessement system in Namibia: its implication for educators and learners. Colloqiuim on HIGCSE and IGCSE. University of Namibia, Windhoek.

Koetsier, J. 1997. Alienation and Paradise in Curriculum 2005. Paper presented at the Kenton Educational Association Conference. Hermanus.

Ministry of Education and Culture (MEC). 1993. *Towards Education for All*. Windhoek: Ginsberg MacMillan.

Ministry of Education and Culture (MEC). 1995. Position Paper on Preprimary Education. Windhoek, Namibia.

Ministry of Education. 1995. White Paper on Education and Training. Cape Town, South Africa (SA).

Ministry of Education. 1997. *Curriculum 2005*. Document unveiled by the Minister of Education, Professor S. Bhengu. Cape Town, South Africa (SA).

Minogue, M. and Molloy, J., eds. 1974. *African Aims & Attitudes: Selected Documents.* London: CUP.

Nyerere, J. K. 1967. *Education for Self-reliance.* Rinck Leodas.

Nzimande, B. 1997. Foreword. In: P. Kallaway et al., eds., *Education after Apartheid.* Cape Town: UCT Press.

Salia-Bao, K. 1989. *Curriculum Development and African Culture.* London: Edward Arnold.

Salia-Bao, K. 1991. *The Namibian Education System under the Colonialists.* Randburg: Hodder and Stoughton Educational.

Sieborger, R. 1997. "How the Outcomes Come Out" – A Personal Account of and Reflections on the Initial Process of Development of Curriculum 2005. Paper presented at Kenton-at-the-Gap Conference. Hermanus.

Sumra, S. 1995. Inequalities and donor aid to education in Tanzania. Presentation to panel on "Donor Aid to Education" in the NASEDEC Conference on "The role of Aid in the Education for All". Oslo. Norway.

UCLES, IGCSE Report on the Examination, November 1993.

UCLES, IGCSE Literature: English, French, Spanish, German syllabus for Examination in 1996.

UCLES, IGCSE History syllabus for Examination in 1996.

Verwoerd, H. F. 1954. Bantu Education: Policy for the immediate future. Statement by the Hon. Dr. H. F. Verwoerd, Minister of Native Affairs, in the Senate of the Parliament of the Union of South Africa.

wa Thiongo, N. 1986. *Decolonising the Mind: The Politics of Language in African Literature.* London: James Currey.

World Declaration of Education for All and Framework for Action to meet Basic Learning Needs. 1990. World Conference on Education for All. Jomtiem, Thailand: Inter-Agency Commission (UNDP, UNESCO, UNICEF, WORLD BANK).

The author

Fhulu Nekhwevha currently teaches Sociology at the University of Fort Hare. Educated at the University of Cape Town (MSocSc) and Cambridge (MA). He taught sociology at the Universities of the Western Cape and North West and lectured in Sociology of Educaton at the University of Namibia. He has been a member of the Council of the South African Sociological Association (1995–1998) and was convenor of the association's Education Working group (1993–1995) and Development Working Group (1995–1997; July 1998–present). He is currently a PhD candidate at the

University of Cape Town and serving a second year as Chairperson of the Kenton
Education Associaton (KEA).

Contact address: Mr Fhulu Nekhwevha, Dept. of Sociology, University of Fort
Hare, P/Bag X1314, Alice 5700, South Africa. E-mail (at University of Fort Hare):
fhulu@ufhcc.ufh.ac.za; E-mail (at University of Cape Town): nekhwevh@southone.
uct.ac.za.

BEYOND THE ENTREPRENEURIAL UNIVERSITY: THE POTENTIAL ROLE OF SOUTH AFRICA'S HISTORICALLY DISADVANTAGED INSTITUTIONS IN RECONSTRUCTION AND DEVELOPMENT

GEORGE SUBOTZKY

Abstract – The author identifies two tendencies affecting higher education. On the one hand, universities and colleges are under pressure to become more market-oriented and to respond to rapid changes in information technology and knowledge production. On the other hand, there is a growing concern that they should work for the benefit of society, promoting social equity and responding to community needs. The author argues that partnerships between the community and institutions of higher education are an effective way of contributing to community development. He describes the potential of South Africa's historically disadvantaged institutions to contribute to reconstruction and development in the aftermath of apartheid.

Zusammenfassung – Der Autor identifiziert zwei Tendenzen, die die Hochschulbildung beeinflussen. Einerseits stehen die Universitäten und Fachhochschulen unter Druck, um martktorientierter zu werden und auf die schnellen Veränderungen in der Informationstechnologie und der Wissensproduktion zu reagieren. Andererseits wird zunehmend Wert darauf gelegt, daß sie nutzbringend für die Gesellschaft sind, die soziale Gleichheit fördern und den Bedürfnissen der Gemeinschaft gerecht werden. Der Autor argumentiert, daß Partnerschaften zwischen der Gemeinschaft und den höheren Bildungseinrichtungen eine effektive Möglichkeit bieten, einen Beitrag zur Entwicklung der Gemeinschaft zu leisten. Er beschreibt das Potential, das die historisch benachteiligten Institutionen in Südafrika besitzen, um zu Wiederaufbau und Entwicklung in der Nachfolge der Apartheid beizutragen.

Résumé – L'auteure identifie deux tendances qui touchent l'éducation des adultes. D'une part, les universités et établissements d'enseignement supérieur subissent une pression qui les contraint à s'orienter davantage sur le marché et à réagir à l'évolution fulgurante des technologies de l'information et à celle de la production des connaissances. D'autre part, on exige de plus en plus que ces établissements agissent pour le bien de la société en favorisant la justice sociale et en répondant aux besoins de la communauté. L'auteure argumente que le partenariat entre communautés et établissements d'enseignement supérieur est un moyen efficace pour contribuer au développement communautaire. Elle décrit les possibilités d'appliquer cette méthode en Afrique du Sud en l'intégrant dans le processus de reconstruction et de développement post-apartheid.

Resumen – El autor identifica dos tendencias que afectan la enseñanza superior. Por una parte, las universidades y escuelas superiores se ven sometidas a la presión de orientarse más hacia el mercado y responder a los rápidos cambios que se producen en la tecnología de la información y producción de conocimientos. Por otra, existe una creciente preocupación por que obre en beneficio de la sociedad, promuevan la justicia social y respondan a las necesidades de las comunidades. El autor sostiene que la cooperación entre la comunidad y los institutos de enseñanza superior es un modo eficaz de contribuir al desarrollo de la comunidad. Describe el potencial que ofrecen las institutiones de Sudáfrica, que historicamente se encontraban en una

508

situación desventajosa, para contribuir a la reconstrucción y desarrollo que tiene lugar en las secuelas que dejó el apartheid.

Резюме - Автор указывает две тенденции, оказывающие влияние на третичное образование. С одной стороны, университеты и колледжи испытывают давление, чтобы стать более ориентированными на рынок и реагировать на быстрые перемены в информационной технологии и производстве знаний. С другой стороны все более возрастает потребность в том, чтобы они работали на благо общества, пропагандируя социальное равенство, а также отвечали на запросы местного населения. Автор утверждает, что партнерское сотрудничество между общественностью и высшими учебными заведениями представляет собой эффективный вклад в развитие общества. Он описывает возможности применения этого подхода в ЮАР в качестве части процесса реконструкции и развития после отмены апартеида.

In the midst of rapidly changing global economic and social conditions, higher education institutions are being increasingly challenged to respond more directly to economic and social needs. The growing demand is for them to emerge from what many perceive to be a persistent inward-looking absorption with the detached pursuit of knowledge for its own sake and to address more directly the widening array of social problems facing humanity under the conditions of late-modernity. As fiscal constraints tighten continuously, rates of social and economic return on higher education expenditure are being intensely scrutinised. In short, public higher education institutions are being held accountable for the effectiveness and efficiency of their contribution to societal needs.

The globalisation of the world's economic and social relations and the rise of the information society have directly impacted on higher education. Rapid innovations in information technology and the necessity for flexible responsiveness to changing market conditions have significantly altered patterns of production. This has changed the modality of knowledge production and has generated the need for more flexible, creative and information-based skills in the modern high-tech workplace. In turn, these changes have implications for the kind of training and research undertaken by higher education institutions.

In response to these developments, the "entrepreneurial" or "market" university has emerged; that is, institutions are exhibiting more and more market-like behaviour. Alongside this, concern has also been growing for the other side of higher education's responsiveness to societal needs, namely, its contribution to social renewal, equity and to addressing the basic needs of the majority. Community service has long been one of the cornerstones of the widely accepted three-fold mission of the modern university, along with teaching and research. In recent times, community-higher education partnerships and community service learning have emerged as an effective operational framework for implementing this. It can be seen that historically disadvantaged institutions in South Africa, which traditionally have fostered close ties with disadvantaged communities and have strong long-standing commitments to community development, could be advantageously placed to actualise these goals.

This paper approaches the conference theme of equity and transformation in education by considering the potential contribution of higher education towards equitable social renewal. It examines these themes through the lens of two related sets of issues alluded to above: firstly, changing global conditions and the inherent tensions – globally and in South Africa – between high-tech development and basic reconstruction and development; and secondly, the impact of these changes on higher education and, in particular, on knowledge production and the relationship between teaching, research and community service.

Two central claims are made in this paper.[1] Firstly, I argue that community service partnerships have considerable potential as the operational basis for fulfilling both institutional and national policy goals of contributing towards social and community development. The second main claim is that South Africa's historically disadvantaged institutions (HDIs – comprising university and technikons, which are technical higher education institutions) potentially hold comparative advantages in contributing towards basic reconstruction and development. This is conditional on building required capacity, assuring quality and increasing institutional efficiency and effectiveness. It is shown that, despite the overwhelming disadvantages suffered by HDIs as a result of apartheid, a small but significant number of excellent programmes have developed which are directed towards the upliftment of the communities with which these institutions share strong historical, political and geographic links. These could provide models for the contribution of higher education to community development.

Claiming this potential role for HDIs should not be interpreted as a call for the perpetuation of the duality and inequalities of the apartheid higher education. Neither does this argument imply that historically advantaged institutions (HAIs) should focus on a global development path and HDIs on reconstruction and development. This would simply reproduce existing disparities. Community-based programmes do of course exist and should be further developed at HAIs. Historically advantaged and disadvantaged institutions are jointly responsible for contributing towards reconstruction and development. On the basis of co-ordinated national planning and regional co-operation, both functions should be strategically addressed at all institutions, with due regard for capacity and equity. This means that the notions of the "market" and the "reconstructive" or community development university refer more to *functions* than *institutional types*. My central contention is that, given the few but

significant areas of strength evident in some of their community-oriented programmes, and on condition that the necessary capacity and quality is achieved,
HDIs potentially enjoy comparative advantages in meeting the stated national
higher education goal of serving community reconstruction and development.

Against the backdrop of global trends and the new national higher education policy framework, I argue that these community-oriented partnership programmes are significant in four respects. First, driven by concerns for social
equity and redress, these innovations represent a complementary alternative
to the hi-tech, market-oriented entrepreneurial university which has developed
in response to globalisation. In this way, the public good, as opposed to the
interests of the market, are served. Second, and directly related to this, community-oriented programmes form the basis of freshly conceptualising and
operationalising the reconstruction and development function of universities.
They thus provide an organisational foundation upon which to address stated
national policy goals and institutional missions, thereby holding the potential
to enhance institutional status, relevance and external effectiveness. Third,
these programmes offer conducive conditions for the potential integration and
mutual enrichment of teaching, research and community service. Fourth and
finally, situated in the social and community context, the knowledge produced
in these programmes constitutes a form of socially distributed, applications-
driven, so-called "Mode 2" knowledge production,[2] which is currently so much
the focus of critical attention (Gibbons et al. 1994; Walshock 1995; Gibbons
1997). A significant difference, however, between knowledge production in
higher education-community partnerships and those with industry is that in
the former, teaching, research and service are (potentially) integrated and
mutually beneficial. By contrast, the strong tendency in higher education-
industry partnerships is towards the fragmentation of teaching and research
(Clark 1991).

I begin by identifying the key changes in the external environment surrounding higher education and the impact which these have had on higher
education. I set out the features of the adaptive responses of higher education to these, both in terms of the growth of entrepreneurialism and the
increasing concern for higher education's contribution to equity and the public
good. I link the tension between these two aspects of the role of higher education with the more fundamental tension within globalisation, namely, the
competing interests of transnational corporations and the basic needs of the
majority poor. The replication of this tension in South Africa's current macro-
economic and higher education policy is then traced. Within this, the position
of the historically disadvantaged institutions is assessed. Case studies of community service programmes, both local and international, are discussed and
the notion of community service is explored. Finally, implications for HDIs
are discussed.

Globalisation and its impact on higher education

Globalisation, the process of intensified transnational economic and social relations leading to complex socio-economic changes, has had a profound impact on both business and higher education. In pursuit of international competitive advantage, governments have encouraged closer links between business and higher education. The production of new knowledge is increasingly occurring within new forms of social organisation (Gibbons et al. 1994; Walshock 1995; Kraak 1995, 1997; Gibbons 1997; Scott 1997). High-tech research is being conducted in collaborative business, government and university-linked consortia, specially established to meet the short-term needs of specific clients or problems. This has had a profound effect on the focus and organisation of higher education research and graduate training in those fields close to the market. As Kraak (1995: 1) observes, "it is this critical nexus between knowledge, innovation and co-operation which provides a new perspective on higher education's relationship with society and the economy".

Gibbons et al. (1994) argue that we are witnessing a fundamental shift from what they term "Mode 1" to "Mode 2" forms of knowledge production. Mode 1 knowledge production refers to research into problems which originate and are solved within the academic context of bounded, homogeneous scientific disciplines. It is conducted within relatively hierarchical organisational structures and governed by standardised peer-based quality control and evaluation.

By contrast, Mode 2 knowledge is application-driven, that is, it is generated within the social and market contexts of its application. Mode 2 knowledge is heterogeneous in that "its solutions entail both theoretical and empirical components and cognitive and non-cognitive elements in novel and creative ways" (Kraak 1995: 8). It is organisationally diverse, typically conducted in industry-higher education partnerships, consortia and multi-disciplinary teams of knowledge workers with diverse backgrounds, rapidly deployed in pursuit of innovative solutions. It is funded from multiple sources, increasingly commissioned by non-statutory and private bodies, and involves new forms of accountability, reflexivity and quality control.

Mode 2 knowledge production does not simply replace Mode 1 disciplinary knowledge production (Kraak 1995). Indeed, the success of its multi-disciplinarity is dependent on drawing from a strong base of disciplinary knowledge. The key point is that this new mode of knowledge production has generated a distinctive form of *social organisation* (Muller 1995). Similarly, Mode 2 knowledge production is not exclusively market-oriented and also arises in the pursuit of solving social and developmental problems. Nonetheless, the dominant context of its application has been in the high-tech industry partnerships on which most of the debate has focused. This paper investigates the organisational and operational framework of knowledge production within community partnerships.

In the context of globalisation and the growth of Mode 2 knowledge production, these developments have led to the rise of the "entrepreneurial" or "market" university (Clark 1997b; Dill 1997; Orr 1997; Scott 1997; Slaughter and Leslie 1997; Tierney 1997). This is characterised by two sets of changes in the epistemological and organisational forms of knowledge production and dissemination, as well as in institutional management style.

The first set of changes involves a shift towards "Mode 2" knowledge production and technology transfer through business-university research partnerships mentioned above. The growing corporate influence in the academy has led to competitive bidding among institutions and, in turn, to the entrepreneurial emphasis on science and technology fields rather than non-commercialisable research. This is accompanied by the commodification of knowledge and the rise of proprietary intellectual rights.

Secondly, and related to this, fiscal constraints have pressurised institutions towards adopting a competitive entrepreneurialism and a managerialist preoccupation with cost effectiveness. This is impacting directly on the nature of work in the academy, with academics increasingly being held accountable for the income they generate (Slaughter and Leslie 1997). Universities are appointing "knowledge workers" or "entrepreneurial scientists" whose role it is to raise these funds (Clark 1995b). New skills are required in marketing, in interdisciplinary and team project management and networking, and in dealing with the media and an increasingly better informed general public. Furthermore, the role of the state in relation to higher education has increasingly shifted from a controlling to a regulatory one. Within this, a tension arises between the concerns of equity and the competitive market paradigm, which is chiefly focused on maximising alternative funding sources and on containing costs.

The tensions underlying globalisation

These global developments and their counterparts in higher education are neither uniform nor disinterested. Ideologically, globalisation can be seen to be the outcome of doctrines aimed at serving the hegemonic interests of world capitalism (Smyth 1995; Chomsky 1997; Kraak 1997; Orr 1997). Following the prescriptions of the neo-liberal Washington Consensus, nations are urged to adopt structural adjustment measures which create conditions conducive to unregulated trade and capital flow and speculative short-term investments. This entails restraining state control of the economy and state spending, and encouraging export-led policies. Ignoring these injunctions purportedly results in loss of favour with potential foreign investors and reduced competitiveness in the global market.

Critiques of neo-liberalism have identified fundamental tensions generated by these doctrines.[3] These have implications for South Africa's macroeconomic policy and, in turn, for its higher education policy and serve as the point of departure in formulating a critical complementary alternative to the marketisation of higher education.

Within neo-liberal globalisation, the increasing determination of national economic policy by transnational corporations (TNCs) has resulted in the decline of national sovereignty (Smyth 1995). Related to this, structural adjustment programmes aim at creating conditions which maximise TNC profits and short-term investment returns, as opposed to the basic needs of the majority poor. By their autonomous nature, TNCs are accountable to no one but their own shareholders. Redistributive policies aimed at meeting basic domestic needs are in fundamental conflict with demands for a political and economic climate conducive to private investment (Chomsky 1997). Vast current global capital flow involving short-term speculative investment can severely damage national short- and long-term interests[4] and redistributive agenda. Further, the pursuit of global competitiveness among developing countries tends to generate a dual internal economy, consisting of a resource-rich export-oriented minority sector which attracts investment, and another sector serving the home market which is increasingly marginalised by the preoccupation with generating high-tech production capacity (Smyth 1995: 44).

It can be seen that these tensions have been replicated in South Africa's emerging post-Apartheid macro-economic policy, and, in turn, in its higher education policy formulation. They derive ultimately from the dual, but integrated social and economic structure of South Africa which was shaped by apartheid. This dual society comprises a relatively advanced political, economic and social order linked to a relatively under-developed one, upon which the former has depended in many critical ways for its existence and reproduction (Wolpe 1995). It is largely determined along racial lines and characterised by extreme disparities in wealth, power and distribution.

Given this duality, the challenge facing the new government's macro-economic policy is to pursue a two-fold development path which simultaneously seeks to position the nation favourably within the competitive global arena and to address the redistributive task of basic reconstruction and development.

The fierce contestation around the two central pillars of the ruling African National Congress' (ANC) macro-economic policy highlights this tension. These are the government's current Growth, Employment and Redistribution policy (GEAR) and the 1994 Reconstruction and Development Programme (RDP).

The GEAR strategy aims at job creation and redistribution through a projected growth rate based on increasing foreign investment and the export-led high-tech competitive engagement in the global information economy. It is designed to create a conducive climate for foreign investment, to win World Bank and IMF favour and to assuage the concerns of local business. It prioritises budget deficit reduction, relaxed foreign exchange control and privatisation. To date, apart from reduction of the budget deficit, it has fallen well short of its targets.

By contrast, the RDP is a redistributive development path focused on meeting the basic needs of the majority of the population. It is premised on growth through redistribution. Despite constant rhetorical commitment to RDP goals, however, severe delivery problems and organisational haphazardness have obstructed its implementation.

The GEAR strategy represents a clear shift from the government's previously unconditional commitment to redistribution and has severely strained relations within the tri-partite alliance between the ANC, the SA Communist Party (SACP) and the Congress of South African Trade Unions. Recent sustained opposition to the GEAR strategy from these quarters is grounded on the argument that it fundamentally favours high-tech global competitiveness at the expense of RDP concerns and the interests of the poor.

Clearly, South Africa must seek a mediating settlement of these tensions and follow a complementary development path which accommodates both global and reconstructive concerns. This entails resisting the uncritical acceptance of the neo-liberal consensus. This is especially so in relation to a strong state role, not only in effecting redistribution, equity and redress, but also in facilitating development along with growth.

This duality is replicated in higher education policy goals (Subotzky 1997b). The White Paper on higher education (Department of Education 1997) states that the purpose of higher education in the South African context is to support both global competitiveness and basic reconstruction. On the one hand, it must "contribute to and support the process of societal transformation outlined in the RDP, with its compelling vision of people-driven development leading to the building of a better quality of life for all" (Department of Education 1997: 1). On the other hand, it must "provide the labour market, in a knowledge-driven and knowledge-dependent society, with the ever-changing high-level competencies and expertise necessary for growth and prosperity of a modern economy" (ibid.).

However, without a grounded sense of how the reconstructive community development function of higher education can be programmatically operationalised, these goals remain unresolved contradictory challenges. As outlined above, there are numerous accounts in the literature which characterise the "market" university. Nonetheless, the policy debates are relatively silent on the notion of the reconstructive development function of higher education, and what this might entail operationally in the South African context.

Significantly for the purposes of this paper, the clearest indication of this is provided in the White Paper which cites community service and service learning as ways of meeting reconstruction and development concerns. The White Paper states that institutions should demonstrate social responsibility and their commitment to the common good by making available expertise and infrastructure for community service programmes. The promotion and development of social responsibility and awareness among students through community service programmes is cited as a national higher education goal. The White Paper expresses receptivity to community service programmes for students and gives in-principle support to feasibility studies and pilot pro-grammes which explore the potential of community service.

Addressing these goals means aligning knowledge production and teaching programmes with the service function. It entails expanding the current focus on Mode 1 disciplinary knowledge production and developing capacity to produce Mode-2 type knowledge which benefits community development. This, as I argue throughout, can be effectively achieved through the organi-sational frame of community service partnerships and programmes, of which community service learning is an integral part. Within this, the conventional definition of scholarship must be expanded, theory and practice must be related, and the legitimacy of other forms of knowledge and the existence of knowledge producers outside the academy must be recognised.

Park (1996) argues convincingly for the expansion of the notion of schol-arship in order to accommodate and reward the teaching, research, outreach and integrative work of women. Drawing from Boyer (1990, 1996), she argues for the redefinition of scholarship in terms of four aspects: discovery (con-ventional research), integration (seeking to capture complex inter-relation-ships), application (service) and teaching.

The scholarship of application links research to service and encourages scholars to consider how knowledge can be responsibly applied to conse-quential problems. This refers to conventional applied research, but Boyer (quoted by Park 1997: 76) goes further to ask whether "social problems *them-selves* [can] define an agenda for scholarly investigation?" (Park 1997) captures the iteration between theory and practice and the importance of knowledge production linked to service as follows:

> Personal experiences and social and political concerns may give rise to intellec-tual analyses which are tested by further experience and experimentation. Theoris-ing suggests new ways of designing environmental policies, treating illnesses, engineering buildings, solving economic problems, and serving local communities; the practical application of ideas, in turn, tests theories and gives rise to new intel-lectual understandings. Thus, rather than devaluing service as trivial, non-intel-lectual or even anti-intellectual, an institution that acknowledged the scholarship of service would value service as [in Boyer's words] "serious, demanding work" which produces as well as applies knowledge (ibid.: 77).

The notions of the scholarship of integration, application and teaching resonate closely with the community-oriented and academic development-related research opportunities which are, I argue below, inherent in community part-nerships.

The position of historically disadvantaged institutions (HDIs)

For HDIs, meeting the goals of service through appropriate knowledge pro-duction entails additional challenges. Considerable institutional changes and organisational development will be required to reverse the imprint of their apartheid past in terms of which they are severely indisposed to functioning as "market" universities. However, my contention is that their potential to contribute to the goals of community development is highlighted in the small but significant range of innovative community-oriented programmes which serve as replicable models.

South Africa's dual society reproduced a corresponding duality in the university system. The racially divided social order was reproduced under grand apartheid through the policy of establishing separate institutions for each racial and ethnic group. A highly unequal set of functionally differentiated institutions emerged, with HDIs fundamentally disadvantaged in a number of ways. The principle function of the historically disadvantaged universities (HDUs)[5] was to provide personnel for the homelands civil service structures and for the embryonic black middle class. A narrow range of programmes was therefore developed in the professional fields associated with these constituencies within the racially divided occupational structure. By contrast, the HAUs provided for the economic, professional, intellectual and cultural needs of the dominant minority.

Despite important differences between them, HDUs share general characteristics which distinguish them from HAUs (EPU 1997; see also Subotzky 1997b for a summary). Their primary function was undergraduate teaching. The HDUs' capacity to engage in market-related research is hindered by: a) the concentration of enrolments in the non-science fields, in teaching-related subjects and at the undergraduate and lower qualifications levels; b) the relatively undeveloped research culture emanating from, among other things, huge numbers of underprepared students and academics who do not incorporate research into their constructions of meaning of what constitutes academic life; c) the comparatively underqualified and junior staff complement and a generally poor quality of teaching; d) inadequate institutional capacity, infrastructure, and support for research; e) their limited capacity to attract alternative funding sources; and f) their isolated location which creates a number of barriers: to academic networking and inter-institutional co-operation; to the recruitment and retention of good quality staff and students; to links and consultancy work with government, NGOs and the private sector (the hallmark of the "market" university); and to gaining access to the power networks which underlie these.

On the other hand, a significant finding of the EPU (1997) study was that, despite these multiple structural, institutional, environmental and resource constraints, HDUs had developed some areas of excellence, particularly in community-based programmes. The department of Family Medicine at Medunsa, for instance, was widely acknowledged as being at the forefront of professional health training in its field. The research and teaching reputation of its staff is internationally recognised. The department has pioneered problem-based teaching and learning in South Africa. Primary health care problems presented in the community shape the curriculum, and student and staff research is directed towards solving these. The masters programme offered by the department has attracted high numbers of students country-wide and from the subcontinent.

Furthermore, a number of interviewees in the EPU study perceived manifold current and potential advantages in HDUs for contributing towards national, regional and especially community development. Many respondents were enthusiastically motivated by unique opportunities for the conduct of research, teaching and outreach activities inherent in the locality. Proximity to disadvantaged communities often offered unparalleled chances to establish development-oriented initiatives in which teaching, research and outreach were related. These were mainly in applied research fields and in some cases involved multi-disciplinary collaborative efforts with other institutions. Indeed, the urban-based HAUs appeared keen to gain access to such research opportunities in these regions. Moreover, collaboration provided opportunities not only for capacity-building through technology and skills transfer from the well resourced HAUs to the relatively isolated HDUs, but also for HDUs to share their accumulated expertise and knowledge of the social and natural environment.

Typical of these opinions were the following comments by interviewees in the EPU study:

> We try to use our disadvantages and change them into advantages . . . especially if you look at our institution in the context of the new dispensation, the RDP and so on. I think we have an ideal opportunity to use our rural environment to do relevant research. Obviously we cannot compete with Wits or Cape Town in nuclear physics, and I don't think we should.
>
> I suppose it's like sitting in the middle of a laboratory. You can just see it. There is just so much we can do. We have got a community. We should be involved in development. I think that should be our whole thrust. After listening to Mandela last night, I felt encouraged again because he said we are going to be a people-based society. If that's what we are going to be, then research in Social Sciences is extremely important.

Thus, in spite of the burden of their apartheid-generated disadvantages and the overwhelming impediments to their institutional effectiveness and academic quality, some centres of excellence and innovation in community-based teaching and research programmes had been developed at HDUs. Building on the advantages inherent in their geographic closeness and strong commitment to impoverished communities, these programmes open windows of opportunity for HDUs to contribute to reconstructive community development. In so doing, they constitute complementary alternatives to the growing market-orientation of higher education.

Mode 2 knowledge is frequently described in terms of how it serves societal needs, both in terms of industrial innovation and social renewal (Gibbons 1994; Kraak 1995). The main thrust of Mode 2 knowledge production is clearly to create organisational arrangements which best serve the needs of companies competing in the high-tech global arena. As Kraak (1995: 8) observes, "the key knowledge areas in which 'Mode 2' is dominant are in the fields of information technology, information theory, artificial intelligence, telecommunications technology, genetic engineering, biotechnology, micro-electronics and advanced materials design". As a result, the market-oriented application of knowledge production overshadows the concerns of social renewal and equity. As Muller (1995: 10) reflects, "What this burgeoning of technology-carried knowledge work will do for communities, solidarity and citizenship is not yet clear. There is much talk of 'virtual community'. But real local communities don't go away: they just become less tied into the knowledge and power networks". My main claim is that community-based programmes, directed as they are towards the solution of social problems, par-ticularly in the health and education fields, represent a potentially significant counter-trend in this regard.

Mode 2 knowledge production can be seen as central to the achievement of the RDP (Kraak and Watters 1995). A case study among various non-health academic departments in higher education institutions in the Western Cape revealed some clear examples of Mode 2 practices in all four disciplines inves-tigated: Engineering, Physics, Business Management and Anthropology (Kraak and Watters 1995). However, of the cases cited as indicative of "Mode 2", many fail to capture *all* of the defining "Mode 2" criteria as specified by Gibbons et al. The authors conclude that a "partial diffusion" of Mode 2 research practices was observable. Given the various political and academic constraints and resistances towards new knowledge production, it is unlikely, in the view of these authors, that "Mode 2" research will flourish unless policy parameters are defined to encourage and facilitate it (Kraak and Watters 1995: 10). The implications are that "the higher education policy framework must seek to deepen these early beginnings, for . . . Mode 2 is critical both to the success of the RDP but also to the rejuvenation of our national economy as a globally competitive and knowledge-intensive resource" (Kraak and Watters 1995: 17).

The emergence of the "entrepreneurial" university has generated a growing worldwide concern about the social purpose of higher education. In the light of evidence of the growing disparity between ivory tower academic norms and societal needs, the contribution of higher education towards the public good and social development is being reviewed (Fairweather 1996; Tierney 1997). New emphasis has been placed on the policy dimension of research, on establishing collaborative linkages with government and the private sector for social development and on the reappraisal of the service and outreach function of higher education (Terenzini 1996; Keller 1997).

Community Service Learning: integrating teaching, research and service

As part of these trends, community service learning (CSL) has expanded rapidly, especially in the USA. It is seen as an increasingly important means of realising the social purpose of higher education (Bringle and Hatcher 1996; Ward and Wolf-Wendel 1997; JET 1998). CSL is defined as "a form of experiential learning in which students engage in activities that address human and community needs together with structured opportunities intentionally designed to promote student learning and development" (Jacoby in Ward and Wolf-Wendel 1997: 1). Its distinguishing feature is the systematic integration of community service into the formal curriculum. CSL is closely associated with problem-based learning (PBL), which is the hallmark of innovative experiential teaching and learning, especially in the Health Sciences.

Originating in mainstream academia during the 1970s, the initial focus of CSL was on service and outreach. During the late 1980s, community priorities and contexts began to be systematically incorporated into the curriculum, especially in those applied, professional and vocational fields with an intrinsic service component. During the 1990s, increasingly in response to the changing conditions outlined above, CSL has been identified as an institution-wide initiative to operationalise the social purpose of higher education.

In South Africa, a strong community service ethos emerged during the 1980s as activist academics sought to direct their scholarly pursuits towards the anti-apartheid struggle and to support the development of a strong civil society (Cooper 1992). Progressive institutions also housed and supported numerous NGOs which rendered a variety of community services. However, as they tended not to conduct formal teaching or research, their presence on campuses and continued donor support was subsequently questioned in the post-1990 period.

Developing community service learning in the current South African context therefore entails transforming this underlying activist tradition and incorporating formal knowledge production and learning within service (Kraak and Watters 1995). CSL, especially in the partnership model, provides a framework for this. Doing so involves a fundamental shift in attitude among those who regard rigour and relevance as mutually exclusive. These, as Cooper (1992) argues, are not contradictory.

Case studies conducted in service-oriented academic departments and units in preparation for the larger forthcoming study mentioned earlier, indicate a growing orientation towards partnerships and community development. While formal research tends to be underdeveloped (especially where the service, clinical and teaching burden is onerous), considerable informal knowledge appears to be produced and disseminated. In some cases, substantial contribution to policy formulation is evident. Context-based curriculum development, however, remains embryonic.

Inquiry-based learning, which underlies CSL, is a particularly effective pedagogy in current times (Clark 1997a). The 21st century workforce will demand complex problem-solving skills amidst growing uncertainty and indeterminacy. The best pedagogical preparation for this is "discovery-based learning experiences" and being educated in a "discovery-rich environment" (Clark 1997b: 294). For these reasons, learning-by-discovery, and teaching and learning by means of research processes should become the norm. Research-based learning should not remain the preserve of the postgraduate level, Clark argues, and should underpin studies at the preadvanced, undergraduate as well as secondary levels. In addition, as Geidt (1997) convincingly demonstrates, community-based learning and research forms an effective method of training adult community workers.

In Clark's view, this "research-teaching-study nexus" will become increasingly important in time. The compatibility between research and teaching "becomes a claim that student involvement in research is an efficacious way to educate throughout the educational system the great mass of students, as well as the elite performers, for the inquiring society into which we are rapidly moving" (1991: 242). In the light of the value of inquiry-based teaching, arguments which assume the schism between teaching and research are regarded by Clark as a false dichotomy.

However, alongside the tendencies to maintain the integration of research and teaching, Clark explains, are a number of developments which fragment the teaching-research-study nexus. These include the massification of higher education and the opening of access to large numbers of preadvanced students and the establishment of teaching-only institutions. In addition, commissioned research, conducted in specialised units as part of the new organisational links between universities and industry, is increasingly removed from university teaching. Increasingly, therefore, in many national systems in which teaching-only institutions developed, it is widely acknowledged that "not all higher education teachers will be researchers" and that "as a counterpart, in and out of the academy, full-time research becomes a career in its own right, without a commitment to teaching and training" (Clark 1991: 111).

Many institutions and faculty experience a fundamental tension between teaching and research (Ramsden 1994; Park 1996; EPU 1997). The reward structure almost exclusively favours conventionally measured research output in terms of peer-reviewed publications. Most academics experience the strain of being paid to teach, whereas the worth of their performance is measured against research output (Tang and Chamberlain 1997). In addition, some faculty clearly enjoy teaching and regard it both as a priority and calling but in most cases, feel the pressure of expectations (Ramsden 1994; Park 1996; EPU 1997).

With this in mind, the prospects for HDUs inherent in their community development partnership programmes take on a new significance. Given their weakly developed research cultures, they provide particularly stark instances of conditions conducive to the fragmentation of teaching and research. However, the community-oriented innovations mentioned earlier create conditions which support, not the full-blown expert-driven advanced-level Humboldtian model, but the potential integration of teaching, research and outreach at all levels in the service of community upliftment.

Ideally, CSL is concerned not only with effective student learning, but also with community development. The notion of partnership is therefore crucial. Where successful, partnerships grounded on mutual relations offer reciprocal benefits. The academy benefits from enhanced student learning and research, staff research (both in the disciplinary fields as well as in the area of teaching and learning) and curriculum development. The community benefits directly from development and from empowering participation in the process. Service, enriched by cutting-edge research findings and community participation, is also enhanced.

In practice, however, this ideal remains elusive. A recent discourse analysis of the current literature on CSL indicates an alarming preoccupation with student outcomes and institutional interests at the expense of reciprocity (Ward and Wolf-Wendel 1997). CSL is perceived predominantly as a vehicle for achieving academic aims and furthering academic interests rather than for pursuing community development. The main purpose of CSL is to meet genuine community needs while simultaneously expanding the educational experience for students. To achieve this, the gap between "needy" communities and "knowing" campuses must be dissolved and the charitable model must be supplanted by the social change and development model, which focuses on the processes of building relationships within stakeholder groups in order to identify and collaboratively address root causes of complex problems (Ward and Wolf-Wendel 1997). Open attitudes, a new partnership-driven paradigm of service learning and the necessary interactive skills on both parts must be developed. Careful planning is also vital to the sustainability of collaborative partnerships. This must include proper supervision, evaluation and assessment. CSL in the partnership model has the potential to play a central role in rethinking the purpose of higher education if it is conceptualised as a way of developing an ethic of care and community involvement (Ward and Wolf-Wendel 1997).

Community-partnership knowledge production involves not only the generation, transfer and application of research findings and available knowledge from the academy. Importantly, it also involves participation by community members in the research process, in setting research agendas based on needs analyses and in controlling and evaluating programme outcomes. It also entails garnering indigenous, tacit and pre-theoretical knowledges. Academics situated in historically disadvantaged institutions and communities have the possible advantage of combining tacit and explicit knowledge of those contexts. They have the potential to assimilate basic and applied knowledge into Mode-2 knowledge (Kraak 1997; Subotzky 1997a).

Two education projects undertaken by faculty at the University of Illinois at Chicago (UIC) provide international cases which illustrate the implications of community partnerships for higher education institutions. Active efforts were made by the College of Education at UIC to nurture collaborative relationships with surrounding schools in the region in order to improve the quality of education. The first partnership aimed at improving learning opportunities by improving teaching methods, which was supported by helping parents to aid their children's educational development and by increasing day care and health programmes. The second aimed at local school council training. Further details need not detain us here, but some of the lessons learnt are illuminating (Braskamp and Wergin 1997).

Those involved in the partnership work quickly learned that:

> Collaborative work often creates a conflict of institutional cultures; that political and community groups want to use the prestige of the university to enhance their agenda; that faculty members often have less *experiential* knowledge of the problem context than do teachers and reformers but compensate by using their theoretical perspectives; that failed experiments outside the academy are more visible than a failed experiment in a laboratory; that compromise is essential; that new forms of communication are needed to reach different audiences; that partnerships can be intellectually exciting and challenging; that faculty scholarship is enhanced; and that continuous support is needed for long-term impact (Braskamp and Wergin 1997: 77–78).

In the view of these authors, the role of the modern university is to become more responsive to social problems and to function as a critical forum for the negotiation of social discourse. In this view, the university is *jointly responsible* for social change in partnership with relevant community bodies. Under this new social contract between higher education and the greater community, the institution becomes an advocate for social justice (Braskamp and Wergin 1997). The success of such ventures depends on a substantial reorientation in the mission and focus of higher education, particularly at research universities.

While there are greater demands to address social ills, the academy remains largely inwardly turned, preoccupied with maximising quantifiable and rewarded publications output. Without including communities in defining research goals and agendas, higher education institutions "will become victimised by their own myopia" (Braskamp and Wergin 1997: 80). Collaborative partnerships do not imply abandoning basic research or compromising rigour. On the contrary, one of the lessons learnt was that faculty involved realised that "their own claims on the truth were rather fragile and incomplete" (ibid.). Likewise, faculty had to learn to bridge the gap between the meaning of research findings and the meaning constructed by those affected by the results, and between academic and political truth.

Echoing the importance of applications-driven scholarship, the authors argue that new forms of scholarship reflect a "knowing-in-action" needed to complement conventional academic knowledge. Academics have to relinquish the notion of the priority of theory-based knowledge over practice-based knowledge. Regarding practice merely as an extension of theory[6] is inadequate to the task of dealing with the complexities of social problems. Forming new partnerships also depends largely on the public commitment of institutional leaders to this end through a variety of supportive measures. Through partnerships, the "research and instructional agenda can be intricately connected to the communities outside the academy" (Braskamp and Wergin 1997:

87). This links academic freedom with social accountability, escaping the insularity of the academy and addressing clamouring social demands.

In the light of these considerations, meaningful involvement in social renewal clearly cannot be separated from institutional transformation. Braskamp and Wergin's account thus highlights the potential strengths and pitfalls of collaborative partnerships in fulfilling the social purpose of higher education.

Conclusion

I have argued in this paper that the higher education-community partnership model provides an operational basis for the production and application of knowledge and skills for community development programmes. HDIs, through their location and focus on community-oriented programmes could become important contributors in this regard.

Cases investigated suggest that community partnership programmes constitute noteworthy sites for the integration of teaching, research and service through the equivalent of "Mode 2"-type knowledge production. They provide institutions (and especially HDIs) with an opportunity to fulfil their contribution towards redistributive development and in this way, give substance to the "reconstructive" function of higher education. These initiatives thus constitute complementary alternatives to the growing dominance of market forces in higher education.

For HDIs to achieve this, fundamental organisational and institutional transformation is necessary. Quality promotion, capacity building and ensuring institutional effectiveness and efficiency are key goals. In the light of prevailing institutional conditions, institutional change is a complex and contested process, and must address the intricacies of organisational culture. Special attention must be given to co-ordinated academic planning, to staff, student and curriculum development and to the building of managerial capacity in HDIs. If achieved, HDIs will be positioned favourably to seize the opportunities before them, to gain status and to become effective contributors to both global and redistributive development.

Notes

1. The paper builds on previous research, publications and presentations (EPU 1997; Subotzky 1997a; Subotzky 1997b), drawing more extensively on current local and international literature, as well as on recently conducted local research. This includes preliminary analysis of interviews which I have recently conducted into community service programmes in the Western Cape, mainly in the health field. These form pilot studies for a major planned collaborative project based at the EPU, UWC on case studies of knowledge production in service of development and, in the light of this, challenges for the building of research capacity. This should yield

524

important detailed insights about the modes of knowledge production in these development-oriented partnerships and the capacities required for this. The present paper therefore represents work in progress.

2. The production and dissemination of knowledge embedded in its application in the social or market context, rather than in the theoretical framework of closed bounded disciplines (Gibbons et al. 1994). This is discussed further below. It should be borne in mind that my principal focus here is not with the epistemological or philosophy of science concerns of whether these activities conform strictly to the Gibbons thesis or not. Instead, I am interested in identifying the organisational features of new knowledge production that address community and reconstruction and development goals.

3. Significantly, critiques of the global neo-liberal consensus are emanating, not only from left-leaning critics, but also from mainstream economists. The seemingly sacred orthodoxy of the World Bank was recently fundamentally questioned from within by its prominent chief economist, Joseph Sitglitz (quoted in Hanlon 1998), who called for an end to "misguided" debt relief policies of the IMF and World Bank. He argued that "the set of policies which underlay the Washington Consensus are neither necessary nor sufficient, either for macro-stability or longer-term development" (ibid.). The goal, he stated, is equitable development "which ensures that all groups in society enjoy the fruits of development, not just the few at the top. And we seek democratic development". Stiglitz contends that "markets are not automatically better" and that "the dogma of liberalism has become an end in itself and not a means to a better financial system" (ibid.).

4. The recent turmoil in the South African financial market bears testimony to the vulnerability of developing countries to the damaging effects of hostile and manipulative short-term currency speculation of this sort.

5. These and subsequent observations relating to HDUs are derived from the findings of a major research project conducted by the Education Policy Unit at the University of the Western Cape (EPU 1997). Primary quantitative and qualitative data was collected and analysed. Interviews were conducting during 1994 with institutional leaders and a representative sample of academic staff comprising 257 interviewees. The discussion focuses on HDUs, as distinct from the historically disadvantaged technikons (HDTs).

6. This attitude is charicatured in the apocryphal story about the university physics professor who was called to a farm to examine a perpetual motion machine developed by the farmer which pumped water uphill endlessly. He was indeed surprised, but dismissed it by saying: "Ah well, it's all very well that it works in practice, but it will *never* work in theory!"

References

Boyer, E. 1990. *Scholarship Reconsidered: Priorities of the Professoriate Princeton.* New Jersey: Carnegie Foundation for the Advancement of Teaching.

Boyer, E. 1996. The Scholarship of Engagement. *Journal of Public Service and Outreach* 9(1), 11–20.

Braskamp, L and Wergin, J. 1997. Universities and the New Social Contract. In: W. G. Tierney, ed., *The Responsive University: Restructuring for High Performance.* Baltimore: Johns Hopkins University.

Bringle, R. G. and Hatcher, J. A. 1996. Implementing Service Learning in Higher Education. *Journal of Higher Education* 67(2): 221–239.

Chomsky, N. 1997. *Neo-liberalism and Global Order: Doctrine and Reality.* Seminar paper presented at the Centre for African Studies. University of Cape Town, 27 May.

Clark, B. R. 1991. The Fragmentation of Research, Teaching, and Study: An Explorative Essay. In: M. Trow and T. Nybom, eds., *University and Society.* London: Jessica Kingsley.

Clark, B. R. 1995a. *Places of Inquiry: Research and Advanced Education in Modern Universities.* Berkeley and Los Angeles: University of California Press.

Clark, B. R. 1995b. Leadership and Innovation in Universities: From Theory to Practice. *Tertiary Education and Management* 1(1): 7–11.

Clark, B. R. 1997a. The Modern Integration of Research Activities with Teaching and Learning. *Journal of Higher Education* 68(3): 241–255, May/June.

Clark, B. R. 1997b. Common Problems and Adaptive Responses in the Universities of the World: Organizing for Change. *Higher Education Policy* 10(3/4).

Cooper, D. 1992. Extension Service Work at University. *Transformation* 18.

Department of Education. 1997. *Education White Paper 3: A Programme for the Transformation of Higher Education.* Pretoria: Government Gazette No 18207, August.

Dill, D. D. 1997. Markets and Higher Education: An Introduction. *Higher Education Policy* 10(3/4).

EPU (Education Policy Unit, University of the Western Cape). 1997. *The Enhancement of Graduate Programmes and Research Capacity at the Historically Black Universities.* Final Research Report. Bellville: Education Policy Unit, University of the Western Cape.

Fairweather, J. 1996. *Faculty Work and Public Trust: Restoring the Value of Teaching and Public Service in American Academic Life.* Allyn and Bacon.

Geidt, J. 1997. *Using Research Processes to Guide the Transformation of Community-based Learning in South Africa.* mimeo.

Gibbons, M., Limoges, C., Nowotny, H., Schwartzman, S., Scott, P. and Trow, M. 1994. *The New Production of Knowledge: The Dynamics of Science and Research in Contemporary Societies.* London: Sage Publications.

Gibbons, M. 1997. What Kinds of University? Choices Concerning Knowledge and Curricula. Paper presented at the CHEPS/OU/CHE Conference on *What Kind of University?* London, June.

Hanlon, J. 1998. The World Bank Speech that Knocked Down Every Pillar. *Electronic Mail & Guardian*, June 23.

Joint Education Trust (JET). 1998. Draft report: *Community Service in Higher Education: A Concept Paper.* Johannesburg: Joint Education Trust.

Keller, G. 1998. Does Higher Education Research Need Revisions? *The Review of Higher Education* (Association for the Study of Higher Education) 21(3).

Kraak, A. and Watters, K. 1995. *Investigating New Knowledge Production: A Western Cape Higher Education Case Study.* Paper commissioned by Taskgroup 2 of the National Commission on Higher Education of South Africa.

Kraak, A. 1995. *Globalisation, the Learning Society and the Case for a Unified National System of Higher Education in South Africa.* Report for Taskgroup 2 of the National Commission on Higher Education.

526

Kraak, A. 1997. Globalisation, Changes in Knowledge Production, and the Transformation of Higher Education. In: N. Cloete et al., eds., *Knowledge, Identity and Curriculum Transformation in Africa*. Cape Town: Maskew Miller Longman.

Muller, J. 1995. *Knowledge and Higher Education*. Report for Taskgroup 2 of the National Commission on Higher Education.

Orr, L. 1997. Globalisaton and the Universities: Towards the "Market University"?. *Social Dynamics* 23(1): 42–64.

Park, S. M. 1997. Research, Teaching, and Service: Why Shouldn't Women's Work Count?. *Journal of Higher Education* 68(1): 46–84.

Ramsden, P. 1994. Describing and Explaining Research Productivity. *Higher Education* 28: 207–226.

SAPSE (South African Post-secondary Education). 1992. *Financial and Related Statements*.

Scott, P. 1997. Changes in Knowledge Production and Dissemination in the Context of global Competition. In: N. Cloete et al., eds., *Knowledge, Identity and Curriculum Transformation in Africa*. Cape Town: Maskew Miller Longman.

Slaughter, S. and Leslie, L. 1997. *Academic Capitalism: Politics, Policies, and the Entrepreneurial University*. Baltimore: Johns Hopkins University.

Smyth, J. 1995. *A Policy Analysis of Higher Education Reform in Australia in the context of Globalisation*. Melbourne Studies in Education, Melbourne: LaTrobe University Press.

Subotzky, G. 1997a. Pursuing both Global Competitiveness and National Redistributive Development: Implications and Opportunities for South Africa's Historically Black Universities. *Social Dynamics 23.1 1997*. Centre for African Studies, University of Cape Town, July.

Subotzky, G. 1997b. Meeting the Dual Demands of Global Competitiveness and Redistributive Development: Constraints and Opportunities for the Historically Black Universities. In: N. Bak (ed.), *Going for the Gap: Reconstituting the Educational Realm*. Cape Town: Juta. 119–134.

Tang, T. and Chamberlain, M. 1997. Attitudes Toward Teaching and Research: Differences Between Administrators and Faculty Members. *Journal of Higher Education* 68(2): 212–227, March/April.

Terenzini, P. 1996. Rediscovering Roots: Public Policy and Higher Education Research. *The Review of Higher Education* (Association for the Study of Higher Education) 20(1).

Tierney, W. G. 1997 (ed.). *The Responsive University: Restructuring for High Performance*. Baltimore: Johns Hopkins University.

Walshock, G. 1996. *Knowledge without Boundaries: What America's Research Universities Can Do for the Economy, the Workplace, and the Community*. San Francisco: Jossey-Bass.

Ward, K and Wolf-Wendel, L. 1997. *A Discourse Analysis of Community-Based Learning: Moving from "I" to "We"*. Paper presented at the Annual Conference of the Association for the Study of Higher Education, Albuquerque, New Mexico, November.

Wolpe, H. 1995. The Debate on University Transformation in South Africa: The Case of the Western Cape. *Comparative Education* 31(2): 275–292.

Wolpe, H. 1996. Educational Policy Research in the Post-Apartheid Transition in South Africa. In: L. Buchert and K. King, eds., *Consultancy and Research in International Education: The New Dynamics*. Bonn: German Foundation for International Development.

The author

Dr George Subotzky is a senior researcher in the Education Policy Unit at the University of the Western Cape which focuses on higher education policy research and analysis. Dr Subotzky has contributed to a number of policy studies, including the National Education Policy Initiative, the ANC's Policy Framework for Education and Training, and the National Commission on Higher Education. He has participated in numerous studies and projects on higher education transformation in South Africa. His main research focus over the last few years has been on the co-ordination of a major three-year study on the *Enhancement of Graduate Programmes and Research Capacity at the Historically Black Universities*. He was principal writer of the Final Report and has presented aspects of the findings of this study at a number of local and international conferences and in various journal publications. His current research interests include: higher education-community partnerships and community service learning; knowledge production; higher education and development; institutional and organisational change management in higher education; policy research methodology; foreign donor aid to education and training; and equity in higher education.

Contact address: Dr George Subotzky, Senior Researcher, Education Policy Unit, University of the Western Cape, Private Bag X17, Bellville, Cape, 7535 South Africa. E-mail: gsubot@epu.uwc.ac.za.

LES SYSTÈMES ÉDUCATIFS À LA RÉUNION ET L'ÎLE MAURICE: QUELLE EFFICACITÉ SOCIALE?

AZZEDINE SI MOUSSA et FRÉDÉRIC TUPIN

Résumé – Les îles Maurice et de la Réunion appliquent des politiques éducatives différentes. Cet article examine dans une optique comparative à la fois l'impact des décisions politiques sur l'éducation et la façon dont les différents systèmes éducatifs sur les deux îles influent sur la démocratisation de l'enseignement. Pour ce faire, les auteurs comparent les parcours éducatifs de différents élèves choisis dans plusieurs écoles mauriciennes et réunionnaises. Au moyen d'une combinaison de méthodes quantitatives et qualitatives, ils peuvent démontrer que les effets sociaux pronostiqués sont affaiblis au cours de l'enseignement. Si l'introduction de l'éducation de masse est indispensable à la démocratisation, il faut reconnaître que les systèmes agissent aussi de façon sélective en fonction de variables comme le sexe, l'âge ou l'origine sociale, par ce qui est transmis quotidiennement dans les écoles.

Abstract – The islands of Mauritius and Réunion have contrasting educational policies. This article examines, from a comparative perspective, not only the impact of political decisions on education but also the way in which the different educational systems in the two islands affect the democratisation of learning. In order to do this, the authors compare the educational trajectories of different pupils from a range of schools in Mauritius and Réunion. Using a combination of quantitative and qualitative approaches, it is possible to show that the expected social effects are moderated in the course of teaching. While the adoption of mass education is a prerequisite for democratisation, it must be recognised that systems also operate selectively with regard to variables such as sex, age or social origin, depending on what transpires in schools on a daily basis.

Zusammenfassung – Die Inseln Mauritius und Réunion praktizieren eine gegensätzliche Bildungspolitik. Dieser Artikel untersucht aus einer vergleichenden Perspektive nicht nur die Auswirkungen politischer Entscheidungen auf dem Gebiet der Bildung, sondern auch in welcher Weise die verschiedenen Bildungssysteme der beiden Inseln die Demokratisierung des Lernens beeinflussen. Zu diesem Zweck vergleichen die Autoren die Bildungslaufbahn von Schülern verschiedener Schulen in Mauritius und Réunion. Durch die Kombination von quantitativen und qualitativen Verfahrensweisen ist es möglich zu zeigen, daß die erwarteten sozialen Ausirkungen im Laufe des Unterrichts abgeschwächt werden. Obwohl die Bildung für die Allgemeinheit eine Voraussetzung für die Demokratisierung ist, muß man sich bewußt werden, daß die Systeme auch selektiv hinsichtlich Geschlecht, Alter oder sozialer Herkunft verfahren, abhangig vom schulischen Tagesablauf.

Resumen – Las Islas de Mauricio y Reunión presentan políticas de educación contrastantes. Desde una perspectiva comparativa, este artículo no sólo examina el impacto de las decisiones políticas sobre la educación, sino también el modo en que los diferentes sistemas educacionales en las dos islas afectan la democratización del aprendizaje. A estos efectos, los autores comparan las trayectorias de educación de diferentes alumnos a partir de una serie de escuelas en Mauricio y Reunión. Usando una combinación de enfoques cuantitativos y cualitativos, es posible demostrar que los efectos sociales esperados se van moderando en el transcurso de la enseñanza. Si bien la adopción de la educación masiva es un requisito previo de la democratización, hay que reconocer que los sistemas también operan de forma selectiva en cuanto a variables tales como género, edad u origen social, dependiendo de lo que suceda diariamente en las escuelas.

Резюме - Остров Маврикий и остров Воссоединения имеют контрастно противоположную политику образования. Эта статья рассматривает со сравнительной точки зрения не только влияние политических решений на образование, но и то, как различные системы образования на двух островах оказывают влияние на демократизацию обучения. С этой целью авторы сравнивают траектории обучения различных учеников из разных школ на острове Маврикий и острове Воссоединения. С помощью комбинации количественных и качественных подходов можно показать, что в ходе обучения модерируются ожидаемые социальные результаты. Зная то, что принятие системы всеобщего образования является необходимым условием демократизации, необходимо признать и то, что системы также работают селективно по отношению к таким параметрам, как пол, возраст и социальное происхождение, в зависимости от того, что ежедневно преподается в школе.

Propos introductifs

Les proximités géographiques, démographiques, historiques, culturelles, . . . de l'Ile Maurice et de l'île de la Réunion ne traduisent pas, pour autant, les spécificités des systèmes éducatifs qui s'y inscrivent. En particulier, les rapports développés par chaque institution – Ecole mauricienne & Ecole réunionnaise – sur la question de l'égalité des chances scolaires divergent de façon notable; à l'île Maurice les élèves sont sélectionnés dès la fin du "cycle primaire" (seuls 60% des élèves entrent au collège) tandis que le second cycle, à la Réunion, s'inscrit dans la politique du"collège pour tous".

La question centrale de cet article consiste à s'interroger sur les *effets sociaux différenciés des politiques éducatives mises en œuvre à l'île Maurice et à la Réunion*. Nous tentons de cerner quel système, in fine, se révèle être le plus socialement sélectif au regard de variables telles que le sexe, l'origine sociale ou l'âge. Il s'agit de se demander si une politique éducative – celle du Rectorat de l'Académie de la Réunion – consistant à ouvrir progressive-ment les portes du second degré à une large proportion d'élèves, indépen-damment de leur origine sociale, porte, en germes, les fruits de procédures tendant à "l'égalisation progressive des chances" comparativement à une politique scolaire socialement plus sélective – celle de l'île Maurice – dès l'entrée du second degré. Autrement dit, comment se traduisent, en termes sociaux, à l'issue des cursus, les choix politiques opérés en amont? Ou, les choix réunionnais sont-ils, dans les faits, réellement plus démocratisants que les choix mauriciens?

Concept central et position du problème: la démocratisation

La question de la démocratisation scolaire revêt un caractère potentiellement original dès lors que l'on s'attache à analyser des phénomènes sociaux mis en scène dans des sociétés insulaires issues d'une histoire post-coloniale.

Si le cas de l'île Maurice – état démocratique autonome, membre du Commonwealth –, et de l'île de la Réunion – département français d'outre-mer –, ne sont pas nécessairement généralisables, il semble néanmoins qu'ils présentent les stigmates de processus, sinon symptomatiques, a minima indicatifs. Leurs histoires tant parallèles que divergentes contiennent les éléments d'une comparaison qui pourrait se révéler fructueuse au plan de l'examen des politiques et des réalités scolaires qui tendent à promouvoir "l'accès au savoir pour tous".

Ces sociétés au sein desquelles on assiste tant à un "télescopage des modèles" (Wolff et Simonin 1996) qu'à une évolution des structures, mesures et réalités scolaires "en accéléré" constituent, hypothétiquement, des cas de figure où les phénomènes de démocratisation sont susceptibles de prendre des formes spécifiques. En toile de fond, la dimension comparative avec les travaux s'attachant à décrire les phénomènes de démocratisation scolaire dans les pays industrialisés reste présente même si, de facto, la confrontation entre système éducatif mauricien et système éducatif réunionnais est mise en exergue.

S'il est impossible d'évoquer ici de façon exhaustive la multitude des traits et phénomènes qui caractérisent ces deux espaces sociaux insulaires (non superposables), quelques points de repères semblent néanmoins nécessaires à la compréhension des phénomènes en présence. A ce titre, on peut citer: le dynamisme démographique, des pyramides des âges caractérisées par des bases étendues, une massification scolaire ultérieure à celle de l'Europe, une organisation économique singulière,[1] un accès tardif à l'autonomie politique et administrative, une histoire récente du peuplement, etc. . . .

Il n'est pas impossible que ces paramètres influent sur les phénomènes d'équité scolaire comparativement à ce qui se produit dans les systèmes éducatifs dont sont issues ces configurations. Cette dimension suppose que l'on redéfinisse le concept de démocratisation à l'aide de quelques travaux "référents" européens qui le délimitent.

Au delà de l'idéal égalitaire républicain affiché par les pays développés durant la seconde moitié du vingtième siècle et ce, dès les lendemains de la seconde guerre mondiale (Prost 1968) les enjeux inhérents à cette question sont multiples. Aussi, si le thème des inégalités d'accès aux études, suivi de celui de l'inégalité de réussite, ont eu un tel succès dans les années soixante, soixante-dix et même quatre-vingts, c'est sans doute parce qu'ils répondaient à une convergence de faits et de prises de position.

Depuis l'après-guerre, l'augmentation numérique de la scolarisation au delà de la scolarité primaire s'est généralisée dans les pays industrialisés (par exemple, Prost 1968); la société doit alors faire face à une scolarisation de masse pour tenter de pérenniser son expansion ou tout au moins, de l'assimiler. Cette question sous-tendue par la problématique du "handicap socioculturel" aboutira à la mise en place de programmes de compensation dans plusieurs pays développés. En France, dans le même espace-temps, l'idée d'une démocratisation de la société fait son chemin et devient un idéal mis en avant par bon nombre de mouvements sociaux. De plus, de façon transversale, les études économiques laissent apparaître une demande croissante de main-d'œuvre qualifiée tandis que les rapports des grandes enquêtes[2] soulignent l'inégalité d'accès aux études (Isambert-Jamati 1990, Van Haecht 1992, par exemple).

Le binôme inégalité des chances/échecs scolaires ainsi dessiné par des réalités sociales et des groupes d'influences différents, aboutira à mettre en évidence le phénomène de la "Reproduction", au sens où Bourdieu et son courant de pensée emploient ce terme.

L'importance symbolique et idéologique de la mise en évidence de ce concept et de ceux qui gravitent dans le même champ, tel celui de la mobilité sociale, des inégalités . . . etc. ainsi que le corpus très important des travaux qui ont eu pour centre ces thèmes,[3] ont conduit, en dehors de la volonté des chercheurs, à systématiser ces conclusions de sorte que dans de nombreux cas, le domaine des constats n'a pas été dépassé pour arriver à la recherche de solutions. C'est en partie ainsi que peu à peu, insidieusement, s'est mise en place l'idée d'une fatalité sociologique face à laquelle "l'acteur", écrasé par "le système", ne pourrait gérer les modalités d'un changement vers une plus grande démocratisation de l'enseignement; "l'acteur" serait en quelque sorte socialement "impuissant".

De tels excès, en dépit des mises au point des chercheurs concernés (Bourdieu 1987, par exemple), nécessitent que ce concept soit affiné et ce, d'autant plus que l'expression de "démocratisation" recouvre, a minima, deux aspects, deux réalités sociales distinctes.

Le concept de démocratisation répond – schématiquement – à deux acceptions (Prost 1992, Langouët 1993, . . .):

• Le premier sens revêt un caractère essentiellement quantitatif; il se superpose avec l'idée d'une ouverture du système éducatif à une fraction de plus en plus grande de la population, c'est à dire qu'il fait référence à un accès progressif à toutes les couches sociales. L'ouverture graduelle du collège à "tous les enfants" dans le système français en constitue, chronologiquement, l'exemple le plus marquant tant par son ampleur que par sa brièveté. Gabriel Langouët parlera de "démographisation" (op. cit., p. 4).

• Le second sens recouvre davantage une dimension "qualitative" puisqu'il correspond à une diminution des écarts scolaires – en termes de parcours et de performances –, entre catégories sociales contrastées. Il s'agit donc, dans cette dernière acception, d'un véritable processus d'égalisation des chances.

Ce distinguo s'avère important en particulier en raison du fait que la "démographisation" n'entraîne pas, automatiquement, d'égalisation des chances, n'aboutit pas nécessairement à une plus grande équité scolaire. Les données statistiques disponibles confirment ce phénomène et si, aux marges, davantage d'élèves et d'étudiants issus des catégories sociales modestes accèdent à un parcours scolaire d'excellence, les flux globaux confirment l'existence de tris à caractère social selon des processus en permanente évolution. Les paliers et modalités de sélection se sont davantage déplacés qu'atténués (Duru-Bellat 1996). Le développement du système scolaire et l'accès progressif de nouvelles couches sociales aux différents degrés de l'enseignement voilent des inégalités de carrières scolaires, socialement déterminées, tenaces non pas quant aux formes qu'elles endossent mais quant à la teneur du fond persistant. Une étude spécifique à la situation réunionnaise confirme cette tendance ainsi que le rôle majeur joué par l'appartenance sociale (Chevillon et Parain 1994).

C'est en ce sens que la comparaison du processus pourrait réunir des conditions assimilées à celles d'un "laboratoire expérimental vivant". Cette dimension, si elle est confirmée, tiendrait tant de la genèse des deux systèmes éducatifs confrontés – mauricien et réunionnais – que des options contrastées retenues en matière de politiques scolaires. Ces politiques se déclinent selon des structures et des modes de fonctionnement différents. Il convient d'en rappeler, ici, les principaux traits.

Structures et modes de fonctionnement

Depuis les années 60, la scolarisation s'est fortement développée à l'Ile Maurice et à la Réunion. Dans le premier cas, c'est le modèle britannique, avec quelques aménagements spécifiques, qui a été suivi tandis que la Réunion, département français d'outre-mer, s'est conformé au modèle national de la scolarité.

A la Réunion, tous les élèves accèdent à l'enseignement secondaire ("collège pour tous"), d'autant que la scolarité est obligatoire jusqu'à 16 ans. En revanche, à Maurice (où la scolarité est obligatoire jusqu'à 12 ans), le CPE (Certificate of Primary Education) joue un rôle sélectif important: la poursuite des études est soumise à la réussite à cet examen. De plus, les élèves sont classés par ordre de mérite en fonction de leurs résultats à cet examen. Le rang de classement détermine l'établissement d'accueil pour les études secondaires. Il existe donc une hiérarchie explicite entre les établissements d'enseignement du secondaire (des établissements "quatre étoiles" aux établissements "une étoile"). Tous les jeunes mauriciens n'accèdent pas à l'enseignement secondaire et on estime que les "bons" établissements accueillent environ 20% des élèves du primaire (Fioux 1998). A la Réunion, la hiérarchie entre les établissements est beaucoup moins discriminante, en raison de l'application de la carte scolaire (scolarisation dans la zone de résidence de l'enfant) mais elle apparaît néanmoins sous d'autres formes (établissements privés "d'élite", dérogations à la sectorisation, Zones d'Education Prioritaires, hétérogénéité/homogénéité des classes au sein d'un même établissement . . .).

Au niveau du second degré, le système réunionnais débute par 4 années de collège, avec des possibilités de filières différentes à partir de la 3ème année, orientées vers l'enseignement général et technologique ou vers l'enseignement professionnel. En fonction de cette première orientation, suivent soit 3 années de lycée (seconde, première, terminale) pour la voie générale et technologique se terminant par l'examen du baccalauréat, soit deux années de préparation au Certificat d'Aptitude Professionnelle (CAP, de moins en moins poursuivi) ou au BEP (Brevet d'Etudes Professionnelles). Ce dernier diplôme permet ensuite de préparer un baccalauréat professionnel. Notons que d'une manière générale, l'orientation dans les différentes filières et durant les différentes étapes de l'enseignement secondaire ne dépend pas de la réussite à un examen mais découle des propositions des professeurs au vu des résultats de l'année et, dans une moindre mesure,[4] des voeux des élèves et/ou des familles.

A Maurice, les cinq années d'enseignement secondaire (Secondary Schools) doivent être validées par la réussite au SC (School Certificate), afin de poursuivre pendant deux années supplémentaires le cycle terminal conclu par l'obtention d'un autre examen, le HSC (Higher School Certificate), qui peut être considéré comme équivalent au baccalauréat français. La voie professionnelle est peu développée, les inscriptions dans les Centres de Formation Professionnelle ne relevant pas d'une orientation scolaire (Tirvassen 1994).

Le système mauricien n'a pas encore la capacité d'accueillir tous les élèves issus du primaire ni de conduire avec des chances équivalentes tous ceux qui entrent dans le secondaire à la qualification du School Certificate. A la Réunion, la sélection existe selon d'autres modalités: les jeunes ne sortent pas tous du système éducatif avec des niveaux de qualification équivalents.

Le schéma ci-après résume le parcours d'une cohorte fictive d'enfants réunionnais et mauriciens dans chacun des systèmes éducatifs considérés. La grille de lecture en est la suivante:

– à la Réunion, sur 100 élèves d'une génération, 98 accèdent à la classe de 6ème, 50 parviennent en classe de seconde et 30 obtiennent finalement un des baccalauréats généraux ou technologiques (la prise en compte des lauréats du baccalauréat professionnel ferait passer cette proportion à 46%);

Tableau 1. Parcours scolaire d'une cohorte fictive.

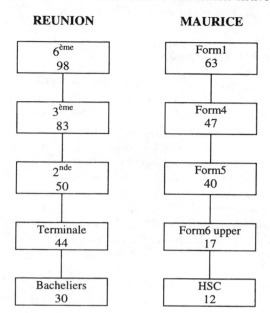

- à l'Ile Maurice, sur 100 élèves d'une génération, 63 accèdent à la Form1 de l'enseignement secondaire (ce chiffre correspond peu ou prou au taux de réussite au CPE), 40 parviennent en Form 5 et 12 obtiennent finalement le HSC.[5]

Sachant que les taux de réussite au SC et au HSC sont de l'ordre de 75%, il existe une différence non négligeable entre le nombre d'inscrits dans les classes préparatoires aux examens du SC et du HSC et le nombre d'élèves qui passent l'examen. Au moins deux facteurs y concourent: la tendance des établissements à présenter leurs meilleurs candidats et des poursuites de scolarité dans l'enseignement secondaire moins systématiques qu'à la Réunion.

Globalement, il apparaît clairement que les choix politiques opérés au plan éducatif se traduisent, dans les faits (et à chaque palier), par une sélectivité plus grande du système éducatif mauricien. Si ce phénomène était hypothétiquement attendu, sa régularité et son ampleur constituent les premiers jalons tangibles d'un processus de sélection sociale. Près d'un jeune réunionnais sur trois poursuit avec succès des études secondaires complètes contre un peu plus d'un élève mauricien sur dix. Par hypothèse, cet écart ne traduit pas une opposition manichéenne des deux curricula réels au regard d'indicateurs traditionnels de l'analyse sociologique tels que le sexe, l'âge et l'origine sociale. En effet, le degré de sélection à l'intérieur de chacun des systèmes varie dès lors qu'on interroge les pratiques des acteurs (personnels de direction, enseignants . . .) au niveau des établissements.

Parcours scolaires selon le sexe

A l'instar de ce que décrivent nombre de travaux (Barton and Walker 1983; Duru-Bellat 1990; Baudelot-Establet 1992; . . .), la variable sexe est discriminante au plan des carrières scolaires. Cet impact prend des formes particulières dans le système éducatif mauricien dès lors que nombre d'établissements ne pratiquent pas la mixité. En effet, si de façon globale, les filles réussissent mieux leur parcours scolaire que les garçons, les écarts se creusent dès l'instant où l'on procède à une analyse par établissement.

A Maurice, de façon globale, les taux de réussite aux examens (admis/présents) sont meilleurs chez les filles que chez les garçons. L'écart est plus important au niveau du CPE (67% pour les filles contre 59% pour les garçons) qu'au niveau du SC (77% contre 74%) et du HSC (74% contre 72%). Parmi les 15 premiers établissements en termes de taux de réussite au SC (taux supérieurs à 93%), figurent 11 collèges de filles. La mixité ne constitue pas pour autant un terroir plus favorable aux garçons. Ainsi, partant des résultats des collèges les plus faibles (taux de réussite au SC inférieurs à 50%), on constate qu'ils sont mixtes et que les résultats différenciés en faveur des filles perdurent. Cette double tendance se poursuit au niveau du HSC.

A La Réunion, les conditions d'enseignement sont radicalement différentes, la mixité des établissements étant la règle. Néanmoins, le sexe reste une variable sociologiquement pertinente: la proportion de filles scolarisées augmente au fil du cursus (57% des élèves de 2nde sont des filles contre 49% en classe de 6ème). Au baccalauréat (général et technologique), les filles sont également plus nombreuses que les garçons à se présenter (59%) et à être

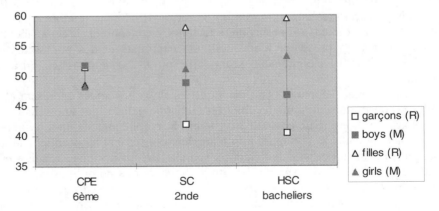

Graphique 1. Proportion de filles et de garçons à différents niveaux de l'enseignement secondaire.

reçues (68% contre 63% pour les garçons). Une différenciation supplémentaire tient aux catégories de baccalauréat: les filières générales et technologiques accueillant davantage de filles que de garçons alors que cette proportion s'inverse dans les filières professionnelles. Le graphique ci-après montre que cette tendance se décline selon des modalités très différentes à Maurice.

Certes, nous pouvons observer que le rapport garçons/filles scolarisés s'inverse du primaire[6] au secondaire et ce, tant à Maurice qu'à la Réunion. Ensuite, si les filles restent au fil des cursus proportionnellement plus nombreuses que les garçons, il apparaît que le système scolaire mauricien crée nettement moins de différences que n'en génère le système réunionnais.

Une première explication de cette différence tient simplement à l'absence de filières professionnelles mauriciennes comparables à celles existant à la Réunion. Mais dans le cas mauricien, il est également intéressant de mettre en relation cette tendance égalisatrice avec les observations suivantes:

- le taux de réussite plus élevé des filles aux différents concours qui jalonnent le parcours scolaire ne conduit pas à une sur-représentation très marquée des filles (elles forment 53% des candidats au HSC);
- la discrimination sexuelle très forte, au détriment des filles, stigmatisée au niveau social et institutionnel (Bunwaree 1997) est surtout caractéristique des milieux sociaux défavorisés, qui sont largement sous-représentés au niveau de l'enseignement secondaire.

La comparaison Maurice/Réunion au regard du sexe trouve ses limites dans les choix contrastés opérés par chacun des deux systèmes éducatifs. A la Réunion, filles et garçons sont placés "objectivement" dans des conditions similaires d'enseignement. A Maurice, l'homogénéité des classes (large absence de classes mixtes) pourrait constituer un facteur discriminant.

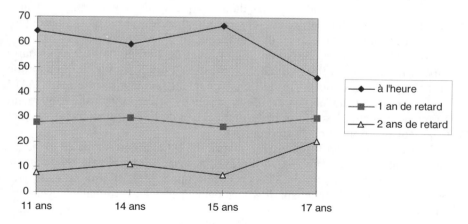

Graphique 2. Retards scolaires des élèves de l'enseignement secondaire à La Réunion (en %).

538

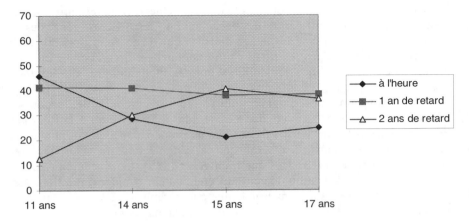

Graphique 3. Retards scolaires des élèves de l'enseignement secondaire à l'Ile Maurice (en %).

L'âge produit des différences

Les systèmes scolaires réunionnais et mauriciens produisent des retards scolaires dans des proportions très différentes. Ceci témoigne de choix de politique éducative particuliers tant en ce qui concerne l'utilisation du redoublement qu'au niveau du mode de certification. Mais les tendances observées dans le graphique suivant constituent également une mesure (partielle) des "performances" de chacun des deux systèmes éducatifs.

Pour faciliter la comparaison, nous nous référons ici au niveau scolaire atteint par les élèves au même âge. Il convient de noter que cet âge ne les situe pas toujours au même palier dans chaque système éducatif. A 11 ans, les élèves réunionnais et mauriciens entrent théoriquement dans l'enseigne-ment secondaire (en classe de 6ème ou en Form1). A 15 ans, l'élève réunionnais accède en classe de 2nde (début de l'enseignement secondaire supérieur) tandis que l'élève mauricien est en Form5, classe de préparation au SC (qui sanctionne la fin de l'enseignement secondaire inférieur). A 17 ans en revanche, les élèves des deux systèmes se retrouvent théoriquement au même niveau, c'est-à-dire la dernière classe de l'enseignement secondaire supérieur (Terminale ou Form6 upper).

Le caractère sélectif du système mauricien est clairement mis en évidence par le graphique. La proportion d'élèves accusant deux ans de retard passe de 13% en Form1 à près de 37% en Form6 upper. A La Réunion, cette pro-portion évolue respectivement de 8% en 6ème à 21% en Terminale. A Maurice, environ 40% des élèves ont un an de retard tout au long de l'enseignement secondaire (contre moins de 30% à La Réunion).

A titre complémentaire et au-delà des informations apportées par le graphique, précisons que la proportion d'élèves "à l'heure" avant le passage du CPE (c'est-à-dire inscrits en dernière année de l'enseignement primaire) est de 56%. A ce même niveau, 38% des élèves ont un an de retard et seuls 6% ont deux ans de retard.

L'examen du CPE constitue donc un premier facteur de retard scolaire mais celui-ci s'accentue considérablement tout au long de l'enseignement secondaire. Le redoublement n'est donc pas uniquement synonyme de "seconde chance" à l'examen: il témoigne aussi d'une discrimination négative. A cet égard, il est symptomatique d'observer que la proportion d'élèves à l'heure "remonte" à près de 25% en Form6 upper.

Ce n'est pas le cas à la Réunion où la proportion d'élèves à l'heure décroît jusqu'à l'accès en troisième (malgré une remontée en fin de cycle liée à une politique régionale de faible redoublement au collège). Notons toutefois que le pourcentage de bacheliers à l'heure atteint 52%, ce qui traduit, comme à l'Ile Maurice, une mise à l'écart du baccalauréat pour des candidats âgés, et de façon cumulative, potentiellement faibles.

Trait majeur à retenir, le redoublement est globalement deux fois plus utilisé à l'Ile Maurice, ce qui, en référence à d'autres travaux en sociologie de l'éducation (Langouët 1985) et par extrapolation, "révèle" l'existence d'un tri à caractère social.

Au plan des "performances" ou de l'efficacité, le nombre de bacheliers à la Réunion comparé à celui des titulaires du HSC à l'Ile Maurice laisse peu de marges à l'interprétation. Même si on formule l'hypothèse heuristique d'une moindre qualité moyenne du baccalauréat français face au HSC, l'argument de la massification invalide l'option de résultats plus positifs à Maurice.

Tri scolaire & tri social

L'analyse comparative de la sélection à caractère social à Maurice et à la Réunion ne peut être menée de façon fiable en raison de l'absence de collecte de données sur l'origine sociale des élèves mauriciens. Bien que ces indicateurs existent au sein des établissements, ils ne font l'objet ni d'une exploitation administrative ni d'une analyse scientifique systématisées. Les témoignages recueillis autoriseraient à attribuer cette tendance aux représentations politiques et culturelles majoritaires des Mauriciens (ultralibéralisme, illusions méritocratiques, etc. . . . .). En revanche, la collecte et l'exploitation des données sur l'origine sociale des élèves relèvent, en France, d'une tradition datant des années 60. L'Académie de la Réunion, depuis sa création en 1985, s'inscrit largement dans cette tradition.

Il ressort de l'analyse de ces données que le système éducatif réunionnais, à l'instar du système national, génère une sélection à caractère social. Cela signifie qu'au delà de la composition sociologique de ce département français d'outre mer largement représentée au plan des catégories sociales[7] défavorisées, l'Ecole renforce les inégalités qui lui préexistent. Le tableau suivant est, de ce point de vue, éloquent:

Tableau 2. Proportion d'élèves selon la catégorie sociale du chef de famille (Académie de La Réunion, année 1997).

Catégorie sociale	En 6ème	En 2nde	Parmi les bacheliers
Très favorisée	7,6	15,1	19,9
Favorisée	7,6	11,7	11,4
Moyenne	22,9	28,2	30,0
Défavorisée	57,9	41,0	36,1
Inconnue, sans objet	4,0	4,1	2,6
Total	100,0	100,0	100,0

Source: Service statistique du Rectorat de l'Académie de la Réunion.

On assiste à une augmentation de la représentation des enfants de catégories sociales très favorisées, favorisées et moyennes au fil du déroulement des carrières scolaires. Ces trois groupes représentent ensemble 38% des élèves en 6ème, 55% en 2nde générale et technologique et 61% des bacheliers de l'enseignement général et technologique. La proportion d'élèves issus des couches sociales les plus favorisées est multipliée par 2,6 de la 6ème au baccalauréat tandis celle des élèves des couches sociales les plus modestes est divisée par 1,6.

A la Réunion, le recrutement des élèves n'est pas soumis à un quelconque rang de sortie à un examen, et reste majoritairement cadré par la carte scolaire. La population scolaire inscrite en collège relève, pour près des deux tiers, de catégories sociales dites défavorisées (enfants d'ouvriers, de salariés agricoles, de personnels de services, de chômeurs, d'inactifs de moins de 65 ans). On ne rencontre que très rarement des établissements à "caractère bourgeois", selon la typologie d'Alain Léger (Léger 1983). Aussi, si la composition sociologique des collèges réunionnais s'égrène selon un continuum qui s'étend de 21% à 84% d'élèves défavorisés inscrits dans l'établissement, reste qu'un seul collège public réunionnais accueille moins de 35% d'élèves socialement défavorisés et que la moyenne académique se situe autour de 60% de collégiens d'origines sociales modestes. Sur les 64 collèges publics implantés dans ce département français, deux tiers accueillent au moins 60% de collégiens "défavorisés" (41/61) et plus de 90% des établissements reçoivent au moins 45% d'élèves répondant à cette appellation.

Les carences statistiques mauriciennes évoquées plus haut ne permettent pas, loin s'en faut, cette précision. Toutefois, le mode de fonctionnement du système éducatif mauricien autorise une prédiction à caractère social qui s'exprime de façon quasi-manichéenne. L'ensemble des acteurs interviewés quelle que soit leur fonction – pédagogique ou institutionnelle – corroborent l'existence de cette sélection à partir des indicateurs suivants:

• *La réussite aux différents examens (CPE, SC, HSC) passe par la fréquentation de cours dits particuliers qui s'apparentent à une école parallèle.*

Or, l'efficacité de ces cours croît avec leur coût. Cette pratique caractérise une tendance lourde des us et coutumes mauriciennes. Tout concourt à renforcer cette tendance: les salaires modestes des enseignants, la course effrénée aux meilleurs établissements puis aux titres de lauréats qui conditionnent l'octroi de bourses d'excellence, l'illusoire corrélation positive entre volume des cours particuliers et résultats, l'amplification des phénomènes de réputation (label du "bon prof" qui a un bon taux de réussite avec les meilleurs élèves) associés à une «marketisation» des cours dits particuliers, certaines autorisations officieuses de dispenser ces cours au sein même des établissements, etc. . . . En fait, le système s'auto-alimente, les professeurs exerçant dans les établissements triés socialement prennent en cours particuliers/collectifs des élèves sélectionnés selon les mêmes critères; la concurrence entre professeurs se développe à l'identique de la concurrence entre établissements; les enseignants obtenant les meilleurs résultats (par la voie du pré-tri) accueillent les meilleurs élèves, confortant ainsi leur image particulièrement au moment des résultats nationaux; l'ensemble génère une reproduction systémique aux allures méritocratiques.

- *La réussite dépend par ailleurs étroitement de l'établissement d'inscription*. Or, seuls quelques cas exceptionnels d'enfants défavorisés fréquentant les collèges les plus prestigieux sont mentionnés. Cette donnée prend toute sa pertinence lorsque l'on sait que tous les établissements mauriciens sont, entre eux, hiérarchisés, et que l'inscription dans tel collège ou tel autre dépend directement du rang de sortie aux examens nationaux. Il est à noter que plus on descend dans la hiérarchie des établissements, plus les effectifs présentés aux examens sont faibles. Il existe une corrélation entre la hiérarchie des établissements établie à l'aune des résultats au SC et HSC et les variables contextuelles de l'établissement. De façon factuelle, la hiérarchie est la suivante:
1) collèges publics d'excellence, collèges confessionnels
2) autres collèges publics
3) collèges privés

Cette classification renvoie aux ressources tant matérielles qu'humaines. Dans les collèges d'Etat, les budgets les plus importants et les enseignants les mieux formés sont la règle, tandis que les collèges privés connaissent des difficultés matérielles majeures et recrutent des enseignants faiblement qualifiés. La logique élitiste et concurrentielle du système consacre et renforce le fossé existant entre les différentes catégories d'établissements. Aux collèges accueillant les classes sociales les plus favorisées, correspondent les établissements les mieux dotés. De surcroît, la composition sociologique des collèges aboutit à faire bénéficier les élèves les plus favorisés des meilleures conditions d'enseignement.

- *Plus on s'élève dans cette hiérarchie, plus les écoles secondaires sont étanches*. Cela signifie qu'excepté pour des enfants de souches sociales favorisées, les possibilités de "surclassement" dans un établissement plus coté sont exclues.

- *L'illusion d'un système juste, donc méritocratique, est renforcée par la médiatisation* – notamment par voie de presse – *des quelques lauréats ayant échappé à la sélection sociale.*

Une recherche bibliographique des rares travaux mauriciens[8] en la matière conforte les pistes qualitatives ainsi tracées. En particulier, une étude menée par le M.E.S (Mauritius Examinations Syndicate) montre l'influence de la situation socio-économique des parents sur la réussite au CPE (M.E.S, 1991). Dans les écoles dont le niveau de performance est jugé élevé ou moyen, cette variable exerce une influence significative derrière les tests "d'aptitude", mais devant les variables contextuelles (attitudes de l'enseignant, niveau de la classe, etc. . . .). Par contre, l'effet des variables sociales est "neutralisé" dans les écoles dont le niveau de performance au C.P.E est jugé faible. Autrement dit, cela signifie que le tri social s'est opéré, au moins en partie, dès l'école primaire. La configuration des écoles à "faible rendement scolaire" en termes de réussite aux examens ne fait que traduire la présence d'un public relativement homogène dont le dénominateur commun consiste à relever des catégories socio-économiques modestes. On comprend pourquoi, dans de telles conditions, la distinction sociale ne peut plus être, statistiquement, pertinente.

Il est à noter qu'un tel phénomène d'homogénéisation sociale du public au sein d'une même école, ou d'un même district ne peut exister avec la même intensité à la Réunion. Si des stratégies de parents et d'enseignants conduisent à modérer les effets égalisateurs de la sectorisation, il n'en demeure pas moins que, sur le sol réunionnais, l'hétérogénéité socio-économique des publics scolaires reste, en moyenne, une caractéristique forte.[9]

Conclusion générale

A l'issue de cette étude comparative, on peut estimer que, même si le système éducatif mauricien et le système éducatif réunionnais produisent des effets sociaux différenciés, ceux-ci ne sont pas aussi tranchés et éloignés que les choix politiques opérés ne le laissaient supposer; cette nuance est révélée par la complémentarité entre approches quantitative et qualitative.

En effet, le système réunionnais, tout en poursuivant des objectifs conjoints de démographisation et de démocratisation, développe une sélection implicite forte. La réalité de ce premier système éducatif met en exergue l'existence d'un hiatus entre curriculum officiel et curriculum caché lié à une zone de forte tension entre pratiques scolaires et directives officielles. Autrement dit, les acteurs éducatifs des collèges et des lycées réunionnais se caractérisent, majoritairement, par des pratiques allant à l'encontre des instructions officielles qui s'inscrivent dans le cadre de "l'école pour tous"; cette tendance centrale restant à moduler d'un établissement à un autre et, parallèlement, d'un enseignant à l'autre.

De fait, il existe – le plus souvent – une «alliance objective» entre les personnels de direction et d'encadrement, les enseignants et les familles favorisées . . . pour ménager un parcours scolaire personnalisé aux élèves de ces catégories sociales qui restent, fréquemment, les meilleurs élèves confiés aux établissements. Cette alliance ou convergence d'intérêt parfois choisie, souvent subie, minore les effets attendus d'une Ecole ouverte à tous (au moins au plan formel). Elle s'exprime sous des formes diverses et complémentaires telles que la constitution de classes homogènes de niveaux, la sélection par les langues – vivantes ou mortes – et les options, les modalités d'orientation, les dérogations à la carte scolaire . . . Il existe donc conjointement, mais de façon souvent contradictoire, des effets de structure et des effets de marge liés aux choix des acteurs sociaux du monde éducatif.

En revanche, le système éducatif mauricien présente une forte cohésion entre politique scolaire et mise en œuvre par les acteurs. Les choix impulsés sont explicitement déclinés et assumés, ils se caractérisent par une politique éducative élitiste qui reçoit l'adhésion de l'immense majorité des enseignants et cadres. L'esprit de compétition est valorisé – voire magnifié –, y compris de la part des professionnels de l'éducation qui encadrent des élèves en grandes difficultés scolaires et sociales. Les familles ayant la meilleure lisibilité du système ne peuvent qu'adhérer à une logique qui favorise et valorise la carrière scolaire de leurs enfants. Les stratégies développées se cristallisent essentiellement autour de la course simultanée aux cours particuliers et aux établissements prestigieux. La cohérence entre instance décisionnelle et pratiques de terrain est donc, de ce point de vue, très forte.

Les effets sociaux différenciés constatés s'exercent sur les trois variables examinées dans le cadre de cette étude: le sexe, l'âge et l'origine sociale. Rappelons que:

- Le système scolaire mauricien, au niveau de l'enseignement secondaire, crée nettement moins de différences relatives au sexe que n'en génère le système réunionnais; cette tendance est à moduler en fonction des catégories sociales d'appartenance.
- Les retards scolaires, plus fréquents à Maurice qu'à La Réunion, témoignent davantage du caractère sélectif de l'Ecole mauricienne que de la promotion de l'étalement des cursus dans l'optique d'une seconde chance.
- Les deux systèmes en présence génèrent une sélection à caractère social, mais dans des proportions différentes. Les deux Ecoles renforcent, par des processus spécifiques, les inégalités sociales qui leur préexistent.

Au plan de l'égalité des chances, la politique éducative réunionnaise mise en place "officiellement" permet à bien davantage d'enfants d'origines sociales défavorisées de "tirer leur épingle du jeu". La différence fondamentale entre les deux systèmes réside donc dans les possibilités potentielles d'accès aux différents paliers d'enseignement. Cette seule confrontation – indépendamment de toutes les autres variables qui diffèrent d'un système insulaire à l'autre – suffit à réactiver le rapport dialectique entre démocratisation quantitative et démocratisation qualitative, entre "démographisation" et démocratisation stricto sensu.

ENCADRE METHODOLOGIQUE

Cette recherche prend appui sur deux types de données, quantitatives et qualitatives, exploitées de façons complémentaires.

Sur le plan quantitatif, les chiffres mentionnés ont été calculés à partir des publications statistiques officielles du Rectorat de l'Académie de La Réunion d'une part, et du Central Statistical Office (CSO) de l'Ile Maurice d'autre part. La publication annuelle du Mauritius Examinations Syndicate (MES) a également été utilisée, pour tous les résultats concernant le CPE, le SC et le HSC.

Sur le plan qualitatif, plus de quarante entretiens ont été menés avec différents acteurs du système éducatif. A la Réunion, nous avons rencontré des proviseurs de lycée, des professeurs principaux en classe de seconde et de Terminale, des principaux et principaux-adjoints de collège et des enseignants en classe de 6ème et de 3ème. A l'Ile Maurice, nous avons également rencontré des chefs d'établissements et des enseignants dans des contextes très différents: collèges d'Etat, confessionnels, privés . . . Ces entretiens "de terrain" ont été complétés par des entrevues avec des responsables administratifs (enseignement secondaire et examens à Maurice, politique rectorale et orientation scolaire à la Réunion) et des universitaires en sciences sociales.

Le principe d'échantillonnage retenu est donc celui de la variété des situations pédagogiques, statutaires et géographiques. Autrement dit, les établissements scolaires visités et les acteurs interviewés se distinguent par des caractéristiques contrastées. Les éléments factuels, les indicateurs, les témoignages recueillis par voie d'entretiens semi-directifs constituent un faisceau cohérent de données qui permet de se prononcer, sinon de façon statistiquement fiable, au moins tendanciellement valide. Notons que la composition de cet échantillon a été perçue par nos interlocuteurs de référence au plan de l'administration comme pouvant donner une image raisonnée des réalités éducatives mauricienne et réunionnaise.

Notes

1. La Réunion bénéficie d'un régime au cœur duquel la protection sociale est forte grâce au vecteur de la solidarité nationale tandis qu'à Maurice – système économique autonome – le modèle adopté relève d'un libéralisme prononcé (bas salaires, zone franche . . .).
2. Institut National d'Etudes Démographiques 1972 (France); Rapport Coleman, 1966, USA; Rapport Plowden, 1967, Grande-Bretagne.
3. Consulter, par exemple, les importantes bibliographies établies par Jean-Claude Forquin dans la série des notes de synthèse qu'il a consacrées à "la sociologie des inégalités d'éducation": "Principales orientations, principaux résultats depuis 1965" puis à "l'approche sociologique de la réussite et de l'échec scolaires: inégalités de réussite et appartenance sociale" (Revue Française de Pédagogie, n° 49 à 53). Ces synthèses concernent tant les travaux français que les travaux anglo-saxons.
4. Ce trait reste à nuancer dès lors que les travaux sur l'orientation montrent l'impact différencié des parents, au plan de l'orientation, en fonction de la catégorie sociale. Nous verrons que ces pratiques sont confirmées par notre enquête.
5. La classe de Form5 correspond à la fin de l'enseignement secondaire. A ce palier, environ 1/3 des élèves réussissent l'examen du SC.

6. A l'issue de ce niveau d'enseignement (CPE/6ème), les proportions filles/garçons sont équivalentes dans les deux îles et donc quasiment superposables sur le graphique.
7. Les catégories sociales ont été regroupées selon les modalités habituellement utilisées dans les publications du Ministère de l'Education Nationale en France. Notons cependant qu'à La Réunion, les professions «instituteurs et assimilés» sont placées par l'INSEE dans la catégorie «très favorisée» en raison du complément de rémunération qui leur est accordé par rapport à la France métropolitaine.
8. La plupart des travaux portant sur le système éducatif mauricien concernent essentiellement le niveau primaire; l'éducation de base constituant la priorité stratégique des pays en voie de développement (voir, par exemple, Chinapah 1983).
9. A la Réunion, l'homogénéité résulte principalement de données exogènes telles que la répartition des groupes socio-économiques par le vecteur de l'habitat; facteur bien évidemment présent à Maurice mais dont l'influence est seconde par rapport au rôle joué par la course aux établissements les plus cotés entraînant une forte mobilité géographique des élèves.

Références

Baudelot, Ch. et Establet, R. 1992. *Allez les filles!* Paris: Ed du Seuil, coll. L'épreuve des faits.

Bourdieu, P. 1987. *Choses dites.* Paris: Ed de Minuit.

Barton, L. and Walker, S., eds., 1983. *Gender Class and Education.* London: Falmer Press.

Bunwaree, S. 1997. Gender, *Education/Training and Development in Mauritius.* Maurice: UNDP Port Louis.

Chinapah, V. 1983. *Participation and Performance in Primary Schooling. A Study of Equality of Educational Opportunity in Mauritius.*

Chevillon, M. et Parain, C. 1994. Parcours scolaires et milieu social à la Réunion. In *Education & Formations*, n° 38. Paris: DEP.

Duru-Bellat, M. 1990. *L'école des filles: quelle formation pour quels rôles sociaux.* Paris: L'Harmattan.

Duru-Bellat, M. 1996. *L'évolution des inégalités sociales dans le système éducatif français.* Paris: Séminaire DEP-IREDU.

Fioux, P. 1998. Enseignement du français et systèmes éducatifs dans les Mascareignes. In *Aspects de la francophonie dans l'Océan Indien*, volume 2. Paolo Carile Editeur.

Forquin, J.-C. 1989. *Ecole et culture, Le point de vue des sociologues britanniques.* Bruxelles: De Boeck.

Isambert-Jamati, V. 1990. Préface de *Sociologie de l'Education, dix ans de recherche.* Paris: INRP/L'Harmattan.

Langouët, G. 1985. *Suffit-il d'innover?* Paris: PUF.

Langouët, G. 1993. Les années 80-90: quelle démocratisation? *L'orientation scolaire et professionnelle* 22(1).

Langouët, G. 1994. *La démocratisation de l'enseignement aujourd'hui.* Paris: E.S.F.

Léger, A. 1983. *Enseignants du secondaire.* Paris: PUF.

546

Mauritius Examinations Syndicate, 1991. *Determinants of Performance in Primary Schools with Special référence to Failures at CPE Level*, UNICEF Report.

Prost, A. 1968. *L'enseignement en France, 1800–1967*, Ed. Armand Colin, Coll U.

Prost, A. 1992. *L'enseignement s'est-il démocratisé?* Paris: PUF.

Tirvassen, R. 1994. Evaluation du système éducatif mauricien et compétences communicationnelles. In *Communication et développement: Le cas de Maurice*. Paris, Didier Erudition.

UNESCO, 1995. Annuaire statistique, Paris.

University of Mauritius. 1988. *The Private Cost of Education*. University of Mauritius/ Ministry of Education.

Van Haecht, A. 1992. *L'école à l'épreuve de la sociologie: questions à la sociologie de l'Education*. Bruxelles: Ed De Boeck/Université.

Virashawny, D. 1984. Le système éducatif mauricien: problèmes et possibilités. In *Etudes créoles*, vol II, n° 1–2, Ottawa.

Wolff, E. and Simonin, J. 1996. Ecole & famille à la Réunion: le téléscopage des modèles. In *Lien social et politiques*. Montréal: Ed. St Martin.

Les auteurs

Azzedine Si Moussa est maître de conférences en sciences de l'éducation à l'Université de La Réunion depuis 1997. Il est actuellement chercheur associé à l'IREDU-CNRS, laboratoire de recherche implanté à Dijon (France). Docteur en économie de l'éducation depuis 1993, il a travaillé à l'Unité européenne d'Eurydice, réseau européen d'information sur l'éducation, en 1996–97. Ses travaux se situent dans le champ de la socio-économie de l'éducation et l'éducation comparée.

Contact address: Faculté des Lettres et Sciences Humaines, 15, avenue René Cassin BP 7151, 97715, St. Denis Messag Cedex 9, La Reunion (France). E-mail: azzedine.simoussa@univ-réunion.fr.

Frédéric Tupin est maître de conférences en sciences de l'éducation à l'Université de La Réunion depuis 1995. Docteur en sociologie de l'éducation (Université de Paris V), il est actuellement membre du LCF (Laboratoire d'études sur les espaces créolophones et francophones, associé au CNRS) de l'Université de La Réunion. Ses travaux portent notamment sur la démocratisation de l'enseignement et les questions sociolinguistiques liées à l'éducation.

Contact address: Faculté des Lettres et Sciences Humaines, 15, avenue René Cassin BP 7151, 97715, St. Denis Messag Cedex 9, La Reunion (France). E-mail: frederic.tupin@univ-réunion.fr.

DISCOURSE, STRUCTURE AND PRACTICE OF CONTINUING EDUCATION: A COMPARISON BETWEEN SWITZERLAND AND GERMANY

KARL WEBER and JÜRGEN WITTPOTH

Abstract – Switzerland and Germany are countries with many similarities in terms of culture, economic development and education. This article compares their continuing education systems and how they have responded to national and international trends. The authors examine the extent of teaching and research in this field, as well as the economic, legal and organizational aspects of continuing education. Among other things, they consider why private providers of continuing education play a far greater role in Switzerland than in Germany.

Zusammenfassung – Die Schweiz und Deutschland sind Länder mit vielen Gemeinsamkeiten bezüglich Kultur, wirtschaftlicher Entwicklung und Bildung. Dieser Artikel vergleicht ihre Weiterbildungssysteme und ihre Reaktionen auf nationale und internationale Trends. Die Autoren untersuchen das Ausmaß des Lehrens und der Forschung auf diesem Gebiet und die wirtschaftlichen, rechtlichen und organisatorischen Aspekte der Weiterbildung. Unter anderem überlegen sie, warum private Anbieter von Weiterbildungsmaßnahmen in der Schweiz eine weitaus größere Rolle spielen als in Deutschland.

Résumé – La Suisse et l'Allemagne présentent de nombreuses similitudes en matière de culture, de développement économique et d'éducation. L'article compare les systèmes d'éducation continue et les réactions aux tendances nationales et internationales dans ces deux pays. Les auteurs étudient l'importance de l'enseignement et de la recherche en éducation continue ainsi que les aspects économiques, juridiques et organisationnels de ce domaine. Ils examinent entre autres les raisons du rôle beaucoup plus important en Suisse qu'en Allemagne des prestataires privés de l'éducation continue.

Resumen – Suiza y Alemania son países que presentan muchas similitudes en términos de cultura, desarrollo económico y educación. Este artículo compara sus sistemas de ampliación de estudios y/o perfeccionamiento profesional y cómo los mismos han respondido a tendencias nacionales e internacionales. Los autores analizan el alcance de la enseñanza e investigación en esta área, así como sus aspectos económicos, legales y organizativos. Entre otras cosas, se ocupan de averiguar por qué los proveedores privados de ampliación de estudios y/o perfeccionamiento profesional juegan un papel mucho más importante en Suiza que en Alemania.

Резюме - Швейцария и Германия - это страны, между которыми много общего в сфере культуры, экономического развития и образования. В статье рассматриваются их системы непрерывного образования и их реакция на национальные и международные тенденции. Авторы рассматривают охват обучения и исследований в этой сфере, а также экономический, правовой и организационный

International Review of Education – Internationale Zeitschrift für Erziehungswissenschaft – Revue Internationale de l'Education **45**(5/6): 547–560, 1999.
© 1999 *Kluwer Academic Publishers. Printed in the Netherlands.*

аспекты непрерывного образования. Кроме всего прочего, авторы рассматривают вопрос, почему частные организации непрерывного образования играют гораздо более важную роль в Швейцарии, чем в Германии.

As regards the scope and type of participation in continuing education, the situation in Switzerland and Germany is very similar at present. The total participation quotas are almost equivalent (G 1994: 42% [vocational: 24%/general: 26%], CH 1992/93: 40% [vocational: 23%/general: 21%]). The disparities in participation also correspond on the whole: appreciably over-represented are younger male employees with good school-leaving certificates, who hold (middle) management positions in large companies or in service enterprises and live in densely populated areas.

On the face of it, this is not surprising since the two countries are comparable in many respects. Not only are the economies developed to a similar degree in Switzerland and Germany, but their pedagogical traditions, the structure of the educational systems and its organisation, the concept behind their vocational training (the "dual system") and the system of professions, are largely the same. Finally, state responsibility for the educational system is federally organised in both countries. The Länder in Germany and the Cantons in Switzerland have considerable autonomy in organising their educational system.

A closer look, however, shows one substantial difference: while the state guarantee of the provision of general continuing education plays a strong role in Germany, it has been of hardly of any significance in Switzerland. This fact is surprising and requires explanation.

To look into this question, we take up the basic theoretical concepts developed by Bourdieu (see *Homo academicus*, for example). We understand continuing education as an area occupied and shaped by various actors. These actors perceive the questions of continuing education in a specific manner and define them. They develop concepts for strategies and endeavour to implement them in the field. The pattern of perception and action that they adopt will largely depend on their position in the field.

On the basis of these general ideas regarding the structure of continuing education, we shall proceed in the following steps to clarify the basic question. First we shall sketch how the profile of international discourse has changed in recent years, and how it was received in the two national contexts. We shall then go on to ask what contribution continuing education research and the profession of continuing educators have made to the development of the discourse. Afterwards, we shall look into the question of whether and how the problem of continuing education is structurally generated in the interaction between education and the social structure, in particular employment. In a fourth step, we describe the legal context in which public discourse on continuing education and structural change are taking place, and, fifthly, how the institutional panoramas in continuing education have been formed on this basis in the continuing education of the two countries. Finally, we summarise the findings under theoretical aspects and go on to formulate questions to further research.

The continuing education discourse

At the **international level** in the seventies, continuing education was considered from two different points of view: in one, the principle of "recurrent education" stood to the fore, which aimed to restructure the entire system of education (cf. e.g. OECD/CERI 1973). At other times it was more a matter of lifelong learning outside institutionalised contexts after leaving school (cf. Faure et al. 1972). These versions constitute not so much competing models as different emphases in the discussion. In the meantime, hardly any recourse was made to recurrence in its original sense and little consideration was given to the continuing education sector as an integral part of an overall system of education (cf. UNESCO 1997, for instance). That a number of these problems can hardly be solved without reforming basic education and integrating it systemically with lifelong learning is a point which is realised by many (cf. Europäische Kommission 1995, for instance).

In **Germany** – at the national educational policy level – from the end of the sixties, it was primarily the recurrence aspect that had been primarily accepted. The criterion for assessing what the educational system had achieved was whether it contributed to securing the country's international competitiveness, and on this basis it was found to be so inadequate that a complete overhaul of the educational system seemed mandatory. At the same time, educational reform was to effect greater equality of opportunity and contribute to further democratisation. Continuing education then came to be viewed as an integral component of a "standard" educational system which was the responsibility of the state. It was left primarily to the radical critics of institutional continuing education to point to "de-schooling" (to speak in Illich's terms), and thus to point to the other, informal dimension of lifelong learning. By the mid-eighties at the latest, the perspective was changed from state responsibility to regulation by market forces, and then continuing education seemed to increasingly being seen as a subsidiary activity with an orientation to qualification requirements in the employment system (cf. Bundesministerium für Bildung und Wissenschaft 1985). Today, there are indications that all references to recurrence have largely been suspended (cf. Dohmen 1997, for example).

In **Switzerland**, the principle of recurrent education was accepted much more guardedly in various respects. At the federal level, the debate started later (middle to end of the seventies) and consensus was lower. There were warnings against "total schooling" and individual responsibility was emphasised as well as the importance of private institutions in continuing educa-tion (cf. Schweizerischer Wissenschaftsrat 1978). Moreover, at an early stage, concern was expressed that recurrent training might possibly lead to aggra-vating rather than lessening social inequality. Unlike in Germany, a reform of the organically formed structure of the education system was apparently not considered necessary. At the beginning of the eighties, recurrent educa-tion was given a new significance, but primarily in view of university reform that would be required in the medium to long-term. Interest focused primarily on the needs of the labour market and industry generally. In the mid-eighties, the federal government started a continuing education initiative to counter the shortage of qualified workers and professionals. Systemic questions like recur-rent education no longer played any part in this program. What was wanted was the promotion of qualifications for specific occupations with already avail-able institutional means. In the meantime, a new debate has started on mod-ularisation, which aims, amongst other things, at an efficient use of resources and a better adaptation of biographical patterns and subsequent occupational qualifications.

A striking fact is that both countries have been extremely selective (depending on "needs") in the way they have taken up the international concept debate. In the days when the reform of education in Germany was dictated by the project of social democrats, there was an almost exclusive fixation on systemic aspects. When the more conservative, economically liberal government took over and the demand for highly qualified workers seemed to have been satisfied, there was a move to extra-institutional dimen-sions of lifelong learning. As regards Switzerland, the striking aspect is the "delay" of about a decade in catching up with international discourse and the generally hesitant attitude towards system reorganisation in the seventies and eighties. A certain scepticism prevails here with regard to the feasibility of educational reform which may be due first of all to the "small-area" and federal organisation of the education system and second to the continuing effectiveness of liberal education traditions. A certain convergence appeared between the two countries from about the mid-eighties in as much as they both favoured free-market principles over state planning and control.

Research and professionalisation in continuing education

From the broad spectrum of very different actors participating in the discus-sion, we now select two special groups. The question here is whether and to what extent the universities and professionals in continuing education con-tribute to the national debates.

In the wake of the expansion of education and the debate on educational reform, in **Germany** adult pedagogics became institutionalised as an inde-pendent field of teaching and research at the universities. This expansion was to provide support to the planned expansion and restructuring of the educational system with relevant research and professional competence. From the mid-sixties, for instance, chairs in continuing education were established at universities and (at the end of the sixties) a diploma course was launched in the faculty of pedagogics, which, amongst other things, served to train teachers in continuing education. There are now about 40 professorships in continuing education and the pedagogic has become one of the big mass disciplines at German universities. It is now possible to train specifically for work in continuing education through both diploma and master's degree courses, as well as other post-graduate courses. While the situation is by no means such that only university-trained people with these qualifications can work in continuing education, the view has gained further acceptance that educators in this field should have training in continuing education.

The establishment of professorships also prepared the ground for the acceptance and generation of new knowledge regarding continuing education. Academic reflection in the field was placed on a systematic and formal basis. A stable academic context for discourse became established in the *Deutsche Gesellschaft für Erziehungswissenschaft*. This gradual creation of expert knowledge was accompanied by the publication of relevant journals (with both theoretical and practical orientation), the expansion of continuing education book publications etc., which contributed to the creation of an autonomous continuing education culture and a debate which reached the public at large.

In **Switzerland**, the degree of institutionalisation in continuing education at the tertiary level is extremely weak. Although the country now has eleven universities, there is only one chair specialising in continuing education. This was established in the sixties in Geneva, a canton with an educational policy under a social-democratic government that has consistently promoted equality of opportunity in education. Accordingly, except in Geneva and – at the post-diploma level – in Bern, qualifications for professional work in continuing education can only be acquired in extra-university and part-time courses which are being offered by very different private and state institutions. As a rule, these are training courses which provide supplementary qualification for teaching on the basis of past professional training.

Under the conditions outlined above, it was not possible to develop continuous research on continuing education and to accumulate knowledge in Switzerland. First of all, the universities do not have the staff for this, and second, sponsoring agencies provide support to research in continuing education only selectively and in a context of changing educational policies. International research and its utilisation in the national context therefore took place not so much through the universities but through professional staff of educational policy actors or through associations. Consequently the conditions for the development of an independent professional culture with its own norms, standards and milieu are still lacking.

A comparison of the two countries shows that in Germany, thanks to the institutionalisation of continuing education at the universities, the debate on continuing education is constantly fed and further developed. In the scientific world, continuing education is also always a matter of public debate. As opposed to this, in Switzerland, public discussion runs much more strongly parallel to educational policy cycles. As a rule, it is generated externally and mostly follows the logic of politics rather than that of science. The entire debate is much more strongly dominated by professional associations, industry and the socio-cultural milieu than in Germany.

Economic and social change as the challenge for education and continuing education

Since the sixties, Germany and Switzerland have been undergoing far-reaching economic changes, which can be essentially summed up in the process of tertiarisation, international networking and a decrease in public funding for education and social welfare. This process of transformation is accompanied by a general and rapid rise in the need for highly qualified manpower. In the discussion of education and continuing education policies, questions of training related to future employment and employability are gaining more importance. This transformation has essentially meant that in the wake of change in the economic structure and the expansion and differentiation of the range of training offered, the relationship between training and employment has taken on added significance. A university degree is still a necessary but increasingly not a sufficient condition for a top professional position. There are indications that longer continuing education courses which end with a diploma have become more important for a successful professional career.

From the fifties, economic growth and changes in the economic structure in **Germany**, resulted in a steep rise in demand for (highly) qualified staff. Until "the Wall" was built between East and West Berlin in 1961, this demand could at least partly be satisfied by immigrants from the GDR. After that, foreign workers were recruited, particularly from southern Europe, who, mostly belonged to the unskilled or semi-skilled group. The employment of foreign workers (about 8% of the population in 1995) thus resulted in the creation of a lower social class in western German society. The people with higher qualifications required in the course of upgrading production and the tertiarisation of education therefore had to be trained in the country itself. This took place, on the one hand, through the expansion of school education and by encouraging higher school leaving certificates in social classes whose children had hitherto enjoyed a merely basic schooling. On top of this, people already in employment were increasingly given further training since knowledge advanced more rapidly than the change of generations on the labour market.

That the reform of education was not exclusively aligned to the needs of the employment system may be attributed to the fact that after 1969 the social democrats came into power. Their major goals included the further democratisation of society and improving equality of opportunity. Both were to be achieved essentially through the reorganisation of the education system. The number of children who went on to secondary schools did in fact increase from 30% (1960) to over 70% (1995). The greater number of better-qualified people encountered a high level of unemployment for the first time in the mid-seventies and then again from the beginning of the eighties. This is still the case today (1997 in western Germany: 11%; eastern Germany: just under 20%). Moreover, conservative-liberal parties have been in power since 1982. Their attempts to strengthen free-market economic principles against state planning and government responsibility thus converge with the continuing oversupply crisis on the labour market.

Also in **Switzerland** a class of poorly educated foreign workers has been steadily created over a number of decades (Levy et al. 1997, from p. 206). Unlike Germany, Switzerland is, however, quite reluctant to grant citizenship and this may at least partly explain the high proportion of foreigners. What is more, foreigners have varying rights and obligations (between permanent residence and 9-month employment) in Switzerland, which means that they are poorly protected against the risk of unemployment. When they have no work, they often prefer to return home rather than stay in Switzerland. These circumstances may well be the reason for the comparatively low unemployment figures in Switzerland in recent years (1997: 5.2%) and explain why employment-related further training programs for the unemployed were only selectively built up.

More interesting is the situation at the other end of the social stratification. Amongst experts and scientists, foreigners are traditionally over-represented. In particular, the universities and private research and development have to rely on foreign professionals. According to employment statistics, in 1996 the quota of foreigners with a tertiary education was the same as the Swiss quota (SAKE (Schweizerische Arbeitskraefteerhebung) 1997). This is attributable, amongst other things, to the fact that Switzerland makes it easy to recruit specialists abroad if it is not possible to find people with the appropriate qualifications inside the country.

Since it is possible to recruit highly specialised people abroad and there is a long tradition of seeking specialized foreign professionals and workers, there has been little local incentive to meet the demand for specialized courses – especially in the case of the universities. This is all the more so because demand is mostly low in any case. For a comparatively small country like Switzerland, this method of providing the country with better qualified people is functionally equivalent and, what is more, an inexpensive alternative, to expanding basic and further education. The fact that Switzerland has retained this alternative to this day weakened pressure from industry to have education expanded and to have the state guarantee continuing education. At the same time, this curbed discussion of the public need for further education.

In this light, it is easy to understand why the expansion of education remained within limits in Switzerland. All the same, the quota of unskilled workers in the population has constantly declined here too in recent years. This can be attributed in particular to mounting demand on the part of women for vocational training and secondary schooling. Amongst people over 25 years of age in 1997, 24% had had no schooling beyond primary school.

These figures make clear that, in coping with economic structural change, the government obviously does not rely only on education but specifically also on migration which is controlled to suit the respective circumstances and labour market situation. This option was favoured by the great legitimacy of educational policy and its effects. Empirical studies made in the seventies and the nineties show that the population was very satisfied with education policy (cf. Schmidtchen 1979 and Hutmacher/Gross 1993).

By comparison, we find that in coping and shaping economic structural change in Germany there was more reliance on education and further education policies than in Switzerland. First of all, in the seventies in Germany, these policies were embedded in the social-democratic model, which burst the limits imposed by economic logic. The governments at the time pushed through the principle of state responsibility also in continuing education. A corresponding reform model had no majority in Switzerland – except in the canton of Geneva. It is therefore not surprising to find – secondly – that quotas in colleges and in university education in Germany grew more rapidly and reached a higher level than in Switzerland. For this reason it can be assumed that endogenous pressure for greater differentiation in continuing education was heavier in Germany than in Switzerland as a consequence of the higher quota of people given training. Thirdly, unlike Germany, Switzerland used its migration policies also as a substitute for education policies.

The legal base of continuing education

Laws are the outcome of a political process. They reflect what is expected of continuing education and the ideas concerning continuing education which have majority support in a society. The laws delimit the field and define procedures to which the actors are to orient themselves when they discuss matters of continuing education policy.

In the course of educational reform and expansion, various laws were passed concerning continuing education in **Germany** from the end of the sixties. In the field of vocational further training, general standards of vocational further training and retraining were agreed at the national level in the *Berufsbildungsgesetz* (1969) (law regulating vocational training). Over and above this, the *Arbeitsförderungsgesetz* (1969) (law on the promotion of employment) created the conditions for obtaining and extending qualifications and for occupational advancement. Following developments on the labour market, the provisions of this law were amended step by step so that they now, in particular, make retraining the unemployed possible. Parallel to this, up to the mid-seventies – because of the federal structure of the country – most of the Länder passed "continuing education laws" which regulate the funding of general continuing education. These laws have made a substantial contribution to the development of a varied continuing education environment in Germany, which has covered an increasing portion of the population, but without creating a clear and comprehensible structure. Accordingly, the current debate on educational policy is dominated by the struggle for legal measures that go further and should have greater transparency and set minimum standards.

In **Switzerland**, an important step was taken in 1973 in legislation regarding continuing education. The Swiss people rejected a change in the constitution which would have given the federal government comprehensive powers in the field of continuing education. After that, several cantons took the initiative in creating the conditions for the promotion of continuing education. Although promotional concepts differ from canton to canton, the state is active in providing subsidies in practically all cases. Its function is to provide information and to coordinate initiatives. Its promotional measures primarily aim to facilitate access to continuing education for disadvantaged groups and, since recently, to support quality assurance. In other words: a network is made available and maintained in the canton with the intention of promoting and supporting voluntary cooperation.

Although the federal government has no comprehensive powers to regulate continuing education, such powers have been anchored in numerous laws. The first relevant law, which must be mentioned here, is the *Berufsbildungsgesetz* (law on vocational training) which regulates basic and further training especially in the industrial sector. Then there is the *Landwirtschaftsgesetz* (law regulating agriculture) which provides regulations regarding basic and further training in agricultural occupations. Recently, it has been made mandatory for the unemployed to take further training in order to make them more employable.

This description makes it clear that in Switzerland the promotion of continuing education with greater state commitment is being used primarily for coping with social problems or for securing standards and privileges in certain occupations, and for defining rules of access to certain areas of activity. The particularist perspective predominates. And in areas where continuing education is of a general nature, state measures restrict themselves to coordination and encouragement.

A comparison shows a striking similarity in the legal bases of the two countries insofar as they relate to the initiatives and the policy of the federal government and especially the vocational sector and employment. There are considerable differences in promotional practices at the cantonal/Länder level. Here it is clear that, in Switzerland, the tradition of the concordance principle – all parties are represented in the government – have forced the cantons to take over a subsidiary role where the continuity of the courses offered must essentially be secured through market forces. In Germany, on the other hand, where there were a few social-democratic governments, it was possible to guarantee educational services throughout the country.

What the two countries have in common is that the regulatory effect of their laws, which differ in quality, must be considered small. Neither in Germany nor in Switzerland is the state capable of regulating this sector of education as a coherent whole or of organising it clearly (to a level comparable to that of the school system). More or less extensive powers with regard to segments of continuing education exist in various ministerial departments, in institutions under public law (the chambers of commerce, for example), in associations, etc. whose policies and courses rarely relate to one another, and which see their own special significance and their legitimation in this very fact.

The structure of continuing education providers

The discussion and the culture of discussion, the interpretation of the problems of continuing education, statutory provisions and the organising power of providers and sponsors determine the conditions under which continuing education providers can become active.

Both in **Germany** and in **Switzerland**, enterprises are most important providers of continuing education with a share of about 30% in each country (cf. Bundesamt für Statistik 1995: Mikrozensus über Weiterbildung; Kuwan et al. 1996). This circumstance suggests that after reaching a certain level, an economic structure can neither survive nor develop further without continuing education.

One striking difference, however, needs to be explained, namely the difference in the position of private schools (including professional associations) in continuing education. In Germany, these manage to recruit only 12% of participants, whereas in Switzerland the figure is 49%. If only general continuing education in Switzerland is considered, the quota is even bigger.

This strong position of private providers conceals one success story and a structural weakness at the same time. In general, vocational and recreational continuing education in Migrosclubschools hold an exceptionally strong position, and are unique even by international comparison. They were founded as language schools after the Second World War by the owner of a now powerful food corporation. The Migrosclubschools have now widened their program and offer their courses everywhere, but mostly only in cities. Many of their courses have been standardised, their language diplomas are internationally recognised, and the development of the decentral branches and their programs is backed by a central professional staff in continuing education. The Migros group subsidises the programs which are more than 70% financed by participants' fees. Their ability to organise and maintain themselves is an outstanding source of power for Migrosclubschools.

The Migrosclubschools were all the more able to develop so well because their strongest competitors – the *Volkshochschulen* (state organised schools of adult education) – are decentrally organised and very loosely connected with one another. They are less professional and have less professional support. At the same time, state authorities are extremely cautious in the promotion of general continuing education (cf. Section 2.4 above). This is not surprising in view of the success of private providers in this sector, which are legitimised by the fact that people are prepared to pay and which perform semi-public functions.

In Germany, on the other hand, the *Volkshochschulen* (about 1000 in number) are the most important continuing education facilities (just under 30%). Their work is funded – on the basis of the already cited laws on continuing education – to a large extent (about two thirds of the costs) out of public moneys (differences between the Länder). In the Länder where extensive regulations apply (mostly under social-democratic governments), the population was everywhere provided with general continuing education courses. There, the municipalities have the obligation to establish *Volkshochschulen* and must (in North Rhine Westphalia) guarantee a minimum number of courses in accordance with the size of the population in the area they serve. There are also other, not public, sponsors of general continuing education courses, but these also receive considerable government support. There are hardly any genuine private providers who can maintain themselves out of attendance fees since only small niches are left over for them at most, which the public sector does not serve or does not do so in a sufficiently "exclusive" manner. In this regard, however, there are certain differences between the Länder.

Theoretical-conceptual synthesis

Our comparative analysis shows that the national and international discourse on continuing education, the formation of institutions amongst providers and the development of participation in continuing education are features which are only very loosely connected.

National public discourse makes use of internationally provided material at the times that suit them and in the way that suits them. This selection is determined by national problems in the relationship between education and work, and the predominant socio-political models, i.e. the policies that are represented and can be carried through by the dominant political forces.

"Below" this level, institutional structures are formed (and reproduce themselves) which, in each country, are based on its particular national traditions, events and balance of power. Their representatives make use of international (sometimes also of national) rhetoric to secure their existence and expansion – the "meaning" which takes shape in practice is drawn from elsewhere. At this level, the debate is used as a tool for maintaining the status quo.

We were quite surprised to find that it is possible to have very similar patterns of participation in continuing education even with quite different provider structures. Although Switzerland started late and only reluctantly joined the international discourse about continuing education, at the present time the Swiss are not less active in the promotion of continuing education than the Germans. The slow beginning in Switzerland is to be partially explained by the lack of a social democratic model of politics (cf. the concordance principle) – which made it difficult initially to create a culture of public responsibility with consequent statutory regulations, establishing continuing education at universities, etc.

Although private schools play a far greater role than in Germany, It would not be appropriate, however, to conclude from all this that the various measures taken in the sector of public responsibility are ineffective. And this not only because participation in general continuing education is a little higher in Germany than in Switzerland. Rather, findings tend to indicate that where the socio-economic conditions exist in Switzerland, the fees charged by private continuing education providers mean that there is hardly any barrier to access. For some participants, in fact, higher fees for continuing education may make it more worthwhile having more of a commitment. If this is the case, and those interested in continuing education make their choice on the basis of the services offered, the question of whether the courses are offered by a private or a public education provider becomes quite meaningless. This argument would carry even more weight if it could be shown that the profile of courses offered by publicly guaranteed continuing education providers is not basically different from that offered by private providers. This is still a question that requires empirical investigation.

From the more theoretical point of view, the problem just outlined can be summarised as follows: to explain continuing education behaviour, in particular as regards participation (and its disparities) under the given socio-economic conditions in Germany and Switzerland, it is not so much the regulatory criteria which are decisive but other criteria which we have not yet studied. The comparison of these two countries hardly yields any empirical evidence to show that public providers of continuing education reach appreciably other social groups, especially disadvantaged people, than private ones. This may well mean that the traditional controversy of public versus private providers has no empirical basis once one allows oneself to look beyond the national context. Nor would there be any assurance that a continuing education system organised on free-market principles would be more effective or efficient.

These finding suggest that the binding nature of continuing education is probably not defined by regulatory mechanisms at the macro level, but rather that it can be assigned to other regulatory contexts. What is meant here is that the contexts and milieu to which the actors belong are steering their continuing education behaviour (the active as well as the passive one) in a normative way, i.e. according to certain rules, and in view of the circumstances given by the respective situation. We are actually thinking of regulations in the occupational, internal company and socio-cultural context. If someone with a skilled occupation wants to train further to become a master after completing basic training, he is normally forced to attend certain courses which have been laid down by a professional organisation and are recognised by the state. For the individual, the question of financing such further training is secondary to his career decision. The arguments could be the same with regard to general continuing education that contributes to coping with the problems of daily life.

Finally, the results of our comparative analysis suggest the hypothesis that from the socio-educational point of view, modern societies require a certain amount of continuing education to maintain themselves. The question of what type of institution should provide this required amount would appear to be secondary.

References

Bourdieu, P. 1988. *Homo academicus*. Frankfurt a.M.: Suhrkamp.

Bundesamt für Statistik. 1995. *Weiterbildung in der Schweiz*. Bern: EDMZ.

Bundesamt für Statistik. 1997. *Schweizerische Arbeitskräfte-Erhebung* (SAKE). Bern: Web-site of the Bundesamt für Statistik.

Bundesministerium für Bildung und Wissenschaft, ed. 1985. *Thesen zur Weiterbildung*. Bonn: Bundesministerium für Bildung und Wissenschaft.

Dohmen, G. 1997. *Das lebenslange Lernen*. Bonn: Bundesministerium für Bildung, Wissenschaft, Forschung und Technologie.

Europäische Kommission. 1995. *Lehren und Lernen. Auf dem Weg zur kognitiven Gesellschaft*. Luxemburg: Amt für amtliche Veröffentlichungen der Europäischen Gesellschaften.

Faure. E. et al. 1972. *Apprendre à être*. Paris: Unesco.

Hutmacher, W. and Gross, D. 1993. *Attemptes priorités et attitudes à l'égard de l'école*. Adliswil: GFS Forschungsinstitut.

Kuwan, H. et al. 1996. *Berichtsystem Weiterbildung VI: integrierter Gesamtbericht zur Weiterbildungssituation in Deutschland*. Bonn: BMBF.

Lévy, R. and Joye, D. et al. 1997. *Tous égaux? De la stratification aux représentation*. Zürich: Seismo.

Migros-Genossenschafts-Bund, Koordinationsstelle der Klubschulen, ed. 1988. *Entwicklungskonzept der Klubschulen*. Zürich: Migros-Genossenschafts-Bund.

OECD/CERI. 1973. *Recurent Education. A Strategy for Lifelong Learning*. Paris: OECD.

Rohrer, C. and Sgier, I. 1995. *Erwachsenenbildungspolitik in der Schweiz: Strukturen, Rechtsgrundlagen, Tendenzen*. Zürich: SVEB.

Schärer, M. 1995. Weiterbildungsforschung in der Schweiz: ein Kurzportrait. *Grundlagen der Weiterbildung (GdWZ)* 6: 218–219.

560

Schmidtchen, G. 1979. *Bildungspolitik aus der Sicht der Stimmbürger*. Bern and Frankfurt a.M.: Paul Haupt Verlag.

Schweizerischer Wissenschaftsrat. 1978. *Dritter Bericht über den Ausbau der schweizerischen Hochschulen*. Bern: EDMZ.

Schweizerischer Wissenschaftsrat. 1981. *Hochschulbildung – Arbeitsmarkt – Beschäftigung*. Bern: EDMZ.

UNESCO. 1997. *Adult Education: The Hamburg Declaration and Agenda for the Future*. Resolutions of the Fifth International Conference on Adult Education (CONFINTEA). Hamburg: UNESCO.

The authors

Karl Weber is in charge of the interdisciplinary Centre for Continuing Education of the University of Berne since its creation in 1990. The main activities in this position include the planning and management of continuous education programmes in cooperation with experts in the various fields concerned, research activities related to continuing education (questions of demand, evaluation), to higher education policy and to sociology of science, and various teaching duties in the fields mentioned above.

Contact address: Prof Dr Karl Weber, Koordinationsstelle für Weiterbildung, Universität Bern, Falkenplatz 16, CH-3012 Bern. E-mail: karl.weber@kwb.unibe.ch.

Jürgen Wittpoth has a chair of Adult Education at the Otto-von-Guericke-University, Magdeburg. His main fields of research are theoretical principles of adult education, functions of continuing education in structural change of society, media in the everyday life of adults and inside of educational processes.

Contact address: Prof Dr Jürgen Wittpoth, Institut für Erziehungswissenschaft, Otto-von-Guericke-Universität Magdeburg, Postfach 4120, D-39016 Magdeburg. E-mail: juergen.wittpoth@gse-w.uni-magdeburg.de.

CRITICAL APPROACHES TO LIFELONG EDUCATION

ROSEMARY PRESTON

Abstract – This paper argues that contemporary interest in lifelong learning can be seen as an artefact of the market. It points out how the attractive vocabulary associated with personal development and empowerment often masks other economic and social purposes. Bearing in mind the social function of education, the author compares the strategies for the promotion of lifelong learning designed for those in "included social categories" with the policies designed for those in marginal and excluded positions. It concludes by challenging its own position by citing positive learner experience in each case.

Zusammenfassung – Dieser Artikel legt dar, daß das heutzutage vorhandene Interesse an lebenslangem Lernen als Produkt des Marktes betrachtet werden kann. Es zeigt auf, wie das attraktive Vokabular, das mit persönlicher Entwicklung und Befähigung in Verbindung gebracht wird, häufig andere wirtschaftliche und soziale Zwecke überdeckt. Unter Betrachtung der sozialen Funktion der Bildung vergleicht die Autorin die Strategien zur Förderung lebenslangen Lernens für Personen in "akzeptierten sozialen Kategorien" mit den Planungen für ausgeschlossene, in gesellschaftlichen Randpositionen lebende Personen. Es endet mit einer Herausforderung seiner eigenen Position, indem es für beide Fälle positive Lernerfahrungen darstellt.

Résumé – Cet article soutient que l'intérêt actuel pour l'éducation tout au long de la vie peut être considéré comme un artefact du marché. Il démontre comment le vocabulaire attrayant appliqué au développement personnel et à l'autonomisation masque souvent d'autres motifs économiques et sociaux. Dans l'optique de la fonction sociale de l'éducation, l'auteure compare les stratégies qui favorisent l'éducation permanente chez les catégories sociales "incluses" aux politiques destinées aux personnes marginalisées et exclues. Elle termine par un questionnement de sa propre position en citant des expériences positives pour les apprenants de chaque catégorie.

Resumen – Este trabajo sostiene que el interés actual en un aprendizaje durante toda la vida puede ser visto como una creación del mercado. Subraya cómo el atractivo vocabulario asociado con desarrollo personal y la adquisición de poder muchas veces enmascara otros propósitos económicos y sociales. Teniendo en cuenta la función social de la educación, la autora compara las estrategias de promoción de un aprendizaje durante toda la vida diseñadas para aquellas «categorías sociales incluidas» con las políticas diseñada para aquellos que se encuentran en posiciones marginadas y excluidas. Finaliza desafiando su propia posición, al citar experiencias de aprendizaje positivas en cada uno de los casos.

Резюме - В этой работе утверждается, что в настоящее время имеющийся интерес к образованию, продолжающемуся всю жизнь, может быть оценен как феномен, искусственно созданный рынком. Статья указывает, что привлекательные слова, связанные с развитием

International Review of Education – Internationale Zeitschrift für Erziehungswissenschaft – Revue Internationale de l'Education **45**(5/6): 561–574, 1999.
© 1999 *Kluwer Academic Publishers. Printed in the Netherlands.*

личности и увеличением возможностей часто скрывают за собой иные экономические и социальные цели. Имея в виду социальную функцию образования, автор сравнивает стратегию пропаганды обучения, продолжающегося всю жизнь, нацеленную на "принятые социальные категории" с политикой, задуманной для людей в убогом и социально исключенном положении. Статья заканчивается опровержением своей собственной позиции, приводя пример позитивного опыта учащегося в каждом из случаев.

The story told in this paper is that of the Janus face of the positivist narratives of lifelong learning for personal fulfilment, democracy, economic and social well-being. As narrative itself, it talks about the different levels of interest that are represented below the surface of the rhetoric of lifelong learning, suggesting ways in which these serve to skew the levels and biases of investment and other resources in the late 20th century. At the present time this approach is not popular. There is little new in the general assumptions made, although their relevance to a variety of specific local and global contexts is quite contemporary. In conclusion, the paper attempts to critique itself, by allowing that there are those for whom the positivist narrative holds true. An alternative approach would have shown the limitations of the claims being made in terms which revealed the possibility of not benefiting from the learning age.

Lifelong learning and the market

Lifelong learning (LLL), it may be argued, is a mechanism of social control mediated by the market. As promoted in this context, the word "learning" does not refer to those reflective incidentally acquired understandings which enable us to navigate our daily lives. In most cases contemporary usage of the term lifelong learning refers to the process of allowing ourselves to be exposed to pre-packaged gobbits of knowledge, allowing ourselves to be assessed on the mastery of that knowledge, accepting the implications of the resulting indicators of our performance for access to the labour market and our resultant positioning within it. Lifelong in some contexts lives up to its promise: the presentation of a variety of opportunities from the cradle to the grave. In other contexts it more narrowly refers to work-related education and training.

Buying courses from birth to the grave is good for business. The more points at which businesses can intervene in planning, resourcing, delivery, assessment and accreditation rating around any packaged learning opportunity, the better for business. Inducing people to buy into the first stage of a succession of interlocking, interdependent commoditised learning opportunities, through a combination of feel-good and feel-guilty mechanisms, as well as career and status incentives, is a powerful tool of the business. At the same time these offerings often omit any reference to the commercial side of provision and systematically mask the appropriation of LLL narratives of seduction intended to attract custom and continuous repeated purchase of the offerings.

The language of learning needs places responsibility for decisions about which package to purchase with the consumer. In an atmosphere of quality assurance and rated credit, together with the rhetoric of participation, this is aimed at the alleviation of doubt about the relevance of the learner's choice. LLL is emerging as a global industry. Evidence of the successful completion of LLL courses is, in certain circumstances related to geographical location or positioning in the labour market, fast becoming a mandatory requirement for advancement in the job market. For those in the business of providing LLL this offers rare opportunities for profit with a mass market guaranteed for the foreseeable future.

What's new? In some cultures, very young children have been reared as a matter of course by people other than their parents. For a long time certificates of skill have been accepted as the passport for admission to different levels of the occupational hierarchy. The more certificates, the higher their currency value, the higher the entry point. For centuries there have been opportunities for work-related training, on and off the job, with and without assessment and certification. There have also been centuries of possibilities for adult education in the community, from basic to advanced levels, with and without assessment and certification. How have things changed with the language of lifelong learning?

Remembering the constants

The universal functions of education, in the broadest sense, relate to the integration and cohesion of societies, and of groups and individuals within them. Early childhood socialisation confers identity, values and preparation for family and community life. More and less organised education outside the home is a preparation for allocation to differentiated social and economic roles, additional to or removed from those in the domestic arena. This differentiation assumes stratification of roles in society. It means that high status roles are preferred to those of low status. The ensuing competition for education and certification means that demand exceeds supply and the provision of lifelong learning is restricted to people who meet sundry qualifying criteria: membership of particular status groups; certification of expertise and experience; the ability to pay for the privilege. Within these regulatory mechanisms, access to education is restricted, with supply tailored to the fluctuating demand for the skills and other qualities which it affords, so enabling only a few to use their education as a platform for mobility and innovation. As a negotiable commodity, education is a direct contributor to the economy, but it also has indirect effects on the structure of society through its impact on the differential quality of labour, productivity and social cohesion.

If the above are essential characteristics of modern education, they hold good whatever form it takes, whatever its mode of delivery. At issue then is how different are the goals being achieved under a form of education which emphasises the social goals of lifelong learning and not solely of education for economic growth.

Education for social well-being, for meeting basic human needs or education as a human right also needs to be taken into account in the process. What are the implications of this for equity and transformation?

The context

It seems sensible to assume that the promotion of a new approach to educational services, lifelong learning in this case, derives from a change in the political, social and/or economic context that makes this desirable. The litanies of the times make us seek an explanation in: technology changing more rapidly than ever and incurring demand for at least some people to have increasingly sophisticated and updatable skills; technologically induced structural unemployment on an unprecedented scale and all it entails (training for labour market re-entry and relocation; the informal and black economy; emiseration, exclusion and unrest). Since these processes developed gradually, over decades, there is a need to examine what more immediate change has occurred in the wider social environment and inspired the adoption of lifelong learning as the promotional banner of the late 20th century. The overarching explanation lies in the shift in the political inspiration of the management of these processes according to the principles of an aggressive neo-liberal market.

It is axiomatic that the workings of such a market will attempt to reduce costs in order to compete. In all states which have introduced neo-liberal economic programmes, the effects of this are tangible in the increased wealth of a decreasing minority, the declining conditions of employment for all but a minority of those in work, and a reduction of living standards for an increasingly large majority.

This has led to the poverty and destitution of a sizeable minority in First World contexts, and has had massive, sometimes catastrophic effects for the majority in Third World contexts (Scott 1994; UNRISD 1994; Watkins 1994). It makes no difference whether these strategies were self-imposed or a requirement of financial deals with the international financial institutions (IFIs). The new beggars on the streets in Western Europe are there for the same reasons as their predecessors a hundred years before and their peers in the less affluent nations. What is different today, compared with the post-World War II welfarist decades, are the varying levels of this emiseration between more and less affluent nations and what this implies for the maintenance of stability and the prevention of the collapse of social order within them.

The World Bank's introduction of a fourth category of nation in its state-of-the-world league tables, the world's poorest nations, is testimony to this process (World Bank 1990), as are UNDP's Human Development, Gender and Human Poverty indices (UNDP 1997). In rich and poor countries the neo-liberal policies are aimed at what are termed stability management strategies. These are said to meet basic needs and provide safety nets against death or disruption resulting from destitution. Amongst these strategies are those that espouse the intention of training the long-term unemployed for labour market re-entry, though it is widely held that the number of jobs is shrinking rapidly under the impact of technology and globalisation.

All this is a far cry from the 1960s language of equitable access to work for all, with education constructed as a key selection mechanism and health as a means of ensuring continuous performance. Referring to more and less affluent nations, a growing literature is heralding the collapse of the global market if strategy to raise the minimally accepted quality of life and to restore greater equity of opportunity are not reintroduced (Hutton 1995 and 1997; Ilon 1994, 1997). Recent fluctuations in the economies of newly affluent Asian states and the continuing collapse of impoverished nations do nothing to deny these ominous warnings.

Back to lifelong learning

For those promoting it, one of the strengths of lifelong learning to date is its ambiguity, the way in which it does not lend itself easily to definition. The attractive term can therefore be applied differently in different contexts, accepted as a universally good thing, without encouraging people to ask the usual critical questions of who exactly has access to it, in what form, under what conditions and who gains what from it. The unifying thread seems to be that the spectrum of provision accessible in any one place should include opportunities for learning at all life stages. I want us to assume that nearly all states make this range of provision, but that the quantity and quality of different modes will vary with their position in the different state-of-the-world league tables. Going back to the constant functions of education, we have also to assume that in all cases, there are accepted mechanisms for selectivity of access to what are variable opportunities of this provision in terms of quality, quantity and outcome. The question is how this is to be managed under the rubric of lifelong learning. Reducing enormously complex processes, we have already accepted the binary of inclusion and exclusion in education. It is there-fore important to examine its implications for lifelong learning at the present time.

Lifelong learning for the included

In today's market, new growth is sought through flexible accumulation, rapid response product customisation and the continuous appropriation of new commodity niches liberated by what is being described as the technologically led compression of space and time (Harvey 1990). It is this that has led to the market domination of commoditised knowledge in cultural sectors of the economy, surpassing the contribution to growth of manufactured products on which it remains dependent (Lash 1990; Stehr 1994). The up-beat language of flexible opportunity for the workforce masks its vulnerability in the face of these changes, camouflaging the recasualisation of labour, including significant proportions of the professional workforce. This has led to enormously increased demands on those still in employment and the growth of managerial cadres to regulate the new structures. Grounded in a rhetoric of decreasing bureaucracy and enhanced flexibility to maintain competitive advantage, it is those in work who carry the bureaucratic function in addition to the responsibility for engaging in learning activities requiring their technical expertise.

The interrelated educational and training implications of this are many. States, in the interest of stability, have to ensure the availability of a quantity of suitable labour at an appropriate price to attract investment, local and international, in the production of goods and services, regardless of where these will be sold. The state no longer assumes that the whole population must acquire such skills. The education/training offered is concentrated on the basic schooling of the young and ever more sophisticated learning strategies are developed for the ever smaller number of graduates who will be able to offer their labour to modern business or to fulfil government administrative and managerial functions. It matters not where these more sophisticated skills are obtained. Indeed the internationalisation of higher level skilling and continuing professional development through the working life, assumes a degree of universal applicability of expertise in both technical and process skills. States, subscribing to the belief that professional development enhances productivity in the work place, are committed to providing firms with incentives to invest in their human capital. For large corporations and parastatal organisations, this may be feasible. For smaller enterprises it is more problematic. How does it work?

Within organisations, core staff have to be skilled in more diverse, often team-based, activities, among them developing the capacities to ensure the quality of the labour they contract and to see that work is executed according to prescribed standards. The growth of the management training industry for public, parastatal and private sectors is a response to this development, with new opportunities in Training Needs Analysis (TNA) and staff development. Simultaneously, competency-based accreditation and career portfolios describing experiential learning and continuing professional development are emerging as key tools in recruitment and promotion. They combine with the trend to outsource recruitment and the management of labour to employment agencies and consultancy brokerage firms, a product of the flattening of core capacity within firms. As a result, eventual providers of a contracted service may not be in direct contact with clients, but only with their own brokering organisations. These organisations may be in direct relations with the client or at one or more removes, as a result of previous sub-contracting (Preston 1996, 1997).

With globalisation, the description of competency is now possible in terms of nationally and internationally interlinked systems for the accreditation of experiential and lifelong learning and continuing professional development (Preston 1996a). Not new, they have developed to such an extent that they are becoming mandatory in applications for employment and promotion from the least to the most skilled sectors of the labour force. In the UK, National Vocational Qualification (NVQ) level 1 specifies a narrow range of prerequisite competencies associated with specific low status work (car parking regulators for example), just as Credit Accumulation and Transfer (CAT) points gained confirm that lawyers and doctors have submitted themselves to the number of days per annum of continuing professional development, required at specific levels if they are to retain membership of their respective professional bodies (Wilson 1995). The ability to link these systems with each other, with the European Credit Transfer Scheme (ECTS) and so with other national systems, including the North American RAMP systems envisages an increasingly sophisticated global system for the classification of flexible and mobile labour at all skill levels (Dalichow 1995). The commercialisation of these systems, across trades and professions, represents an infinity of new opportunities in educational commoditisation, quite separate from either teaching or learning, while for employers and contractors of labour, they claim to offer kite marks of applicant credibility.

There are several dilemmas. The award of qualifications and credit on the basis of the level and length of the learning experience may say little about the quality of learning achieved, without attention being paid to additional personalised information about related process and substantive skill acquisition. Casualisation and the precisely specified accreditation of narrowly defined process or technical skills, where these are described, may combine to reduce the scope for further development, in anticipation of what might be unpredictable workplace requirements and the difficulty of anticipating the most appropriate form of flexible, variable and progressive career development. In these circumstances, workers, manual and professional alike, find themselves in circumstances where conditions of employment are being steadily eroded. They find themselves on a treadmill as they try to develop strategies to meet domestic financial commitments. Without time or money to invest in training or other personal development, deskilling ensues as they rehash old knowledge and skill to meet the minimal terms of reference of new work. In time there comes the mechanistic repetition of tasks, not on the endless manufacturing conveyor belt of the past, but in equally controlled working contexts, where they work for diverse employers at their places of

568

work, or on-line at home. As the cost of CPD, accreditation and portfolio preparation is borne increasingly by individuals, rather than by employers, those unable to purchase certificates of recognition, whatever the status of their occupational expertise, run the risk of initial or continuing exclusion from a work force in which the supply of labour is far in excess of demand.

As the complexity of integrating and scheduling the increasing number of small inputs grows, so the professions of fixed term, multi-task project and programme management are becoming important. In a lego-world, their task is to put together the interlocking blocks of any scheme. Those contracted to such schemes are responsible for the co-ordination of the parts and are liable for costs incurred should there be a failure in syncopation. However, although inspired by claims of organisational efficiency, the downsizing of client organisations may leave them without the capacity either to manage the logistics of these out-sourced processes or to evaluate expertise in the range of skills required, offered and purchased, or even to assess the quality of output. This can lead to a secondary contracting spiral of commoditised quality management and the hiring of consultant regulators, evaluators and appraisers, trained to ensure the successful operation of the "package".

Under the rhetoric of liberalisation and consumer choice, these processes represent a narrowing of loci of overall political and economic control. There is continuing homogeneity of purpose, and of capital accumulation, in what appears to be increasingly heterogeneous endeavour, as new commodifiable space is seized. There is nothing new in the systemic need for the exploitation and control of labour, and the ways in which this is achieved vary only in detail, with the locus of task to be performed and the nature of the goods or services to be produced. The maintenance of a multi-national, multi-skilled labour surplus is essential to an aggressive global market, whether output is manufactured or cultural. It is a prerequisite for the weakening of labour organisations, the reduction of pay and the by-passing of supplementary entitlements such as pensions and health care.

The systems of learning and competency accreditation, being adopted world-wide, are new mechanisms for this control of labour, particularly casualised labour, differentiating in fine detail, within formerly broad bands (skilled and unskilled, etc), those fit for work at increasingly specific tasks. In the process, there is an increased appropriation of the processes of teaching and learning, a reification of intellectual output which complies with standardised forms and a rejection of that which does not. Performance in educational and training systems continues to dictate labour market eligibility and occupational status. It now regulates survival in work as well. Failure to comply with self-funded professional development requirements, across trades and professions, becomes attributable to the individuals concerned. It is not seen as a product of the increasingly vulnerable social and economic positions in which they are placed. In this, the reconfigured knowledge exchanged at conferences becomes of secondary importance to the growing need for academicians to be seen to invest in diverse forms of personal development, among them the presentation and publication of conference papers, provided that this is through market-approved, quality-assured media.

The emphasis on technocratic, outcomes-oriented planning and evaluation, with the short-termism in which it is couched, legitimates the growing loss of institutional memory and the decontextualisation of seemingly fragmented experience. Hidden in the language of organisational learning, learning organisation and learning society, it masks the opportunity costs of stressful over- and under-employment and its impact on social reproduction, in the shorter and longer term. It hides the old politics of partiality on which the system is based with its historically derived gender, ethnic and status biases. It appropriates critique. After the fashion of the capitalist market, the function of education and training, in whatever form, continues to be cohesion and control over ever increasing amounts of time of individuals included in the system. As such it assures that the quality of human resources will meet its prescribed purposes, whatever the loss of autonomy. The alternative is exclusion. Until recently, the continuity of liberal arts educational opportunities (for those who could pay) without accreditation presented the softer face of lifelong learning for included groups, seemingly in tune with the humanistic spirit of the vocabulary, masking these trends in work-related provision. The mainstreaming of these initiatives, through commoditised quality control, assessment and accreditation mechanisms, is bringing an end to this. It is coming close to denying the status of learning to any activity that is not processed in this particular manner.

Lifelong learning for inclusion

An alternative track to lifelong learning is that which seeks to enable those on the margins to increase their toeholds within the included sectors of their societies. Across diverse sectors of the labour market, it caters to those in low status employment wanting to improve their positions, the would-be employed, the informal sector worker and subsistence producer. It combines, separately and together, basic skill training for those out of school, market-oriented initial and continuing skill development, some higher education and strategies for people to come to some understanding of the political dynamic of their predicament and methods of using this knowledge to change the quality of their life. With the exception of higher education, this provision of LLL is characterised by its irregular distribution, combined typically with low levels of short-term project-related funding. Such schemes may be funded and/or managed by international institutions, states, local governments and/or international and local voluntary sector organisations. In spite of evidence doubting the capacity of these initiatives to improve significantly the quality of the dwindling social capital of people in this category or their economic opportunities (Field 1998), the majority of developmental initiatives supported in this way involve education and training of some kind. All claim to be about alleviating poverty or holding it at bay. In more and less affluent nations, the granting of funds for such purposes usually depends on a stated commitment to the objectives of social inclusion. They also require some evidence that the skills being imparted will enhance learner competitiveness when selling their own labour and its products (Preston 1996). Here the language of participation is double-edged. Under one guise it refers to learner empowerment as a product of increased understanding and skill. Under another, it refers to the process of signing on for a course and enabling a fee to be paid to its providers, either by the student or from government or voluntary sector sources. Access refers as much to persuading identified client categories to overcome personal inhibitions and cultural barriers to registration, as it does to the provision of such opportunity within a manageable time/distance price ratio. In more affluent countries (I am thinking of the UK and elsewhere in Western Europe) the new category of the non-learner, the majority of the population who as yet do not enrol on such courses, is becoming a new way of defining and scapegoating members of marginal and excluded underclasses. Incentives (possibilities of work experience and certification) and sticks (the withdrawal of benefits) are being used to encourage course registration and new (privatised) bureaucracies are being created to further the process. In the UK they include the University for Industry and a learning bank.

In less affluent and turbulent societies the aid regime regulates the activities that can be developed by implementing bodies, state or NGO, within different types of programme and the modes of expertise to be enhanced. The aim of its constituent organisations to support each other's work means that it has an increasingly uniform agenda. In common is the expectation that when acquired skills come to be applied in the interests of generating income, there will be a market either for them in their own right or for what they produce. A prerequisite of most of these initiatives is the purchase of either means of production or its inputs or both (sewing machines, sheet metal, bread ovens, day-old chicks). In impoverished communities this has an implication for access to credit against the expectation that income will be sufficient to pay off loans. Failure to account for cultural expectations of reciprocity may mean that there is never any product to sell or service to provide, or that what is produced cannot compete with cheap manufactures imported at below cost prices. In this circumstance, failure to pay off loans, however modest, may result in the project exacerbating destitution rather than reducing it.

At the interface of lifelong learning for included and marginal categories are the project implementers, facilitators and trainers who work on such schemes. Committed to helping the poor and usually only marginally less poor and poorly educated themselves, they may give their services for free. Often they are minimally trained to the point that this itself is a deterrent for sustained participation on the part of recruits to the activity in question. When they are trained, increasingly, because states are concerned with assuring the quality of public services, this is becoming subject to the same processes of quality regulation, assessment and accreditation as more mainstream professional development services. From here, with the more affluent states spearheading the move, it is but a short step to the prescriptive regulation of the whole activity. How close we are to this is already manifest with some regional offices of multilateral organisations regulating the timing to the day and minute of interim monitoring and evaluation of country programmes through the control of their computers. Under these circumstances, there is minimal scope for sustained autonomous action to transform marginality into greater social inclusion and more secure economic participation, while sponsored activity may work, with rare exceptions, to prevent it.

Lifelong learning and exclusion

For those positioned beyond the margins, within insecure residence entitlements, no access to paid work, and living on hand-outs from whatever source, lifelong learning has different implications. For some, learning provision and consumption becomes a surrogate for work, a means of furthering understanding without prospect of its application in mainstream communities (Preston 1991). The extent to which its currency influences the structuring and positioning of the excluded group is another matter. Typically, refugee communities will intitiate schooling for their children as soon as they have a roof over their heads, no matter how precarious their physical or economic circumstances. Where basic education is otherwise available, they will hold classes to prevent the loss of language and culture of countries of origin. Thereafter they will fight for assisting organisations to provide materials and texts and for the means of recognition of the qualifications they award. Suffering a shortage of teachers, they will lobby for training of teaching personnel, however rudimentary, and also for the means of teaching adults the basic skills. In the process, those involved establish themselves as significant actors within the community hierarchy, and they become a significant factor in the relations between the community and those on the outside who are sympathetic to the causes being promoted. Their goal is unlikely to be integration in the host society. It may be integration, including employment, after return to places of origin, depending on the relevance of the prevailing political situation to their plight. Otherwise, education in these circumstances is a means of maintaining self-respect and creating a daily purpose in life.

With the economically excluded in poorer states, there is neither the option of subsistence production nor the production of petty commodities within domestic or community arenas. Without supporting networks to provide such options the life is one of dispossession. The extent to which there is support from within the excluded community, depends on its resources. Certainly, in more and less affluent states, the renaissance or development of systems of non-monetary exchange may take place organically as mechanisms for self-sufficiency have been learned. The extent to which, self-taught, the excluded survive without interference from institutions of state varies with what is seen to be the implications of what they are doing for the dominant economy or for the destabilisation of the wider social order.

Equity and transformation for whom?

The above picture is very negative, based on a portrayal of the ways in which vested interests structure the form and incidence of lifelong learning in different environments. But people are rational beings. They would not buy into this process without perceiving that it offered them intrinsic as well as instrumental returns for their investment in doing so. In Sao Paolo (Brazil), Nelly Stromquist (1997) describes the positive reports of the impact of minimal exposure to the MOVA literacy programme by slum women, interestingly structured by the extent of their childhood exposure to school. Over the same period, Cathy Preston and Ravi Thiara (1997) find that Asian women in Coventry (UK) cautiously exult in their new perceptions of themselves and their capacities after a participatory learning experience for women returners. In neither case do more than a tiny minority seek to change their social position by committing themselves to further study. For all some transformation had occurred, some hope of greater equity in the domestic and social worlds. Transformation can also occur when part-time students following higher degrees consider in wonderment their own personal journeys and seek to explain the extent of their self-motivation or social pressure in their decision to enrol on arduous and protracted courses entailing heavy demands on time, which is their scarcest resource. For some the process becomes self defeating. As for many of those exposed to all kinds of less elevated programmes, it confirms their sense of limited capacity as far as education and training is concerned. For others it is a means of knowing and better understanding the world. For a few it leads to further related action to increase these awakened capacities.

References

Dalichow, F. 1995. Foreseeing global systems: checking the potential of the European Community Course Credit Transfer System (ECTS). Paper presented to the INCED Conference *Restricting freedom? International credit transfer and skill recognition in the late twentieth century, 3–6* July, 1995, Manchester College, Oxford.

Field, J. 1998. *Combating Exclusion Through Adult Learning*. Paris: OECD.

Harvey, D. H. 1991. *The Condition of Post Modernity*. Oxford: Basil Blackwell.

Hutton, Will. 1995. *The State We're In*. London: Jonathan Cape.

Hutton, Will. 1997. *The State to Come*. London: Vintage.

Ilon, Lynn. 1994. Structural Adjustment and Education: Adapting to a Growing Global Market. *International Journal of Education in Development* 14(2): 95–108.

Ilon, Lynn. September 1997. Stabilising market conditions through education. Paper presented to the fourth Oxford International conference on education and development, *Education and Geo-political change.*

Lash, S. 1990. *The Sociology of Post-modernism.* London: Routledge.

Preston, C and Tiara, R. 1997. Self-defence: forgotten women learning in urban Britain. Paper presented to *Transitions in Gender and Education*, the first International Gender and Education Conference, University of Warwick, March 1997.

Preston, Rosemary. 1991. The provision of education to refugees in places of temporary assylum: some implications for development. *Comparative Education* 27(1): 61–81.

Preston, Rosemary. 1996. Consultancy Research and Human Development. In: L. Buchert and K. King, eds., *Consultancy and Research in International Education: The New Dynamics* (39–152). Bonn: NORRAG/DSE.

Preston, Rosemary. 1996a. Restricting freedom? International credit transfer and skill recognition in the late twentieth century, 3–6 July, 1995, Manchester College, Oxford. *Conference report*, University of Warwick, INCED, p. 10.

Preston, Rosemary. 1997. Knowledge Societies and Planetary Cultures: International Consultancy in Human Development. *International Journal of Educational Development* 17(1).

Scott, J. 1994. *Poverty and Wealth: Citizenship, Deprivation and Privilege.* London: Longman.

Stehr, N. 1994. *Knowledge Societies.* London: Routledge.

Stromquist, Nelly. 1997. *Literacy for Citizenship: Gender, Grassroots and Dynamics in Brazil.* New York: State University of New York Press.

UNDP. 1997. *Human Development Report.* Oxford: Oxford University Press.

UNRISD. 1995. *States of Disarray: The Social Effects of Globalisation.* Geneva: UNRISD.

Watkins, K. 1995. *The Oxfam Poverty Report.* Oxford: Oxfam.

Wilson, P. 1995. Lasers in the jungle somewhere: credits, qualifications and the skills market place. Paper presented to the INCED Conference *Restricting freedom? International credit transfer and skill recognition in the late twentieth century, 3–6 July, 1995, Manchester College, Oxford.*

World Bank. 1990. *World Development Report.* Washington DC: World Bank.

The author

Rosemary Preston is Director of the International Centre for Education in Development, University of Warwick, UK. She has worked in education and international development focussing on human resources and labour and war-related migration in Latin America, the South Pacific and Southern Africa. Recent writing addresses the influences of globalisation and the restructuring of the international labour market and its implications for professional development and learning. She is co-editor of *Gender and Education* and *Compare* and recent past Chair of the British Association of International and Comparative Education.

Contact address: Dr Rosemary Preston, International Centre for Education in Development, Department of Continuing Education, University of Warwick, Coventry CV4 7AL, UK. E-mail: R.A.Preston@Warwick.ac.uk.

LIFELONG LEARNING WITHIN HIGHER EDUCATION IN SOUTH AFRICA: EMANCIPATORY POTENTIAL?

SHIRLEY WALTERS

Abstract – In South Africa under apartheid higher education was inaccessible to the majority. This article argues that in the new South Africa there is an opportunity to redress this situation and promote equity though lifelong learning. This would involve greatly widening access and providing programmes to develop broadly applicable abilities such as computer literacy and problem-solving skills, which would increase the economic competitiveness and personal empowerment of learners. At the same time, the author argues, new educational approaches are needed to promote active citizenship.

Zusammenfassung – In Südafrika war die höhere Bildung während der Apartheid für die Mehrheit nicht zugänglich. Dieser Artikel argumentiert, daß im neuen Südafrika die Möglichkeit besteht, diesen Zustand zu ändern und die Gleichheit durch lebenslanges Lernen zu fördern. Dies würde bedeuten, den Zugang erheblich auszuweiten und Programme bereitzustellen, um auf vielen Gebieten anwendbare Fähigkeiten zu entwickeln, wie beispielsweise der Umgang mit Computern und Problembewältigung, was die wirtschaftliche Wettbewerbsfähigkeit und die persönliche Autonomisierung der Lernenden erhöhen würde. Laut dem Autor sind gleichzeitige neue Verfahrensweisen in der Bildung erforderlich, um die aktive Staatsbürgerschaft zu fördern.

Résumé – Sous le régime sud-africain de l'apartheid, l'enseignement supérieur était inaccessible à la majorité des élèves. Cet article affirme que la nouvelle Afrique du Sud renferme la possibilité de redresser cette situation et de favoriser l'équité au moyen de l'éducation permanente. Cette démarche exigerait un accès sensiblement élargi et des programmes qui développent les compétences applicables dans de nombreux domaines, comme l'initiation à l'informatique ou la gestion des conflits, ce qui favoriserait la compétitivité économique et l'autonomisation individuelle des apprenants. L'auteur constate par ailleurs que de nouvelles approches éducatives sont nécessaires pour promouvoir une citoyenneté active.

Resumen – En Sudáfrica, bajo el apartheid la enseñanza superior era inaccesible para la mayoría de sus habitantes. Este artículo sostiene que en la nueva Sudáfrica existe una oportunidad de remediar esta situación y de promover la justicia social con el aprendizaje durante toda la vida. Esto implicaría una gran ampliación del acceso y de la oferta de programas destinados a desarrollar habilidades de aplicación general, tales como el uso de ordenadores y la aptitud general de resolver problemas, que incrementarían la competitividad económica y la adquisición de poder de los participantes. Al mismo tiempo, argumenta el autor, se necesitan nuevo enfoques educacionales para promover una ciudadanía activa.

Резюме - В ЮАР при системе апартеида высшее образование было для большинства недоступным. В статье утверждается, что в новой Южной Африке имеется возможность изменить эту ситуацию и

International Review of Education – Internationale Zeitschrift für Erziehungswissenschaft – Revue Internationale de l'Education **45**(5/6): 575–587, 1999.
© 1999 *Kluwer Academic Publishers. Printed in the Netherlands.*

стремиться к равенству путем обучения в течение всей жизни. В
рамки этого входило бы значительное увеличение доступности, а
также предоставление программ для развития навыков с широкой
сферой применения - таких, как компьютерная грамотность и навыки
по решению проблем. Это улучшило бы экономическую
конкурентоспособность обучающихся и их личные возможности. В то
же время автор утверждает, что необходим новый просветительский
подход для развития активного гражданского участия в жизни
страны.

There are growing numbers of calls being made on higher education institutions to reform themselves and to take lifelong learning seriously. For example,
the draft *Declaration and Framework for Action* of the World Conference
on Higher Education (UNESCO, Paris, October 1998) have several references
to the importance of lifelong learning for higher education. The documents
urge States "to develop higher education institutions to include lifelong
learning approaches, giving learners optimal range of choice and a flexibility of entry and exit points within the system, and redefine the roles accordingly. . . ."

In South Africa, as in many other parts of the world, lifelong learning
has become part of the policy framework for education across the board. As
far as higher education is concerned, the National Commission on Higher
Education (1996) both implicitly and explicitly urges institutions to take
lifelong learning seriously. It states:

> A further challenge is to move the higher education system in the direction of
> becoming an open learning system which is organised for use by learners at dif-
> ferent times, in different ways and for different purposes at various stages of their
> lives and careers – a system that promotes lifelong learning, not merely at the
> margins for small groups of "mature" students, but in its basic shape and struc-
> ture. (1996: 119)

In this paper I discuss critically what lifelong learning may mean for a university within a context of an increasing drive to the marketisation of higher
education. I argue that lifelong learning needs to be qualified in relation to
its social and universal purposes if it is to avoid being primarily an instrument of "the market" and if it is to contribute to emancipatory social goals
at local, regional and global levels.

Background

Higher education in South Africa is undergoing radical restructuring and
this has major implications for every aspect of university life. The universi-

ties in the country are in different stages of institutional renewal in order to align themselves with the new policies and other national and international imperatives. Some of these include the rethinking of knowledge organisation from disciplines to programmes, increasing participation of students a wider spectrum of social groups and classes, and the necessity of being more responsive to societal needs. As in many parts of the world, massification and diversification are required without the expectation that resources will increase substantially, therefore innovative approaches to learning and teaching are required.

In South Africa there are 21 universities with gross inequalities between historically black (HBUs) and historically white universities (HWUs) for a population of 40 million people. In 1959 the Extension of Universities Act was introduced which created universities for particular ethnic groups. The majority of black universities are located in the rural areas and the former privileged, dominantly white institutions in urban areas. Vast discrepancies have existed in financing, material resources, staffing, undergraduate teaching loads, quality of students, availability of courses, and so on, between HBUs and HWUs. At their conception the HBUs were planned to provide a supply of civil servants for the apartheid bureaucracies, and this led to their having heavy concentrations on courses in public administration, education, religion, the humanities and little provision of the teaching of the natural sciences, engineering and related disciplines. Also post-graduate programmes, research and publication remain poorly developed in most of these institutions. University education as a whole has been largely geared to school leavers.

Compounding South Africa's legacy of exclusion and inequality, the national and international trend of diminishing resources and increased demands, gives an added critical dimension to the present situation. South African institutions are tenuously balancing the question of access, equity and quality within an increasingly competitive economic environment. Holding the tension between attainment of social equality, academic quality and economic development is one of the major challenges facing higher education. This tension is present in the National Commission on Higher Education Report and in the new legislation on Higher Education.

Lifelong learning: a concept with diverse meanings

Driven by the imperatives of late capitalism, lifelong learning has become a key concept in the thinking about education and training worldwide. Candy (no date) points to the extraordinarily rapid pace of social, technological, cultural, economic, legal and educational changes throughout the world, combined with the increasing global connectedness of many societies and economies, which emphasise the need for people who are adaptable and responsive to these new circumstances. In short, he calls for a system which is capable of delivering lifelong learning. The even more dramatic changes in the South African society render it particularly important for the South African educational system, including the higher education system, to produce lifelong learners and to provide for continuing learning throughout life. The imperatives for lifelong learning in South African are driven by its reinsertion into the global economy and by the political and social necessities of equity and redress after the years of colonialism and apartheid.

By its nature, lifelong learning is cross-sectoral; it is not limited to formal education but includes adult community education and workplace-based learning, along with access to other learning opportunities including libraries and electronically transmitted and stored data. In fact, lifelong learning includes all sorts and levels of learning irrespective of its content, form or location. As Candy states, the embracing and endorsing of principles of lifelong learning has implications for all aspects and facets of education and training.

Reading education policy documents in various parts of the world, including South Africa, lifelong learning often seems a panacea: it will help career development, cure unemployment, encourage flexibility and change, raise personal and national competitiveness, help personal development etc. It has become "policy speak" which assumes multiple meanings and interpretations. As Soobrayan (1997) argues, at one extreme, it is employed as a conceptual framework which presents a comprehensive and particular understanding of educational priorities, the strategies required to address these and a fundamental assertion of a radically different and distinct pedagogy. At another level, its more simple expression places emphasis on the temporal plane, making education available throughout the life cycle. In this form, the major questions posed relate to access and provision rooted in a discourse of equity. In this latter dimension there is no explicit focus on pedagogy; the main emphasis is on expanding present education provision.

It is not possible here to present a history of the concept and to elaborate the competing ideological tenets and understandings of the term, but it is essential that we recognise that lifelong learning can mean different things to different people. Very briefly, the argumentation for lifelong learning has varied in the course of history. It has addressed the needs of production (worker), society (citizen) and culture (human being) to different degrees at different times. In adopting the term we need to clarify its meaning based on our analysis of the political, social, cultural and economic needs of the country and how we see the university serving those needs.

Put very simply, there are two different and important theoretical and ideological strands in lifelong learning. They are the human capital school with its legacy for neo-liberal ideology, and the humanistic school which is concerned with a social democratic, holistic approach to education and training. The human capital school talks of education in terms of the market and investment in human capital and reduces education to the needs of the economy. Lifelong learning historically has been more closely associated with the humanistic strand which considers education from the perspective of the individual and the democratic citizen. Within the debates about lifelong learning both strands exist, but the drive to the marketization of education and training within a human capital perspective holds sway both globally and, increasingly, in South Africa.

In South Africa there has been a rigorous debate about the apparently opposite goals of economic growth and the need to achieve social justice in terms of notions of equity and redress. There has been a convincing argument that we must recognise the competing claims of both equality and economic growth, which inevitably are in tension. In the South African context equality cannot be achieved without economic development and economic development amongst the majority of people cannot be achieved without striving to achieve equality. Therefore, for the majority to benefit, an approach to economic and social development must recognise the interrelatedness of society and the economy where human values not human capital predominate.

Lifelong learning and its consequences for Higher Education

It is customary to divide the work of higher education into three domains: teaching, research and community service. In each of these three areas, the purpose is to promote or facilitate learning. Candy (no date) argues that since learning is never finished, it follows that the mandate of the university must be to foster and support lifelong learning in each of the domains. If this argument is accepted, it has significant implications for many aspects of higher education. Broadly speaking, there are two implications to the above recommendations:

- those to do with providing learning opportunities throughout life, including articulation with learning contexts beyond the institution, and
- those to do with assisting staff, students and graduates to develop the skills and attributes of lifelong learners.

The *provision of learning opportunities throughout life* challenges the traditional culture of the university which has privileged the provision of education to students of between 18 and 24 years and the notion of contact-based teaching. Provision to older students has most commonly been in the form of post-graduate studies to a relatively small group. Particularly amongst the historically black universities (HBUs) in South Africa there has been a large part-time provision to older students who attended classes in the evenings. While this has occurred, at times on large scale, the part-time provision has not challenged the dominant culture of services to students at universities which assume that all students are young. Also, the dominant picture of teaching has privileged a notion of contact-based provision as opposed to notions of open learning which emphasise flexible, student centred approaches to delivery.

Candy talks about "downwards linkages," "sideways linkages" and "forward linkages" when discussing the provision of lifelong learning opportunities. The "downward linkages" refer to the university's relationship to the school sector, with adult education and with various bridging courses. The "sideways linkages" refer to the relationship that higher education institutions enjoy with contexts where part of the learning occurs in the home, the workplace or the community. And the "forward linkages" refers to the relationships with graduates through postgraduate studies or, more commonly, through continuing professional education programmes, public lecture series and various forms of outreach.

Accepting such a model as a guiding principle would have significant implications for higher education. For instance, in terms of "downward linkages", it would imply multiple entry pathways from school and from adult education programmes and recognition of prior learning. With respect of "sideways linkages" it would mean that those in geographically remote areas would have access to higher learning through flexible delivery. It would also imply that learners could obtain academic credit not only for studies completed elsewhere, but for a variety of learning undertaken at work, in home and through self-directed efforts. Finally, under "forward linkages" such an approach would mean not only greater ease of access to postgraduate and continuing professional education, but that institutions of higher education would increasingly be viewed as forms of "community learning centres", whose lecture theatres, laboratories and libraries might be used more intensively than they are at present. Overall such radically enhanced access to and use of higher education would have significant flow-on-effects to all parts of the culture and life of higher education institutions. This would need to occur without losing the distinctiveness of higher education.

On the theme of developing learners through higher education, Candy (no date: 6) elaborates usefully by drawing on an influential study in Australia which was "to identify whether and in what ways the content, structure, teaching modes and assessment procedures of undergraduate degrees, and the activities of student support services, are designed to lead to the formation of attributes which both enable and encourage graduates to become lifelong learners". The study accepted that lifelong education can be based on both instrumental values such as the need to maintain professional currency and to have an internationally competitive workforce, and on more liberal and humane considerations such as the enrichment of society and people's fulfilment as individual citizens. The study found that undergraduate courses which enhance lifelong learning have five basic characteristics:

1) they provide a systematic introduction to the field of study;
2) they offer a comparative or contextual framework for viewing the field of study;
3) they seek to broaden the student and provide generic skills;
4) they offer some freedom of choice and flexibility of structure; and
5) they provide for the incremental development of self-directed learning.

They also pointed to teaching methods that encourage graduates to become lifelong learners. They have the following characteristics:

1) they make use of peer-assisted and self-directed learning;
2) the include experiential and real-world learning;
3) they make use of resource-based and problem-based learning;
4) they encourage the development of reflective practice and critical self-awareness; and
5) as appropriate, they make use of open learning and alternative delivery mechanisms.

Lifelong learning as an organising principle, which strives to produce lifelong learners and to provide for continuing learning throughout life, can thus be seen to have many implications for the system as a whole, for individual institutions, for courses or programmes of study, and ultimately for individual members of both academic and support staff.

Candy's elaboration of lifelong learning in higher education is very useful, but it focuses primarily on the teaching and learning processes which highlight the needs of individual learners. While this is important, the approach will not necessarily challenge a market-driven human capital view of higher education. His approach does not highlight sufficiently the social and universal purposes of lifelong learning. As Tedesco (1997: 183) argues, "Uncertainty has become the most widespread manner of describing the future, and the social or political assurances of a "better future" have paled considerably". In response to what some refer to as a "profound crisis in the meaning of existence of each human being and of each society on the Planet" (Arruda 1996), growing numbers of people are arguing for a reassertion of the importance of social and universal purposes which encourage active citizenship at national and global levels.

Education for active citizenship

"The Mumbai Statement on Lifelong Learning, Active Citizenship and the Reform of Higher Education" (1998: 2) captures succinctly some of the critical concerns. It states:

> We see the purpose of lifelong learning as democratic citizenship, recognizing that democratic citizenship depends on such factors as effective economic development, attention to the demands of the least powerful in our societies, and on the impact of industrial processes on the caring capacity of our common home, the planet. The notion of citizenship is important in terms of connecting individuals and groups to the structures of social, political and economic activity in both local and global contexts. Democratic citizenship highlights the importance of women and men as agents of history in all aspects of their lives.

The notion of citizenship is a concept which is undergoing radical redefinition under pressure from globalizing economies on the one hand and social movements of ecologists and feminists on the other. Korsgaard (1997) presents a useful synopsis of some of the major contemporary issues relating to the notion of "citizenship". He states that the emergence of the modern understanding of citizenship in the West was associated with the advent of capitalism and of centralised nation states in the sixteenth to seventeenth centuries. Citizenship was finally given voice as a massively influential political concept in the seventeenth and eighteenth centuries by the historical events of the English, American and French Revolutions. The "natural rights" and "Rights of Man" announced by these revolutions, their concepts of "liberty, equality, fraternity" and their attempts to found the modern nation state constitutionally on the will of the people, helped construct the modern Western conception of citizenship. However, globalization of the economy and the creation of economic blocs are beginning to challenge national sovereignty and citizenship. The emergence of a strong European Union is one good example of this where citizenship of the EU and one of the member countries may be in tension at different times.

In addition, feminism in modern society challenges the masculine structures of the state, the market and civil society; feminists challenge men in modern society to recognise the existence of a patriarchal order and of the manifold ways in which they both dominate women's lives and benefit from doing so. In effect, feminism challenges men to accept a duty to act against the patriarchal order in which women are second class citizens and to act for a society of equal citizenship.

Also the ecological movements are concerned with rights – the rights of non-humans (animals, the environment, nature etc). Of course nature's rights imply duties for humans. Ecologists also champion nature and the environment on behalf of posterity. Thus generations of humans as yet unborn are assumed to have the rights to an environment at least as resource-rich and as un-degraded and undamaged as the one the present generation inherited. The "rights of future generations" are thus deemed to impose duties of environmental "stewardship" on all individuals, communities, organisations, and nations. Thus, ecology challenges the dominant paradigm of citizenship in two ways: it expands its sphere beyond the national state to the global level and vice versa; also it expands it beyond the present generation and requires us to consider the inter-generational dimension of our sociality and our moral and citizenship duties.

In South Africa, the notion of citizenship is also hotly contested. It is only recently that South African citizenship has been deracialised while economic status is still highly racialised with nearly 95% of the poor being black, 5% coloured and less than 1% Indian or white. South Africa is forging a new national identity after the previous government sought to systematically fragment the population by declaring that there were "many nations in one". Simultaneously, South Africa's political and economic position in the southern

African region is being emphasised as the imperative to forge a strong economic bloc in the region is stressed. There are some calls for a wider identification of citizens with the region. On a local level though, there is growing xenophobia as unemployment, poor housing, and crime are being blamed, for example, on Mozambicans, Malawians and Zambians. Thus, South Africa is both building a nation at a time when the nation state is being de-emphasised in many parts of the world and simultaneously building a consciousness of being a citizen of the region and the continent at a time when economic hardships and the legacies of apartheid tend to promote xenophobia amongst the citizens.

In addition, there are what Mamdani (1998) refers to as two types of political identities in Africa i.e. "civic" and "ethnic" identities which were recognised by the colonial states. Civic identity was the identity of the citizen. It was racially defined and the rights of the "civilized", who were the settlers, were written into civil law and enforced through the central state. The rights of the natives were defined by ancestral codes. Natives were obliged to follow the customs of their ethnic group and were enforced as "customary" law by a native authority. The local state spoke the language of culture, not rights. Mamdani describes how "settler" and "native" citizenship in post-apartheid South Africa is unequal – civic citizenship is deracialised but ethnic citizenship remains unreformed. He poses the challenge of moving beyond "ethnic" and "civic" citizenship to a common citizenship which "transcends the political divide between settlers and natives, between ethnic and civic citizenship, and (which) forge(s) a single citizenship for all".

Clearly the notion of citizenship is a "site of struggle" where global and local interests try to influence its meaning within specific contexts.Therefore, education for citizenship will also be an area of contestation. According to Paolo Freire:

> Citizenship is the exercise of being oneself in the context of the state. It is a social construction; it doesn't appear by chance. Either the masses impose themselves through struggle or citizenship doesn't exist. The dominated classes need to democratize citizenship. A literacy program must include political aims to build citizenship; the capacity to understand the world, to establish relations between fact and problems demands the politicization of persons, the political comprehension of the world, permanent curiosity, the right to participate, mobilize, and organize grassroots groups. It demands going beyond common sense to change reality, to overcome domination, and to invent solidarity. (quoted in Stromquist 1997: 217)

While Freire is referring to the importance of adult learners in literacy classes building democratic citizenship, there seems to be no reason why the argument should not hold for learners within higher education. One of the biggest dangers currently is that the discourses of the market and business become increasingly hegemonic. In the South African context while there is formal democracy there most certainly is not equality. There is still a long trek, under conditions that by no means guarantee a happy outcome, to achieve a truly democratic, nonracist, nonsexist society.

Universities in South Africa have an important role to play in ensuring that people, particularly the poor, black people and women are supported in their attainment of active citizenship. But how can this be done?

Lifelong learning for active citizenship is in part a debate about curriculum. As Muller states, "nothing is more urgent than a clear and dispassionate view of who or what the South African citizen is, or could be. . . . This in turn focuses the question: what kind of curriculum do we therefore need in order best to foster this citizen-to-be?"

Education for citizenship has a long history. As Comeliau (1997: 33) says, "Torrents of ink have flowed on the new imperatives for education in the context of globalization: we need to know how to manage and calculate, we must develop advanced technological knowledge, we must acquire 'flexibility', learn foreign languages and be receptive to 'intercultural' dialogue, and so forth". But he states that is not enough. He, like many others, argues that alternatives must be found to the crucial conditions for survival, equilibrium and full development of human societies. While it is essential to train good engineers, financiers, technicians and specialists in many fields, it is important that a dominant view of economic globalization "that there is no alternative" must be changed to "there must be an alternative" (DAWN 1998).

This search for alternatives is not seen as a disembodied intellectual exercise, but one which is the collective work of social groups which is both an intellectual and a political task. As Comeliau argues, "the requirements of this new education (are) a collective awareness of the real issues involved in long-term development (which are very different from those of growth) and progressive training for the many tasks needed to respond to them" (1997: 34).

Higher education institutions, along with other institutions in the society, are intimately involved in the transformation of the society and have to make hard political and economic choices. They too are characterised by the same struggles as exist in the broader society as social forces vie for preeminence. As educators within higher education we do not work in isolated national contexts. An illustration of this is given by Buchbinder et al. (1996) who describe very usefully how the North American Free Trade Agreement (NAFTA) has serious implications for higher education and the trans-national delivery of programmes. In their article they begin to explore the intersection of knowledge, capital and technology in this context. While it is set in Canada it has relevance for other regions. The point they make is that higher education no longer can be considered a national concern as universities particularly in the developed north actively pursue markets around the world. In this process curricula are being dislodged from the local base and the prospects of ahistorical, decontextualised curricula grow ever stronger. This is potentially a serious problem.

As Muller (1997: 195) argues, "The importance of not losing sight of the local can never be minimised". He continues:

Citizenship in a plural and diverse world consists in mastering the various skills of autonomy, but retaining, or constructing, some or other local home to actually live in, in a meaningful and fulfilling way. Autonomy without a home lacks relevance, one might say, but this time a personal relevance not easily reducible to group or national relevance. It is at the juncture of cosmopolitan and local, of autonomy and relevance, that a new sense of citizenship for a runaway world will be constructed.

Developments within higher education reflect the impact of globalization on the curricula, the teaching and learning processes and the employment practices (e.g. the increasing casualisation of employment). Lifelong learning for active citizenship requires higher educators to work collaboratively across regions in order to take on the pedagogical and political challenges of creating alternatives which can build on the positive aspects of globalization. As Buchbinder et al. (1996) urge, "we need to be working to ensure that we are not moving uncritically to the tune of the contemporary pied piper: the tune of global capital". Educators and learners within higher education would need to engage along with other activists with issues like those described by Arruda (1996: 30):

> We are seeking to connect critically the micro with the macro and, in the search for a vision of the world which will be both utopic and viable, point to an horizon of a cooperative globalization, built by individuals and societies that have become active and conscious subjects, personally and collectively, of their own development.

The consideration of the emancipatory possibilities of lifelong learning in higher education therefore is a political question as much as a pedagogical one.

Lifelong learning in higher education: emancipatory potential?

I have argued that we need to understand and clarify the meaning we give to lifelong learning based on our analysis of political, social, cultural and economic needs of the society and how we see the higher education institutions responding to those needs. I have suggested that lifelong learning presents a comprehensive and particular understanding of educational priorities which responds to South Africa's history of exclusion and inequality. If we adopt Candy's definition of lifelong learning which insists on "developing lifelong learners" and "creating lifelong learning opportunities" essential issues of redress and equity can be addressed. On the one hand, access can be radically enhanced, and on the other, generic capabilities are developed which can support individuals ability to continue to learn throughout life.

In the South African context where higher education has been so inaccessible to the majority and there has been so little emphasis in general on generic capabilities such as language, computer and information literacy, critical problem solving, and so on, the attainment of accessible, quality learner-centred, flexible approaches to teaching and learning which take seriously the South African Qualifications Authority's critical cross field outcomes, would be a major achievement. It would certainly contribute to the individual development of black women and men learners and their own competitiveness in the job market thus enhancing their economic and personal empowerment. While this is critically important, I have argued that this is not enough.

In addition, major curricula interventions are required to assert lifelong learning for active citizenship. As quoted above in the Mumbai Statement, the notion of citizenship is important in terms of connecting individuals and groups to the structures of social, political and economic activity in both local and global contexts and to emphasising the importance of women and men as agents of history in all aspects of their lives.

In South Africa the original Reconstruction and Development Programme (1994) provides a useful frame of reference for constructing curricula which strive to enhance possibilities for equal citizenship amongst the rich and poor, black and white, men and women. The struggle over economic, political and social priorities that are raging in South Africa, and elsewhere, around "there is no alternative" and "there must be an alternative", becomes a crucial curriculum issue for learners and educators in the higher education system. Lifelong learning for active citizenship is therefore both about pedagogy and politics which requires local and global cooperative actions of solidarity to build alternatives which emphasise human values rather than human capital. It seems that the emancipatory potential of lifelong learning will only be fully realised through collective struggles across national and regional boundaries, where some of the benefits of globalization, like the new communications technologies, can be used to forge new visions of a world which are both "utopic and viable".

The world's poor are increasingly being left to their own devices. Lifelong learning which is to have emancipatory potential has to challenge this reality in every way that it can.

References

African National Congress. 1994. *The Reconstruction and Development Programme: A Policy Framework.* Johannesburg: ANC.

Arruda, M. 1996. Globalization and Civil Society: Rethinking Cooperativism in the Context of Active Citizenship. A Paper of the Institute of Alternative Policies for the Southern Cone of Latin America, Brazil, December, 1996.

Badat, S., Zenariah, B. and Wolpe, H. 1995. The Post-secondary Education System: Towards Policy Formulation for Equality and Development. In: *Higher Education Financing Conference, Background Reading and Conference Papers.* Johannesburg, January 1995.

Buchbinder, H. and Pinayur, Rajagopal. 1996. Canadian Universities: The Impact of Free Trade and Globalization. *Higher Education* 31: 283–299.

Candy, P. C. 1996. Lifelong Learning and the University Sector, a discussion paper for the National Commission on Higher Education.

Comeliau, Christian. 1997. The Challenges of Globalization. *Prospects* XXV11(1), March 1997.

DAWN. 1997. From "There is No Alternative" to "There Must be an Alternative", South African Development Education Project. Bellville: University of Western Cape.

Gustavsson, Bernt. 1997. Lifelong Learning Reconsidered. In: Shirley Walters, ed., *Globalization, Adult Education and Training*. London: Zed Books.

Holford, J., Griffin, C. and Jarvis, P. 1997. Lifelong Learning: Reality, Rhetoric, and Public Policy. Conference Proceedings 4–6 July 1997, University of Surrey, Department of Educational Studies, England.

International Review of Education. Vol. 40, Nos. 3–4, 1994. Special Issue on Lifelong Education, edited by Paul Bélanger and Ettore Gelpi.

Korsgaard. O. 1997. Adult Learning between Global Economy and National Democracy. In *Adult Learning and the Challenges for the 21st Century*. Denmark: Association for World Education.

Mamdani, M. 1998. When Does a Settler Become a Native? Inaugural Lecture, University of Cape Town, 13 May 1998.

Muller, J. 1997. Citizenship and Curriculum. In: N. Cloete, J. Muller, M. W. Makgoba and D. Ekong, eds., *Knowledge, Identity and Curriculum Transformation in Africa*. Cape Town: Maskew Miller Longman.

National Commission on Higher Education. 1996. *A Framework for Transformation*. NCHE Report. Pretoria: NCHE.

Soobrayan, B. 1997. From Apartheid Education to Lifelong Learning: Assessing the Ameliorative Potential of Emerging Education Policy in South Africa. Paper presented at Lifelong Learning Conference, July 1997, University of Surrey, England.

Stromquist, N. 1997. *Literacy for Citizenship State*. Albany: State University of New York Press.

Tedesco, J C. 1997. Editorial. *Prospects* XXV11(1), March 1997.

UNESCO Institute of Education. 1998. *The Mumbai Statement on Lifelong Learning, Active Citizenship and the Reform of Higher Education*. Hamburg: UIE.

The author

Shirley Walters is professor of adult and continuing education at the University of the Western Cape, South Africa. She has been seconded to direct the University Mission Initiative on Lifelong Learning out of the Vice Chancellor's office. As a result of this work the university has decided to adopt lifelong learning as an important framework for repositioning the institution.

Contact address: Prof. Shirley Walers, University of the Western Cape, Private Bag X17, Bellville 7530, South Africa. E-mail: ferris@iafrica.com.

UNDERSTANDING THE EXPERIENCES OF BEGINNING SECONDARY SCHOOL TEACHERS

EDMUND Z. MAZIBUKO

Abstract – This paper reports a study which sought to obtain deeper insights into the experiences of beginning secondary school teachers in Swaziland during 1997. Out of a sample of 48 beginning teachers, 28 participated in the study. They were invited to complete a questionnaire and were also visited in their schools where they were interviewed and observed during teaching practice. The paper describes the experiences of these teachers. The study found that, while there were several common concerns and experiences during the first year of teaching, there were also some significant different experiences. The paper discusses some implications of the study for teacher education.

Zusammenfassung – Dieses Dokument berichtet über eine Studie, die zum Ziel hatte, einen tieferen Einblick in die Erfahrungen neu ausgebildeter Lehrer an weiterführenden Schulen in Swaziland im Jahre 1997 zu gewähren. Von 48 neu ausgebildeten Lehrern nahmen 28 an der Studie teil. Sie wurden gebeten, einen Fragebogen auszufüllen und wurden auch in ihren Schulen besucht, wo sie interviewt und bei der Ausübung ihrer Lehrtätigkeit beobachtet wurden. Das Dokument beschreibt die Erfahrungen dieser Lehrer. Die Studie ergab, daß es zwar viele gemeinsame Belange und Erfahrungen im ersten Lehrjahr gab, jedoch auch einige deutlich unterschiedliche Erfahrungen vorhanden waren. Das Dokument erläutert einige Punkte bezüglich der Bedeutung der Studie für die Ausbildung von Lehrern.

Résumé – Cet article présente une étude qui se proposait d'analyser en profondeur les expériences vécues par les débutants de l'enseignement secondaire au Swaziland au cours de l'année 1997. Sur un échantillon de 48 enseignants débutants, 28 ont participé à l'étude. Ces derniers ont été invités à remplir un questionnaire, ainsi que intérrogés et observés dans leur pratique pédagogique lors d'une visite de classe. L'article décrit l'expérience de ces enseignants. L'étude établit que, tout en partageant plusieurs préoccupations et expériences communes au cours de cette première année d'enseignement, ils la vivent partiellement de façon sensiblement différente. L'article examine diverses conclusions de l'étude à intégrer dans la formation des enseignants.

Resumen – Este trabajo informa sobre un estudio que buscaba obtener conocimientos más profundos de las experiencias hechas por docentes principiantes de la educación secundaria en Swazilandia durante 1997. De una muestra de 48 docentes principiantes, 28 participaron del estudio. Fueron invitados a completar un cuestionario y además se les visitó en sus escuelas donde fueron entrevistados y observados durante su práctica de enseñanza. El trabajo describe las experiencias hechas por estos docentes. El estudio llega a la conclusión de que, pese a que existan algunas preocupaciones y experiencias comunes durante el primer año de enseñanza, también se registran varias experiencias significantemente diferentes. El papel discute algunas consecuencias que estos resultados tienen para la formación de docentes.

International Review of Education – Internationale Zeitschrift für Erziehungswissenschaft – Revue Internationale de l'Education 45(5/6): 589–602, 1999.
© 1999 *Kluwer Academic Publishers. Printed in the Netherlands.*

Резюме - Этот труд рассказывает об исследовании, которое ставило своей целью получение более глубокого понимания того, что испытывали начинающие учителя средней школы в Свазиленде в 1997 году. Из общей группы 48 начинающих учителей в исследовании приняли участие 28. Их попросили ответить на вопросы анкеты, а, кроме того, их посетили в их школах, где с ними проводились беседы и проводилось наблюдение за их практикой проведения учебного процесса. В документе описывается опыт этих учителей. В результате исследования было установлено, что в течение первого года обучения, несмотря на некоторые общие проблемы и связанный с ними опыт, имел место также и значительный опыт другого характера. В работе рассматриваются некоторые выводы, полученные в ходе исследования, по отношению к обучению учителей.

Background

The study reported in this paper involved a group of beginning teachers who had just graduated from the Post-Graduate Certificate of Education (PGCE) programme of the University of Swaziland. Swaziland is an independent country on the south eastern part of Africa. It is a landlocked country, surrounded by the Republic of South Africa on the north, western and southern part, and the Republic of Mozambique on the eastern side. In size, the country is about 17300 square kilometres, with a population approaching a million.

About a quarter of the national budget is allocated to the Ministry of Education. In the last decade, the country has witnessed rapid expansion in both primary and secondary education, causing a lot of strain on resources and facilities. This expansion affects the quality of education provision. In 1987 there were about 400 primary schools and about 150 secondary schools. In 1997, the number of primary schools had increased to about 500 and there are about 200 secondary schools. The task of producing teachers for the country's schools rests with the university and the four colleges. There are three teacher training institutions, one training secondary school teachers, and the other two produce primary school teachers. The College of Technology (SCOT) is responsible for the preparation of secondary teachers in the commercial and vocational fields. At the university, the Faculty of Agriculture trains agriculture and economics teachers for secondary schools, and the Faculty of Education trains both primary and secondary degree students, and post-graduate certificate in education (PGCE) teachers in both the humanities and sciences. A few students study outside the country, mainly in the Republic of South Africa.

In recent years, there has been an over-production of primary and secondary school teachers, particularly in the humanities. There is a shortage of teachers in the sciences because teachers often leave teaching and pursue other more financially attractive professions. The training institutions do not meet the demands of the schools for science teachers, basically because there are few school leavers who qualify for admission in the tertiary institutions to pursue science courses.

Except for science teachers, graduates from the colleges and university have found it increasingly difficult to get teaching posts. It is now common for graduates to have to wait a considerable time after graduation before getting their first appointment. The posting of teachers rests with the Teaching Service Commission (TSC), which has often been criticized for failing to absorb the newly graduated teachers in the country's schools. The Teaching Service Commission has therefore resolved that teachers should seek out teaching positions for themselves in schools because teachers posted by the TSC are sometimes turned away by the headteachers on the grounds that there were no teaching positions available at the school (*Times of Swaziland*, February 23, 1998).

A survey of the graduates from the teacher training institutions (Mazibuko 1996a) revealed that a number of primary and secondary school teacher graduates were likely to join the ranks of the unemployed after graduation. The survey also revealed that some of those who were lucky to get teaching positions found themselves teaching subjects they were not qualified to teach or they taught at levels they were not qualified to teach. Mazibuko found that about 27 Secondary Teacher Diploma (STD) holders from a sample of 45 taught at primary school level, and about 10 PGCE graduates out of a sample of 60 taught primary school classes. A number of B.Ed (Primary) graduates were also holding positions of authority either as headteachers or deputy headteachers of secondary/high schools.

The survey also found that teaching positions were available in the remote and rural schools, but recently qualified teachers were often not interested in teaching in these schools. An additional factor was that these schools often also lacked suitable accommodation and facilities.

There is considerable competition for teaching posts in secondary schools, given the fact that there are a number of centres of production. Mazibuko (1996b) found that of the 40 graduates of the B.Ed (P) programme between 1994–1996, ten obtained positions as high school headteachers, eight as teachers at high school level, ten as college lecturers, and twelve were located in private schools. The common practice with most B. Ed (P) graduates was to avoid working in government primary schools because of the relatively poor incentives and promotion structure. A B.Ed (P) degree holder does not benefit at all by serving as a headteacher of a primary school, since this position is not financially rewarded.

Over the past few years, the author has been involved in the PGCE programme in the University of Swaziland, and has conducted surveys of PGCE graduates regarding their success in obtaining work and their experiences as beginning teachers. The PGCE graduates hold degrees in different disciplines before joining the Faculty of Education for the one year PGCE full-time course. The course is also offered in a 2 year part-time mode, though this is being phased out.

The PGCE full-time programme is an intensive programme. Candidates take eleven courses in the Foundations and Curriculum areas. A number of courses taken within the PGCE are similar to those taken by the B.Ed (S) students and the students sit for the same assessment and end of year examinations. The PGCE students are also expected to complete a total of twelve weeks teaching practice. The first teaching practice covers four weeks, usually in February, and the last is about eight weeks and is completed after the examinations in May.

Technically, the students have not graduated until they complete and pass teaching practice, which normally finishes at the end of July, when the posting of graduates begins. However, in some cases graduates are posted as soon as they finish their exams, and they are supervised in the schools to which they are appointed. There are a number of problems associated with this practice.

Assuming that all graduates are employed when they finish teaching practice in July, by mid December, these teachers have been in the field for at least four months. At the time of graduation in October each year, most teachers have already been in their teaching positions for approximately 3–5 months, depending on when they were posted.

The researcher designed a questionnaire drawing on key issues in the literature on beginning teaching, and also incorporating factors which had particular relevance to Swaziland. This questionnaire was used to survey one cohort of these students. This was done approximately three months after they entered employment as teachers. The results from the surveys of graduates who have recently graduated and joined the market have been reported elsewhere (Mazibuko 1996a).

The aim of the present study was to go further than conducting a survey of the graduates. The aim here is to gain deeper insights and understandings of the experiences of recently qualified and beginning teachers. This necessitated going beyond the data obtained through the initial survey and using different approachs. About 28 recent graduates of the PGCE programme of the University of Swaziland were followed up, after the initial survey. This paper reports work in progress on these beginning teachers.

Literature

There has been a lot of research activity centred around the workplace conditions and the professional socialization of new teachers. Much of this research have been concentrated in the West (Grossman 1990; Bullough 1989; Feiman-Nemser 1983; Lortie 1975). One of the common conclusion from these studies is the overwhelming isolation of beginning teachers. An earlier study by Lortie (1975) concluded that the structural organization of schools constrained the frequency and nature of collegial interaction. Beginning teachers are not given enough supervision and they are often given responsibilities and tasks that could only realistically be carried out by experienced teachers. Hence, the first year of teaching seems to be a very difficult year for teachers.

Methodology

This research began in February 1997. This was a good time for the start of the research because schools in Swaziland open in the third week of January. The researcher was responsible for the compiling, distribution and collection of the questionnaires and also for visiting the teachers and observing their lessons.

The study began with sending letters of introduction to potential participating beginning teachers and requesting their participation in the research. Letters were also sent to the headteachers of the schools explaining the research project. The teachers who responded were visited in their schools. Arrangements were made to administer the questionnaires, and to observe them teach and to interview them concerning their experiences as beginning teachers.

After the classroom observation, the researcher invited the beginning teachers to identify significant experiences and events about beginning teaching that were obvious during the class activities. In some schools, headteachers were also interviewed to draw on their experiences of working with beginning teachers.

Data for the study came from a number of sources and a number of techniques were used. However, emphasis was placed on the information acquired during discussions with the beginning teachers who were requested to comment on their experiences. Their concepts and modes of expression were used in the recording of data. At the end of the time spent with the beginning teachers, some formal structure was added for obtaining their perceptions on a few direct questions. The method used to analyze and synthesis data was similar to one used for analysing qualitative data.

Following the principles for interpretive case study research (see Eisner 1991; Strauss 1987) individual stories were written for each of the beginning teachers. The researcher confirmed the results of the analysis with each of the beginning teachers. These cases are discussed in another paper (Mazibuko 1996a).

Graduation and becoming a teacher

Graduation seemed to be an important stage in the process of becoming a teacher amongst the beginning teachers involved in the study. Most beginning teachers pointed out that graduation was a stage in which their status as teachers was validated. The students finished their course in May, and some got posted as soon as they finished their exams (though teaching practice was still outstanding). Students had to wait until October to graduate. Even though the students would have completed other requirements and were eligible to teach, the graduation ceremony had some significance in their lives.

One beginning teacher expressed his feelings clearly when he said:

> When I started teaching, I felt I was still a student. I didn't feel like a real teacher. You finish exams and go straight to a classroom. But after graduation, I went back to class with all the confidence that I was now a teacher.

Some of the beginning teachers remarked that having teaching practice at the end of the course gave rise to a number of problems. One of the problems they cited was that even in cases where they obtained teaching positions before they completed teaching practice, they still lacked confidence in themselves. One beginning teacher remarked;

> I got this teaching position in May. But you know, I am not really comfortable. You people keep on coming to check us. What if I fail T.P? The kids also are aware that I am not a "real" teacher. Even though I tell them that I am here to stay, they still regard me as a practising teacher.

The above illustrates the problem associated with the practice of employing the graduates before they complete all the requirements for graduation. In some cases the graduates fail teaching practice, and they are allowed to repeat it and to graduate the following year.

The schools

There are many changes that are taking place in the country's schools. In primary schools there is the issue of continuous assessment which the teachers are trying to halt. Continuous assessment will soon be introduced in the secondary schools. There are frequent changes in some subjects in terms of curriculum materials. These developments have an impact on student teachers and beginning teachers. Beginning teachers are also over-worked in the schools. Besides the heavy teaching load, they are also expected to take part in extra curricular activities. All the beginning teachers reported high levels of stress caused by the amount of work they are required to do. Moreover, the teachers reported that the PGCE course did not adequately prepare them for some of the things they were expected to do in schools.

> It's theory, theory all the time. We also spend a lot of time running from this lecture to the other. There is very little time to reflect and think about what we discuss in our lectures. What happens in schools is different from what we learn in some courses. I wish we spent some time in schools as part of our training.

It is clear from the above conversation that beginning teachers are overwhelmed by the amount of work they find themselves doing in schools. Above all, these teachers felt that the course did not prepare them enough for the challenges they meet in schools.

It should be emphasized that beginning teachers did not have the same experiences in all schools. Some schools were well organized and there was support for beginning teachers. The following is an example, though this is not common;

> The headteacher is very supportive. He also encourages his staff to make sure that they help me. The teachers are also good. They are ready to help. The teaching load is average. I am told that this will be increased in future. I am trying my best to be effective because I don't want to disappoint the headteacher and the other teachers. Teachers produce good results here. That is how they are judged.

Some schools are well equipped in terms of teaching resources, while others are very poor and uninviting places to teach. The beginning teachers were found in all sorts of schools. As one beginning teacher pointed out;

> I am lucky to be here. At least I have a job. My friends are unemployed. But as you can see, there is no chalkboard here. The kids do not have desks and chairs. It's hard. The kids do not have textbooks. They depend on the teacher.

The beginning teachers are aware that they are unevenly distributed in schools across the country. They are also aware that they have to teach students who in the end sit for the same public examinations despite the fact that some come from deprived environments. Sometimes beginning teachers feel embarrassed to tell their friends where they are teaching:

> I feel embarrassed to tell my friends where I teach. It is a remote school. There is no decent accommodation. I can't even invite my friends to visit me (laughing). Maybe I am lucky to be here – some of my friends turned down such schools. I think the school is neglected by the Ministry. There are no resources for teachers.

Five beginning teachers had been fortunate to obtain teaching positions in urban schools. They described their schools as good, parents were very supportive and they expect high academic standards. A number of beginning teachers were in schools that could be classified as average in terms of their performance. The majority were in rural schools and in schools with relatively inexperienced teachers. In one school, the only experienced person was the headteacher, all the other teachers were beginning teachers (some from the other colleges).

One of the major problems facing beginning teachers was knowing the schools in which they were placed. This was a major problem for the teachers, because their major focus was in getting the work done rather than knowing the school environment.

There is no doubt that the location of the school and the wealth of the parents who send the kids to the school have an impact on the beginning teachers. In some of the desperate cases, some beginning teachers pointed out that they had to spend a considerable amount of their own meagre resources and money to get the resources they need for their classes.

In some schools, headteachers were very strict with the use of resources and photocopying facilities:

> We are always told that there is no money. The headteacher doesn't seem to be supportive at all. When I ask to photocopy some notes for the students, I am told that I should use the chalkboard. Sometimes you may want to photocopy a chapter from that book for your students. Can you copy that on the board? I am not sure whether this is the job I would like to do for the rest of my life.

Getting started as a beginning teacher

Asked to comment about the first few weeks of teaching, the teachers had much to say. A number of teachers used terms such as *"boring"*, *"daunting"*, *"difficult"*, *"stressful"*, *"frightening"*. They all pointed out that beginning teaching was different from their first teaching practice experience. One beginning teacher described it as;

> A matter of sink or swim. It's a new school, new people around, its demanding. It is scary in case I did something wrong. Preparing daily lesson plans for the different classes I teach takes time.

During the first few weeks, stress levels were high because beginning teachers were generally conscientious, enthusiastic and hardworking. They wanted to do their best. They put in long hours from Monday to Friday and often spent a great deal of the weekend planning and preparing their lessons. Beginning teachers were extremely busy people during their first year of teaching.

While all beginning teachers carried a heavy load, those with family responsibilities were overburdened.

One beginning teacher lamented:

> I am at school from about 8.00 am to 4.00 pm. When I get home I have my own family to look after. On most nights I am up until 11.00 pm doing school work. I also have to work on weekends. It's just like being at university with assignments to submit, except that the family is here needing my attention.

School supervisors and mentors

In most of the schools where the beginning teachers were located, there was no formal system of supervising and mentoring. The beginning teachers reported that the mentoring role was voluntary, depending on whether the beginning teacher was able to make friends from the experienced teachers. Most beginning teachers reported that some friendly teachers in their schools were helpful as mentors. Some beginning teachers reported that they were being isolated in their schools. The old teachers were not prepared to help them. One teacher who was successful in making friends said:

> I make initiative to ask for help. I talk to all the teachers. After a few weeks I was friendly to most and they were all very helpful in many ways.

Some of the teachers had a different experience.

> You are just thrown there and expected to learn for yourself. There was no help at all. One teacher told me that I had to find my way, she had the same experience.

One other observation was that experienced teachers were generally very busy people who found it difficult to find the time to provide a great deal of help to the beginning teachers.

In all schools there were no formal induction programs for the new teachers. It is important to highlight that though a number of teachers in the study referred to the concept of induction, they indicated that there was little support and the part that other teachers played in their orientation to the new environment was minimal.

Knowing other teachers in the school

The task of getting to know other teachers in a school proved to be a difficult task for some beginning teachers. This proved to be more difficult in the large schools where there were many teachers and the patterns of interaction were limited. One beginning teacher remarked:

> How can you meet other people if your have a big teaching load? By the end of the day you are flat out and you only want to have a rest.

The students also pointed out that the older staff members have well established social groups and in some cases they found it hard to join some of these groups. The exception seemed to be in situations where there were a number of beginning teachers in a school. One beginning teacher remarked:

> I did not necessarily know the other beginning teachers. I saw them at the university but we were not really friends. But we have since been brought together by the predicament we are in.

Some beginning teachers pointed out that they found that it was easier to know the teachers in their departments than the teachers in other areas. A study by McLaughlin (1993) observed that departments vary widely, even within a single building. In some cases, teachers who work literally across the corridor from one another but work in different departments experience their workplace in critically different ways. A few of the beginning teachers got teaching positions in the schools in which they had done their teaching practice. This was an advantage for them in that they knew the school routine and many of the staff. By way of contrast, a teacher who came into a school half way through the year found things difficult because routines and interaction patterns were already well established.

The curriculum and teaching approaches

Most beginning teachers found the task of teaching daunting. There were a number of differences in the approaches followed by the schools. Teachers found daily lesson planning demanding, particularly in cases where they taught different levels.

Some beginning teachers talked extensively about the learning they were engaged in. They made reference to the fact that their subject matter knowledge need to improve.

> What we study at university is not really relevant to the school. One has to learn new things here. You just feel that you don't have the required knowledge.

This view was echoed by many beginning teachers who felt that the university course should concentrate more on giving students a deeper knowledge of the subject matter relevant to the schools. Some students even suggested that there should be more handling of the content particularly in their PGCE course, though some were mindful of the fact that the programme was already overcrowded. With reference to the pedagogical knowledge, a number of students pointed out that they were well equipped with useful skills, though they highlighted that sometimes the theory they got from the university was not applicable in practice.

While there was not a great deal of discussion about teaching styles, it was clear that beginning teachers were reflecting on their practice. One teacher remarked:

> I have to revise the lesson because the students forgot a lot of what I taught.

Another teacher was excited about the achievements in her class.

> I was pleased that the lesson objectives were achieved. The students' responses revealed that they understood the major concepts.

Another teacher felt that it was hard to teach without a detailed knowledge of the children, so she made an attempt to know the children in her class. She remarked that this exercise was very helpful because she was able to understand individual needs of the learners.

School routines and practices

Beginning teachers found themselves engaged in a number of administrative routines in the school. They were concerned that some of these routines were a problem to them because they did not have the necessarily skills. Some wondered if it would not have been helpful to deal with these issues during their training.

> We were not told how to correct and manage a class register. Not to mention some financial management skills. I keep money for sports, books, films, etc. Besides, there are a number of other things one has to do. On our last staff meeting, I wrote the minutes. It was a daunting task.

When one beginning teacher was asked to lead the assembly for the week, she found it very stressful. She was conscious that she would be the focus of the school for the week. She was mindful of her appearance during this week.

Classroom management and student discipline

Most beginning teachers talked at length about classroom management and student discipline. Some felt that classroom management was easier than expected. Most beginning teachers felt that there were a number of problems in their schools and this affected their teaching. One beginning teacher felt that he spent a lot of time dealing with classroom management problems rather than getting down to the actual process of teaching.

> The big boys are a menace. They make a lot of fun on anything. It's hard to control them. Some think I am just a young girl. I am old.

Another beginning teacher mentioned that discipline in his school was a serious problem. The students did not respect the teachers and in some cases students refused to be punished by beginning teachers. This was very stressful for some teachers who remarked that if teaching was characterized by such students indiscipline, they were not so sure if they would last in the teaching profession.

The joy and frustration associated with teaching

During the interview sessions, the beginning teachers were asked to indicate what their biggest joy had been during their first year of teaching. Most of the responses focused on achievements related to teaching. These included; *my lesson had gone very well and the students had learnt something*; *the students responded very well*; *the students made progress; the student's attitudes changed after the lesson*, and so on.

With reference to the biggest frustration associated with their work, the beginning teachers raised several concerns. Most pointed out that they were frustrated when the students were not responding and learning. The difficult students who were also very disruptive were also frustrating the teachers. A number of female teachers felt that the boys in their classes demanded more attention than the girls. Beginning teachers also pointed out that being unable to achieve their goals and also failing to establish effective relationships with staff was also a major source of frustration.

Lessons for the Faculty of Education

At the end of the interviews respondents were asked what would be the most important message(s) that they would like to convey to the Faculty of Education who are responsible for their teacher preparation course. Most of the students highlighted that the course was generally good, but felt that there was so much taught that in the end they don't have time to think about the issues discussed in their lectures. Some teachers felt that there was need for more practice in the courses instead of the focus on theory as it is the case in a number of courses. Beginning teachers also felt that there was need for more school exposure and experience during the course. Most beginning teachers noted that learning to teach occurred in two distinct contexts: the University lecture and the classroom and they identified elements of conflict between the two contexts, which need to be addressed.

Beginning teachers felt that some time needed to be spent on practical issues like how to mark a register, manage school finances, and the development of skills related to the extra curricular offerings in schools. A number of students mentioned that some courses need to be dropped to pave the way for a course of physical education and maybe music education. Some of the beginning teachers were asked to be sports masters and to lead the school choir and they did not have the necessary training.

Conclusion

The emphasis in this paper has been on the experiences of a number of beginning teachers at a time when relatively few manage to get positions immediately after graduation. The paper discussed experiences of a group of teachers who managed to get teaching positions. One of the major findings of the study has been to show the difficulties faced by the beginning teachers in their first year of teaching. Beginning teachers are overwhelmingly isolated in schools. There is very little interaction between new teachers and experienced teachers. Paradoxically, these new teachers are sometimes given the same complex set of responsibilities and tasks as experienced teachers. These difficulties affect the performance of these teachers and they also destroy the enthusiasm to teach. It would help beginning teachers if the schools that give them appointments can offer these teachers support, and if they can provide induction programmes for the new teachers. The study found that it was rare for beginning teachers to join a lively and supportive community of practice where mentors guide the novices through the difficult periods of their chosen profession.

Feiman-Nemser (1983) observed that while such isolation leaves room for self-expression, it also narrows the range of alternatives that will be tried and increases the likelihood that the novice will misinterpret successes and failures. Beginning teachers need to learn a lot about how things happen in schools. It is in this regard that the PGCE course needs to be evaluated to ensure that it meets the needs of the students and the schools where they are teaching. The evidence from this study indicates that the experiences of these teachers in Swaziland was not very encouraging and that this should be of concern to those preparing them for teaching, to those employing the teachers, and to those responsible for the development of the teaching profession. Clearly, it is necessary to rethink the experiences that beginning teachers have in schools if we are concerned with addressing issues of equity and transformation in education.

References

Bullough, R. 1989. *First-year Teacher: A Case Study*. New York: Teachers' College Press.

Eisner, E. W. 1991. *The Enlightened Eye: Qualitative Inquiry and the Development of Educational Practice*. New York: Macmillan.

Feiman-Nemser, S. 1983. Learning to Teach. In: L. Shulman and G. Sykes, eds., *Handbook of Teaching and Policy*. New York: Longman.

Grossman, P. and Slodoisky, S. 1995. Content as Context: The Role of School Subjects in Secondary School Teaching. *Educational Research* 24(8): 5–11.

Grossman, P. 1990. *The Making of a Teacher. Teacher Knowledge and Teacher Education*. New York: Teachers College Press.

Lortie, D. 1975. *Schoolteacher. A Sociological Study*. Chicago: University of Chicago Press.

Mazibuko E. Z. 1996a. *A Survey of the Graduates o the Faculty of Education*. Research Paper. UNISWA, Kwaluseni.

Mazibuko, E. Z. 1996b. *The Destination of the Graduates from the BEd (Primary) and BEd (Secondary) Programmes*. Research Paper. UNISWA, Kwaluseni.

McLaughlin, M. 1993. What matters most in teachers' workplace context? In: J. Little and M. McLaughlin, eds., *Teachers' Work: Individuals, Colleagues, and Contexts*. New York: Teachers College Press.

Strauss, A. L. 1987. *Qualitative Analysis for Social Scientists*. Cambridge: Cambridge University Press.

Times of Swaziland, February 23, 1998.

The author

Edmund Zizwe Mazibuko earned an M.Ed from the University of Wales and a PhD in Education from Edith Cowan University. He is a Lecturer in History Education and Head of the Department of Curriculum and Teaching, University of Swaziland. His research interest is in the teaching and learning of history, teaching practices and knowledge construction.

Contact address: Dr Edmund Mazibuko, University of Swaziland, Private Bag 4, Kwaluseni, Swaziland. E-mail: EDMUND@uniswac1.uniswa.sz.

POSTCOLONIALISM AND COMPARATIVE EDUCATION

LEON TIKLY

Abstract – The article considers the relevance of recent developments in postcolonial theory for comparative education research. The article starts with an account of these developments. This account is then used as a basis for a critical discussion of previous theoretical frameworks that have been used by comparative researchers to explain the colonial legacy. The implications of adopting a postcolonial approach in comparative education are discussed in relation to issues of race, culture, language and the curriculum. The article concludes by arguing that a consideration of the postcolonial condition is necessary for developing a more holistic and less eurocentric understanding of the relationship between globalisation and education.

Zusammenfassung – Der Artikel betrachtet die Bedeutung jüngster Entwicklungen in der postkolonialen Theorie für die vergleichende Bildungsforschung. Der Artikel beginnt mit einem Bericht über diese Entwicklungen. Dieser Bericht wird dann als Grundlage für eine kritische Diskussion über die früheren theoretischen Rahmenbedingungen, die von vergleichenden Forschern verwendet wurden, um die koloniale Hinterlassenschaft zu erklären, verwendet. Die Bedeutung der Verwendung einer postkolonialen Verfahrensweise in der vergleichenden Bildung wird in bezug auf Rasse, Kultur, Sprache und Lehrplan diskutiert. Der Artikel endet mit dem Argument, daß eine Betrachtung der postkolonialen Bedingungen für die Entwicklung eines mehr holistischen und weniger eurozentrischen Verständnisses der Beziehung zwischen Globalisierung und Bildung notwendig ist.

Résumé – L'article analyse l'importance de l'évolution récente de la théorie postcoloniale pour la recherche en éducation comparative. Il commence par dresser le bilan de l'évolution récente de la théorie postcoloniale, qui sert ensuite de fondement à une analyse critique des cadres théoriques antérieurs utilisés par les chercheurs comparatifs pour expliquer l'héritage colonial. Il étudie alors les conséquences de l'adoption d'une approche postcoloniale en éducation comparative par rapport aux questions de race, de culture, de langue et aux programmes. Il conclut en affirmant que l'étude de la situation postcoloniale est nécessaire pour élaborer une notion plus holistique et moins eurocentrique de la relation entre mondialisation et éducation.

Resumen – Este artículo considera la relevancia que revisten los desarrollos recientes en la teoría postcolonial para la investigación de la educación comparativa. El trabajo comienza con un recuento de los últimos desarrollos en teoría postcolonial, que sirve de base para una discusión crítica de los marcos teóricos previos usados por los investigadores comparativos para explicar el legado colonial. Las consecuencias que ha tenido la adopción de un enfoque postcolonial en la educación comparativa se discuten en relación con temas tales como razas, culturas, lenguas y planes de estudio. El artículo termina argumentando que es necesario tener en cuenta la condición postcolonial para desarrollar una comprensión más holística y menos eurocéntrica de las relaciones existentes entre la globalización y la educación.

International Review of Education – Internationale Zeitschrift für Erziehungswissenschaft – Revue Internationale de l'Education **45**(5/6): 603–621, 1999.
© 1999 *Kluwer Academic Publishers. Printed in the Netherlands.*

604

Резюме - Статья рассматривает применимость новейших разработок в постколониальной теории по сравнительным образовательным исследованиям. Статья начинается с обзора этих разработок. Этот обзор затем используется в качестве критической дискуссии о предыдущих теоретических схемах, которые использовались сравнительными исследователями, объясняющими наследие колониализма. По отношению к вопросам расы, культуры, языка и программы обучения рассматриваются результаты принятия постколониального подхода. Статья заканчивается утверждением, что принятие во внимание постколониального условия является

Recent years have seen the development of "postcolonial studies" as a sub-discipline of literary and cultural studies. The emergence of this sub-discipline reflects a renewed interest in the historical legacy of European colonialism within the arts and social sceinces. According to the authors of the recent *Post-Colonial Studies Reader* (Ashcroft, Griffiths and Tiffin 1995) postcolonial theory "involves discussion of the following kinds of experience: migration, slavery, suppression, resistance, representation, difference, race, gender, and the responses to the influential master discourses of imperial Europe". The authors point out that discussion of these issues should include themes and perspectives of older colonial and anti-colonial texts. What is distinctive about recent postcolonial theory, however, is that it attempts to reinterpret the colonial experience in the light of developments in postmodernist and poststrucuturalist thought.

The aim of this article is to consider the relevance of these recent theoretical developments for comparative and international education (CIE) research. The article was motivated by the following concerns. Firstly, although much valuable research has been undertaken about the colonial legacy in education, there has been little effort in recent years to develop the *theoretical* dimensions of this work. To the extent that existing texts on CIE *have* addressed the theoretical aspects of colonialism, this has often been done in relation to some variant of dependency theory, which has increasingly been subject to criticism. More recent developments such as the use of globalisation theory in CIE have often neglected to adequately theorise the colonial legacy.

Secondly, and related to the above, although some writers on education have begun to incorporate a postcolonial perspective into their work this literature has remained marginal in relation to the CIE canon and the implications of recent postcolonial studies for CIE (and indeed for education more generally) have not been discussed in any systematic way.

Thirdly, much of the recent literature on education in formally colonised countries has been weighted towards economic concerns. This reflects the post-Jomtein emphases on access and quality in relation to basic education in the context of deepening austerity and structural adjustment programmes. It also reflects the hegemony of what Samoff (1992) has described as the "intellectual-financial" complex in education research (i.e. the dominance of the research priorities, discourses and agendas of the major donors and financial institutions in education). One implication of this emphasis has been the relative neglect of "non-economic" concerns including those around race, culture, language and identity. This is despite the central role that these issues continue to play in shaping education policy, particularly in the context of the resurgence of ethnic nationalisms and conflict in Africa, Eastern Europe and elsewhere.

The article starts with a summary of the key aspects of recent developments in postcolonial theory. The purpose here is not to provide an exhaustive account of the field but rather to outline a theoretical approach that is useful for critical discussion of educational issues in subsequent sections. Although the work of several authors has been influential the writing of Stuart Hall (1996a, b) and of Ania Loomba (1998) has been found particularly helpful.

The meaning of postcolonialism

At the most general level the term "postcolonial" is used to describe a global "condition" or shift in the cultural, political and economic arrangements that arise from the experiences of European colonialism both in former colonised and colonising countries. Importantly, it is used not just to describe specific developments or events related to colonialism and its aftermath but also to signify an *epistemological* shift in the way that these events are described and interpreted. There is much debate, however, concerning the meaning of the term. These debates have centred on issues relating to the durability of relations of colonialism and dependency in the modern age and the extent to which those at the "bottom" in terms of class, caste and gender have witnessed any improvement in their situation in the "postcolonial" period. There is also dispute regarding whether or not "postcolonialism" proves too homogenising a term given the diverse experiences and histories of formally colonised countries (McLintock 1992; Loomba 1998).

Rather than using the term "postcolonialism" as a yardstick by which to compare the nature and extent of colonialism and de-colonisation in different countries, the approach adopted here is to use the term to signify a general "*process* of disengagement with the whole colonial syndrome which takes many forms" (Hulme 1995) and "the contestation of colonial domination and of the legacies of colonialism" (Loomba 1998: 12). If the term is understood at this level of abstraction it is possible to keep in mind the global experience of European colonialism as a general referent whilst leaving room for the careful study of the effects of colonialism in specific contexts.

Understanding postcolonialism as a process also helps to draw attention to an important element of postcolonial theory, namely the move away from the modernist pre-occupation with the nation state. For writers such as Hall (1996a) and Loomba (1998), postcolonialism should be seen as an aspect of the emergence over several centuries of the system of global capitalism. For the purposes of our discussion, this view of postcolonialism has three important implications. Firstly it serves to underline the point that colonialism is not "over" in the sense of an epochal shift, but that its modalities and effects are being transformed as a consequence of globalisation. Secondly, it allows for a consideration of the experiences of colonialism both in former colonised and colonising countries, i.e. to the "ways in which colonialism was never simply external to the societies of the imperial metropolis [but] was always inscribed deeply within them" (Hall 1996a: 246).

Thirdly, it draws attention to the central role that European colonisation of countries outside of Europe has played in defining the postcolonial condition. This is not to underplay the historical significance or contemporary relevance of other forms of colonialism (Russian colonialism in Eastern Europe or Japanese colonialism in Asia for example). It is simply to recognise that the process of European expansionism since the sixteenth century has been particularly instrumental in the development of contemporary global markets.

Implicit in Hulme's characterisation of postcolonialism as a process is a more subtle change of emphasis not only in the content of what postcolonialism is seeking to describe but also in the way that colonialism is *understood* and narrativised. In keeping with postmodern and in particular, poststructuralist emphases, postcolonial theory provides a critique of the "metanarratives" of the European Enlightenment. Thus according to Hall:

> This [postcolonial] re-narrativisation displaces the "story" of capitalist modernity from its European centering to its dispersed global peripheries; from peaceful evolution to imposed violence; from the transition from feudalism to capitalism (which played such a talismanic role in, for example, Western Marxism) to the formation of the world market (Hall 1996a: 250).

This re-narrativisation then involves a reconceptualisation of colonialism not as a sub-plot of some "grander" (European) narrative, but as a violent event central to the developing new relationships of globalisation and global capitalism. Crucially it also signals an "epistemic shift" (i.e. a renegotiation of the ground base of knowledge on which European, modernist accounts of colonialism were premised). This involves going beyond the "binary oppositions" by means of which colonialism has been studied in the past such as those between "coloniser" and "colonised", "First" and "Third World" and "Black" and "White". The consequence of this shift has been the development of a more contingent and complex view of colonial culture, politics and identities.

On the one hand this has been achieved by focusing on the "unstable", "hybrid" and "fractured" nature of colonial and postcolonial identities.

Spivak's (1985) work, for example, draws attention to the implication of a variety of factors – colonialism, patriarchy and caste – in the formation of different subject positions amongst the colonised. Similarly, Hall's (1992: 254) work provides a critique of the essentialised "black subject" and seeks to recognise the "extraordinary diversity of subject positions, social experiences and cultural identities which compose the category 'black'".

On the other hand postcolonial theory also seeks to deepen understanding of the coloniser/colonised relationship by drawing attention to processes of transcultural "mixing" and exchange and to the complexities of diasporic identification. In his (1993) book *The Black Atlantic*, for example, Gilroy considers how cultural forms, identities and modalities of resistance to colonialism have developed as an aspect of the emergence of the African Diaspora. Other phenomena, such as the formation of exiled and refugee communities have contributed to this process as well. In this respect, postcolonialism is concerned with what Hall describes as the "transverse" linkages between and across nation state frontiers in addition to the more traditional "vertical" relationships between coloniser and colonised.

Although there are clear overlaps between postcolonialism and postmodernism in terms of the epistemological critique of enlightenment thought, there are also important divergences. Chief amongst these is the view expressed by some postcolonial writers concerning the Eurocentric nature of postmodernism. Extending Said's earlier critique of Foucault (Said 1978), the authors of the influential postcolonial text, *Past the Last Post*, have argued that postmodernism represents a new form of Western global hegemony. In other words postmodernism "inevitably proscribes certain cultures as being 'backward' and marginal" whilst presenting itself as "a neo-universalism to which these other cultures may aspire" (Adam and Tiffin 1991). Eurocentricism is also demonstrated by the late recognition on the part of some postmodernists that their critique of modernist thought had long been pre-empted by anti-colonialist (and feminist) authors (Williams and Chrisman 1994; Loomba 1998; Appiah 1992; Young 1992).

Turning now to criticisms of postcolonial theory, some authors have argued that postcolonial theory neglects an analysis of the possibilities for economic and political change. For Shohat the problem lies in the tendency of postcolonial theory to "dissolve polititical resistance" because it "posits no clear domination and calls for no clear resistance". Rather than signifying a move away from political struggle, however, writers such as Hall (1992, 1996a) and Loomba (1998) have argued that postcolonial theory leads towards a more contingent and strategic view of what political struggle entails. In explicating his position, Hall (1992: 244) gives the Gulf war as an example of a typical "postcolonial event".

What the Gulf war provided was not the clarifying political experience of "lines . . . drawn in the sand" but the difficulties that arose in opposing the western war in the desert when manifestly the situation in the Gulf involved both the atrocities

608

which the Alliance committed in defence of Western oil interests under UN cover against the people of Iraq (in whose historic "under-development" the West is deeply implicated); and the atrocities committed against his own people and against the best interests of the region, not to speak of those of the Kurds and the Marsh Arabs, by Saddam Hussein.

For some postcolonial writers the work of Antonio Gramsci on political struggle and on hegemony has provided a means for reinserting a concern with political agency into their work. The attraction of Gramsi's ideas lies in his "open" form of Marxism which allows for a theorisation of the ways in which different factors, including "race", class and gender, become implicated in the operation of both hegemony and counter-hegemony (see Hall 1996b; Barrett 1991, for example). There are, however, dangers in assuming that one "epoch" of political struggle according to the old binaries (exemplified by the struggles for national liberation in Africa and elsewhere) has simply been replaced by new, more subtle forms of hegemony and counter-hegemony. If, as argued above, one views postcolonialism as a process, then it is crucial to understand how old binaries (for example between "First World/Third World", "Black and White") continue to be re-inscribed upon and to articulate with, new modalities for understanding and engaging with the political level. It also underlines the necessity of taking seriously the work of the earlier theorists of national liberation (Parry 1995).

For Dirlik (1994), the problem with postcolonial theory is the way that he believes it grossly underplays "capitalism's structuring of the modern world" in a way that makes postcolonialism complicitous in "the consecration of hegemony". Indeed it is often the case that the emergence of global capitalism is bracketed to one side in much postcolonial literature and this can in part at least be related to the emergence of postcolonial studies as a sub-discipline of literary and cultural studies. Some postcolonial writers, however, have attempted to engage with Dirlik's critique and to take seriously the importance of the economic domain. Loomba (1998: 249), for example, has argued that it is debatable as to whether the neglect of economic considerations in the work of other postcolonial critics makes them "agents of global capitalism". Rather, she draws attention to the way that "narratives of women, colonised peoples, non-Europeans *revise* our understanding of colonialism, capitalism and modernity: these global narratives do not disappear but can now be read differently".

Implicit in the above view of postcolonialism is the denial of the post-structuralist assumption that there is "nothing outside of the text" and the acknowledgement of the existence of the "non-discursive", material realm. Indeed, a key concept within postcolonial theory is that of "articulation" which is used to designate the contingent and context-bound relationship between these two spheres (Grossberg 1996; Slack 1996). Also related to the above is a rejection of some approaches towards both postcolonialism and postmodernism that privilege the "local" at the expense of the "global" (exemplified in the rather glib slogan "think globally, act locally"). As Hall (1996a) has argued, it is not a question of the global fragmenting into the local but rather of the global and the local being repositioned in relation to each other. In this understanding, political struggle should not be confined to the sphere of immediate experience but should seek to engage with politics at the global and national levels as well.

Postcolonialism and comparative education

The aim of this section is to critically discuss the relevance of postcolonial theory for CIE research. Rather than claiming that postcolonial theory provides an all-embracing framework for comparison, it will be argued that it provides a new "critical idiom" (Loomba 1998) through which the master discourses of CIE can be re-narrativised. This re-narrativisation involves both a reconsideration of the content of the CIE canon and the theoretical perspectives used. The section will start with a look at how more recent postcolonial theory relates to existing accounts of colonialism in education. Attention will then turn to a consideration of some of the possibilities opened up by more recent postcolonial theory for CIE research. The article will conclude by arguing that postcolonial theory provides a necessary basis for developing a less Eurocentric and more comprehensive account of the effects of globalisation on education.

Colonialism and the CIE canon

There have of course been many attempts to write and theorise about the colonial legacy in education within CIE. Critical writing on this theme reached its apotheosis during the 1970s and early 1980s in the context of the ongoing movement towards independence in Africa, Asia and elsewhere. Much of this literature was based either explicitly or implicitly on some version of dependency theory (see for example, Carnoy 1974; Altbach and Kelly 1978; Watson et al. 1982; Watson et al. 1984). The work provided a valuable critique of human capital and modernisation theory, which had treated the colonial relationship as unproblematic. It also greatly enriched understanding of the relationship between colonialism, neo-colonialism and education through providing detailed case study material. As this work developed it began to integrate theories of the state within an overall dependency framework (Fagerlind and Saha 1989; Carnoy and Samoff 1990).

Important criticisms have, however, subsequently been directed at dependency theory and its use in CIE and these have been discussed at length elsewhere (see Hettne 1990; Martinussen 1997; Fagerlind and Saha 1989). From the perspective of recent postcolonial work, the limitations of dependency theory may be summarised as follows. Firstly, it is fundamentally an *economic* theory of underdevelopment and as such does not lend itself easily to an analysis of issues of race, culture, language and identity. Secondly, it tends to portray the relationship between colonised and colonisers as one of omnipotence to the extent that little attention is given to the contradictory effects of colonial education or to the development of forms of educational alternatives and cultural resistance. Thirdly, as a modernist discourse it works exclusively within the binary oppositions of colonised and colonisers, centre and periphery and uses as its fundamental unit of analysis the nation state. This has had further implications.

To begin with, with some notable exceptions (see for example, Watson et al. 1984), work within the dependency mould has focused on the effects of colonialism on education in colonised countries and has neglected its effects on the education systems of colonising nations. In other words, little attention was paid to the ways in which the colonial legacy "worked its way back" to the imperial centre through migration and the implications of these processes for education. Further, although dependency theory does have as a central referent a notion of global relationships, the potential opened up for understanding the transnational aspects of educational policy has often gone unexplored within the CIE literature. This is because of the tendency to examine the effects of colonial education at the national level through the use of country case studies.

There were other attempts during the 1980s to account for the colonial legacy in education that largely fell outside of the dependency paradigm. Some researchers, for example, working within a socio-anthropological paradigm made use of a concept of "cultural identity" in order to explain the role of education in reproducing cultural patterns in the postcolonial period (Brock and Tulasiewicz et al. 1985). In contrast, Mangan et al. (1988) used a historical approach to try to understand the contradictory effects of British imperial education on the political socialisation of both the colonised and colonisers. Like many of the dependency studies, these texts as examples of their genre, have provided valuable case study material although they maintain the emphasis on the nation state as the primary unit of analysis and pay less heed to the transcultural and global aspects of the colonial legacy. The texts are also problematic because they employ an essentialised view of culture as a "whole way of life" into which children are "assimilated" through forms of socialisation. As will be discussed below, more recent approaches would contest the notion of any "fixed" identity and would seek to examine how terms such as race, culture and language are themselves discursively constructed and are constitutive of social realities and of identities.

Postcolonialism and CIE research

This section will explore some of the implications for research that arise from a consideration of the postcolonial condition. The intention here is to raise questions and to open debate rather than to imply closure. The choice of areas and the issues raised are therefore intended as being illustrative only.

i) *Racism and education policy*

The publication of *Orientalism* by Edward Said marked the beginning of a concern within postcolonial theory with the analysis of colonialism and of racism as discursive practice. Subsequently, writers in education have used a similar strategy to analyse changing discourses concerning race, culture and education in countries as diverse as England (Rattansi 1992), South Africa (Tikly 1995a, 1997), the USA (McCarthy and Crichlow et al. 1993) and Australia (Knight, Smith and Sachs 1990). Such an approach has, however, made only a limited impact as a basis for comparison between countries (Mangan et al. 1993; Carrim 1995; Gundara 1990) despite its potential contribution to the CIE canon.

Firstly, such an approach lends itself to an understanding of "racism" as a category of comparative research. Traditionally, where issues of race, culture and difference have been concerned, comparativists have felt more comfortable working within a pluralist, multicultural framework based on the socio-anthropological reading of colonialism described above. Within this framework, inequality is rarely seen as the result of racist discourses and practices despite the centrality of these within the colonial project as a whole. The understanding of racism implied by more recent postcolonial literatures differs, however, from previous structuralist accounts. These differences have been described in some detail elsewhere (see Wetherell and Potter 1992; Donald and Rattansi 1992 for example). In brief, recent postcolonial theory starts from an understanding of racism as discursive practice. That is to say, it tries to understand how individual and group identities are constructed in discourse, often in quite contradictory and changing ways and how these constructions have operated hegemonically to legitimate inequalities and the colonial project.

The recent work by Mangan et al. on the imperial curriculum provides an example of the application of such an approach comparatively and historically. The contributors to this volume discuss how racial stereotypes of the non-European Other were constructed in imperial text books. The book demonstrates the "infinite diversity" of these constructions depending on the time and context of their location and also their contradictory nature (how, for example, the colonised could come in for selective praise as well as scorn in the eyes of Europeans). Of relevance here is that the book is concerned not only with the impact of racist constructions on the colonised, but also on how they profoundly influenced the learning experiences of children in the imperial centre. In his own contribution and drawing on the work of Jan Mohammed, Mangan, describes how these constructions then fed into an "Manichean allegory" (i.e. a field of diverse yet interchangeable oppositions between white and black, good and evil, superiority and inferiority). This allegory "functions as the currency for the entire colonial discursive project" and serves to legitimate the economic exploitation of the colonised.

Many commentators have remarked, however, upon a shift in the nature of European racism during the second half of the twentieth century away from an overt "biological" essentialism (based on supposed biological differences) towards a more subtle, cultural essentialism (in which cultural differences are used as a basis for legitimating inequality) (see for example, Wetherell and Potter 1992; Tikly 1994; Carrim 1995). In part this shift can be attributed to the extent to which biological accounts of difference have been challenged and discredited (although such accounts still play a prominent role in "common sense" racism). The shift can also be related, however, to the changing hegemonic function of racist accounts of difference in these postcolonial times. In many wealthier industrialised countries for instance, cultural essentialism has been used in dominant discourse primarily to maintain the "insider-outsider" binary or "the alien wedge within" (Hall 1983; Rasool 1998).

One area of relevance then is to deepen understanding of how different groups are constructed in the curricula, textbooks and policy discourses of contemporary societies and how these legitimise continuing inequalities. This type of analysis need not of course confine itself to a consideration of how groups of European origin continue to preserve their hegemony in Europe, Australia, North America and elsewhere. If we are to take account of the complexities of the postcolonial condition, then attention also needs to be given to how non-European elites defined by ethnicity, cast, class and gender also legitimise their dominance over other groups through their control over education systems.

Besides playing a hegemonic role in relation to dominant groups within the education systems of specific countries, cultural essentialism is also apparent at the global level in many of the policy discourses of multilateral agencies and in the international media. For example, Samoff has criticised the school effectiveness paradigm adopted by multilateral funders of African education on the grounds that it is premised on a new kind of modernisation theory. According to Samoff, the discourse of school effectiveness "insists now as it did 30 years ago that the causes of Africa's problems are to be found within Africa: its people, resources, capital, skills, psychological orientation, child-rearing practices and more". This observation leads him to assert that "just as poverty is to be explained by the characteristics and inabilities of the poor, so the explanation of problems of African education are to be found within and around African schools" (1992: 30). The implication for comparative research arising out of this kind of analysis is to question the extent to which culturally essentialist constructions play a role in legitimising global economic arrangements such as the imposition of structural adjustment policies, the tolerance of Third World debt or uneven terms of trade between North and South.

ii) *Culture, language and curriculum*
In the above section, the focus was on the possibilities for deconstruction opened up by the application of recent postcolonial theory to CIE. As mentioned in the previous section, however, postcolonial theory has also histori-

cally been concerned with the development of alternatives to colonialism. This has implications for curriculum development. The struggle against colonial domination has often involved a rejection of imposed educational patterns and the establishment of alternative forms of provision. The history of South African education provides rich examples of this. What is interesting about these examples for comparative researchers is that forms of resistance have often assumed a diasporic dimension.

For example, Kallaway et al. (1984) draw attention to the role that Garveyism and the American school movement played in the growth of African nationalism during the first half of the 19th century. Indeed, the rich exchange of ideas between the African Diaspora in the USA and elsewhere was an important ingredient in the ferment of black consciousness during the 1970s and 1980s. Further, in 1979 the ANC established a school for South African refugees in Morogoro, Tanzani. The author worked as a science teacher at the school between 1987 and 1989. An important goal of the school was to develop an alternative to apartheid education. The school was staffed not only by South African exiles (who had subsequently lived and developed skills in many other parts of the world), but by representatives of the international community. The cultural and educational forms that emerged at the school were both hybrid and global. Students and teachers from the school have subsequently directly participated in the development of education policy in the new South Africa. These examples do not fit easily with traditional ways of understanding the role of different cultures in the curriculum. Rather than present curriculum politics as a binary opposition between two opposing and essentialised cultures, as many pluralist models do, they are suggestive of more complex processes of transcultural mixing in which the boundaries between cultural forms and identities are fluid rather than fixed.

These observations are of direct relevance for curriculum reconstruction elsewhere. Firstly, in many parts of the previously colonised world, governments are still grappling with the highly contested and complex process of developing curricula that are more suited to the cultures and histories of the local population. Some of the complexities of this process have recently been captured by Bray (1993, 1994). Exponents of curricula reform have often had to contend with the vested interests of local elites, a lack of resources and the hegemony of western culture and forms of knowledge in an increasingly global world. This hegemony and the subsequent interpretation and hybridisation of cultural forms (processes in which education systems have been so deeply implicated) have made it increasingly difficult to define what a more culturally "relevant" curriculum might entail.

Secondly, the example of the ANC School in Tanzania also draws attention to another dimension of the postcolonial condition that has implications for an essentialised view of culture in the curriculum, namely the issue of refugee communities. As of January 1998 the United Nations High Commission on Refugees estimated that there were 22.3 million refugees, returnees or people displaced within their own countries (UNHCR 1998). What the

SOMAFCO experience demonstrated was not only the potential benefits for curriculum development that the transcultural context of refugee education affords but also the difficulties involved in defining a common identity given the diversity represented not only by the refugee community but by the host community as well.

Thirdly, during the 1980s and 1990s "cultural restorationists" in Britain, the USA, Australia and elsewhere in the more industrialised world sought to challenge the inroads that multiculturalists had made into the curriculum and set about reinserting a "traditional" (read Eurocentric) view of knowledge (McCarthy and Crichlow et al. 1993; Chitty and Mac an Ghaill 1995; Knight, Smith and Sachs et al. 1990). Apart from heralding the triumph of a conservative, nationalistic and essentialist worldview these events also brought into sharp relief the crisis of the multicultural movement in education. Faced with the charge of cultural relativism from the right, this crisis was in important respects an epistemological one and is worth outlining briefly below.

One historical response to white, European cultural hegemony in the colonial curriculum has been one of *substituting* one conception of reality and "truth" with another, black or non-European view. For Steve Biko and his black consciousness colleagues in South Africa, for example, the solution to the Eurocentric curriculum lay simply in replacing existing "White truth" based on Eurocentric norms and values with a "Black truth" based on African humanism (Tikly 1995b). Similar strategies of replacing parts of the existing curriculum with new material based on positive representations of black experiences and cultures were adopted by proponents of "black studies" in the USA, Britain and elsewhere during the 1970s and 1980s.

However understandable such efforts may have been in the context of their time, they were also problematic in that they were based on the same false premise as the approaches they criticise i.e. that it is possible to present a "single, uncontestable, objective and accurate" representation of reality (Rattansi 1993) (Ironically, such approaches were also unpopular in the USA with black parents because they were perceived to deny children access to the formal, academic curriculum (Stone 1984)).

A second strategy, favoured by multiculturalists in particular, has been to *add* new multicultural material to the formal curriculum (A similar approach has also sometimes been adopted by governments of newly independent countries). This approach has been criticised, however, on the grounds that it actually serves to legitimise Eurocentric curricula by leaving unchallenged the underlying norms and values embedded within them (McCarthy 1993). Rather, drawing on the related work of several scholars (McCarthy 1993; Said 1993; Giroux 1997; Taylor et al. 1993), it is possible to outline an alternative approach, more congruent with recent postcolonial theory, that engages with the existing canons in the curriculum. This new approach has three interrelated aspects.

The first aspect involves acknowledging the place of black and non-European scholars within the canon and, therefore, within the school curriculum. In the words of Mathew Arnold, it is to acknowledge that the "best that has been thought and said" within the disciplines necessarily includes work of black and non-European scholars and intellectuals. The second aspect involves understanding and engaging with the complex and interrelated process of canonisation and curriculum design themselves. This necessarily involves focusing on the production, distribution and legitimisation (canonisation) of "official knowledge" (Apple 1993) across a number of institutional sites (the academy, the school, research institutes, government departments, publishing houses, examination boards etc.). It is only on the basis of an understanding of the micro-processes by which certain forms of knowledge become "official" and others not that a politics of transformation involving the democratisation of knowledge production can be advanced. The third aspect involves demonstrating the relationality and interconnectedness of western and other forms of knowledge, i.e. to recognise, following Bernal (1987), how the very notion of "westernness" is itself a construct and how western forms of knowledge and "civilisation" are directly indebted to older, non-European forms.

To date research of this nature has focused largely on the USA and the UK, although Altbach's (1984) study on the *Distribution of Knowledge in the Third World* goes some way towards identifying these processes in wider context. The key point from a postcolonial perspective, however, is that largely as a result of the colonial legacy, these processes are global in nature and need to be analysed as such.

Similar arguments to those advanced above have been made concerning language policy in education. Space does not permit for a full discussion of this complex area so only certain aspects will be highlighted. The importance of language in relation to postcolonial theory is that it is a fundamental site of struggle over meaning and by implication the nature of social reality and of identity. One of the most significant legacies of colonialism in education then has been the hegemony and subsequent globalisation of the languages of the colonisers and the underdevelopment of indigenous languages (Tollefson et al. 1995; Ashcroft, Griffiths and Tiffin 1989).

There have been two broad responses to this hegemony within the postcolonial literature. The first response exemplified by writers such as Ngugi wa Thiong'o (1995) has been to reject the colonial language as a medium of communication and instruction and to promote indigenous languages in their place. As critics have subsequently pointed out, however, this approach relies on an essentialised view of traditional culture as something that can be "restored" (Ashcroft, Griffiths and Tiffin 1997; Pennycook 1995). A second response has been to start from the recognition of linguistic and cultural identity as contested and contingent and it is this view that is more consistent with the complexities of the postcolonial condition.

For, example, in a recent paper, Naz Rasool (1998) has described the issues surrounding linguistic human rights in the context of mass migration of peoples and the hybridisation of indigenous cultures as an aspect of globalisation. On the one hand he describes the tremendous possibilities opened up for language choice for migrant and formally colonised groups of people in relation to ever-changing geographical demographies. On the other hand, he points to the difficulties of language planning in relation to these groups. He demonstrates how the issue of language choice for specific communities in former colonised and colonising countries is heavily contingent on a number of factors including their social status within the country in question. Interestingly, from the point of view of this article, he also describes how language maintenance policies and rights of migrant groups also need to be understood transnationally, i.e. as an aspect of the status of specific languages in the country of origin.

A further example of the application of postcolonial theory to language policy concerns recent responses to the globalisation of English as a colonial language. In the past the predominant debate has been between conservatives (who have wanted to preserve Standard English within the "traditional" curriculum) and pluralists (who have wanted to accord different *Englishes* equal status within the education system). For more recent postcolonial scholars, however, the problem with the pluralist position is that it fails to acknowledge the relationship between different versions of the English language and discursive power. For them the issue is more one of emphasising the *process* of reading the texts. This involves a greater sensitivity to the relationship between Standard English and global hegemonic discourses than pluralist models allow for and recognition of the relative power and position of learners in relation to these discourses. They also place emphasis on language as a site of struggle and on how English has been used "against the grain", as a means of the empire "writing back" to the centre (Ashcroft, Griffiths and Tiffin 1989). The implication for comparative language policy research is to recognise how counter-hegemonic discourses can be "formed in English" (Pennycook 1995: 52).

Conclusion: Postcolonialism and the globalisation of education

During the 1990s globalisation theory has increasingly been used as a framework for comparative analysis. Indeed, so popular has it become that it now operates as a "master narrative" within the CIE canon in a similar way that dependency theory did in previous decades. At a general level, as Green (1997: 130) has observed, globalisation theory has three major elements to it. The economic element emphasises the increasing significance of global market forces and transnational corporations over national economies, the globalisation of labour markets and a new international division of labour. The political element considers the demise of the nation state as an aspect of the new power of international capital and of the development of supra-national trading blocks and organisations. The cultural element looks at "the emergence of the borderless world where national cultures are transformed by global communications and cultural hybridisation".

Different authors have, however, emphasised different aspects of globalisation depending upon their particular "take" on the theory and on the theme(s) that they have wished to illuminate. Accepting Green's account of globalisation, it would seem that globalisation theory provides a promising framework for the exploration of postcolonial issues. What is striking about this literature, however, is that very little attention is in fact given to the colonial legacy. This neglect has the following implications.

Firstly, a large body of the literature on globalisation and education and in particular that literature informed by a postmodern reading of the world takes as its point of reference Western industrialised countries and (occasionally) their Significant Others, namely the newly industrialised countries of the Pacific Rim. Where the education systems of developing countries are mentioned this is often as an aberration to the European "norm" either in respect to their origins or to the extent to which they demonstrate "postmodern" characteristics. Thus in Green's (1997) and Cowan's (1996) work, for example, the education systems of formerly colonised countries are presented as variants on "modern" education systems (which are defined as having their roots in the processes of state formation in Europe). Eurocentricism is also evident within this body of literature in relation to the choice of themes discussed such as the implications of the information superhighway for learning or the crisis of the modernist (read European) curriculum and pedagogy.

Secondly, where globalisation theory has been applied to the developing world economic concerns have often predominated (with some notable exceptions, see for example Phillipson 1998; Crossley 1996). The upshot is that many issues relating to race, culture, diaspora and identity are either ignored or marginalised. What is required then is a postcolonial re-reading of globalisation theory in education. This would start from the perspective that the colonial legacy is central to the ongoing processes of globalisation in education rather than marginal to it. That is to say that it is impossible to understand globalisation in education without recognising the role that colonial and postcolonial education systems have played in the spread of western cultural forms and languages and the implication of these systems in the processes of cultural mixing and hybridisation (They have, of course, also played a key role in relation to the developing global economy and political systems although these are aspects that have not been dealt with explicitly in this article).

In conclusion, a note of caution. Attention has been given to the *theoretical* contribution that an appreciation of the postcolonial condition can make to the CIE canon. Clearly, however, there are also implications to be drawn for the *processes* of comparative research although space has not permitted a full exploration of these issues. This is to acknowledge that there is a necessary dialectic between theory and research and that the development of a fuller understanding of the colonial legacy in education is intimately tied up with the politics of inclusion and exclusion within the knowledge production process itself.

618

Acknowledgement

I would like to acknowledge the help of a number of people who provided critical comments and advice on earlier drafts. In particular I would like to thank Richard Sergeant, Jenny Douglas, Clare Tikly and Glen Rikowski.

References

Adam, I. and Tiffin, H. eds. 1991. *Past the Last Post*. Hemel Hempstead: Harvester Wheatsheaf.

Altbach, P. and Kelly, G. 1978. *Education and Colonialism*. London: Transaction Books.

Altbach, P. 1984. The Distribution of Knowledge in the Third World: A Case Study in Neocolonialism. In: P. Altbach and G. Kelly, eds., *Education and the Colonial Experience* (Second revised edition) (229–251). London: Transaction Books.

Appiah, K. A. 1992. *In My Father's House: Africa in the Philosophy of Culture*. London: Methuen.

Apple, M. 1993. *Official Knowledge: Democratic Education in a Conservative Age*. London: Routledge.

Ashcroft, A., Griffiths, G. and Tiffin, H. 1989. *The Empire Writes Back: Theory and Practice in Post-colonial Literatures*. London: Routledge.

Ashcroft, B., Griffiths, G. and Tiffin, H. eds. 1995. *The Post-colonial Studies Reader*. London: Routledge.

Barrett, M. 1991. *The Politics of Truth: From Marx to Foucault*. Cambridge: Polity Press.

Bernal, M. 1987. *Black Athena: The Afroasiatic Roots of Classical Civilisation* Vol. I. London: Free Association Books.

Bray, M. 1993. Education and the Vestiges of Colonialism: Self-determination, Neocolonialism and Dependency in the South Pacific. *Comparative Education* 29(3): 333–348.

Bray, M. 1994. Decolonisation and Education: New Paradigms for the Remnants of Empire. *Compare* 24(1): 37–51.

Brock, C. and Tulasiewicz, W. eds. 1985. *Cultural Identity and Educational Policy*. London: Croom Helm.

Carnoy, M. 1974. *Education as Cultural Imperialism*. New York: David McKay.

Carnoy, M. and Samoff, J. 1990. *Education and Social Transition in the Third World*. New Jersey: Princeton University Press.

Carrim, N. 1995. From Race to Ethnicity: Shifts in the Educational Discourses of South Africa and Britain in the 1990s. *Compare* 25(1): 17–33.

Chitty, C. and Mac an Ghaill, M. 1995. *Reconstruction of a Discourse*. University of Birmingham: Educational Review Publications.

Cowan, R. 1996. Last past the Post: Comparative Education, Modernity and perhaps Post-Modernity. *Comparative Education* 32(2): 151–170.

Crossley, M. 1996. Issues and Trends in Qualitative Research: Potential for Developing Countries. *International Journal of Education Development* 16(4): 439–448.

Dirlik, A. 1994. The Postcolonial Aura. *Citical Inquiry* 20, Winter 1994: 328–356.

Donald, J. and Rattansi, A. eds. 1992. *"Race," Culture and Difference*. London: Sage.

Fagerlind, I. and Saha, L. 1989. *Education and National Development: A Comparative Perspective*. Oxford: Pergamon.

Gilroy, P. 1993. *The Black Atlantic: Modernity and Double Consciousness*. London: Verso.

Giroux, H. 1997. *Pedagogy and the Politics of Hope: Theory, Culture and Schooling, a Critical Reader*. Oxford: Westview Press.

Green, A. 1997. *Education, Globalization and the Nation State*. London: Macmillan Press.

Grossberg, L. 1996. On Postmodernism and Articulation: An Interview With Stuart Hall. In: D. Morley and K. Chen, eds., *Stuart Hall: Critical Dialogues in Cultural Studies* (131–150). London: Routledge.

Gundara, J. 1990. Societal Diversities and the Issue of "The Other". *Oxford Review of Education* 16(1): 97–109.

Hall, S. 1983. The Great Moving Right Show. In: S. Hall and M. Jacques, eds., *The Politics of Thatcherism* (19–39). London: Lawrence and Wishart.

Hall, S. 1992. New Ethnicities. In: J. Donald and A. Rattansi, eds., *"Race," Culture and Difference* (252–259). London: Sage.

Hall, S. 1996a. "When was the Post-Colonial"? Thinking at the Limit. In: I. Chamber, and L. Curti, eds., *The Post-colonial Question: Common Skies, Divided Horizons* (242–260). London: Routledge.

Hall, S. 1996b. Gramsci's Relevance for the Study of Race and Ethnicity. In: D. Morley and K. Chen, eds., *Stuart Hall: Critical Dialogues in Cultural Studies* (411–440). London: Routledge.

Hettne, B. 1990. *Development Theory and the Three Worlds*. Harlow: Longman.

Hulme, P. 1995. Including America. *Ariel* 26(1).

Kallaway, P. ed. 1984. *Apartheid and Education: The Education of Black South Africans*. Johannesburg: Ravan Press.

Knight, J., Smith, R. and Sachs, J. 1990. Deconstructing Hegemony: Multicultural Policy and a Populist Response. In: S. Ball, ed., *Foucault and Education: Disciplines and Knowledge* (133–152). London: Routledge.

Loomba, A. 1998. *Colonialism/Postcolonialism*. London: Routledge.

Mangan. J. 1988. *Benefits Bestowed? Education and British Imperialism*. Manchester: Manchester University Press.

Mangan, J. 1993. Images of Confident Control: Stereotypes in Imperial Discourse. In: J. Mangan, ed., *The Imperial Curriculum: Racial Images and Education in the British Colonial Experinece* (6–22). London: Routledge.

Mangan, J. ed. 1993. *The Imperial Curriculum: Racial Images and Education in the British Colonial Experinece*. London: Routledge.

620

Martinussen, J. 1997. *Society State and Market: a Guide to Competing Theories of Development*. London: Zed Books.

McCarthy, C. 1993. After the Canon. In: C. McCarthy and W. Crichlow, eds. *Race, Identity and Representation in Education* (289–305). London: Routledge.

McCarthy, C. and Crichlow, W. eds. 1993. *Race, Identity and Representation in Education*. London: Routledge.

McLintock, A. 1992. The Angel of Progress: The Pitfalls of the Term "Post-Colonialism. *Social Text*, Spring 1992: 1–15.

Ngugi wa Thiong'o. 1995. On the Abolition of the English Department. In: B. Ashcroft, G. Griffiths and H. Tiffin, eds., *The Post-colonial Studies Reader* (438–442). London: Routledge.

Parry, B. 1995. Problems in Current Theories of Colonial Discourse. In: B. Ashcroft, G. Griffiths and H. Tiffin, eds., *The Post-colonial Studies Reader* (36–44). London: Routledge.

Pennycook, A. 1995. English in the World/The World in English. In; J. Tollefson, ed., *Power and Inequality in Language Education* (34–58). Cambridge: Cambridge University Press.

Phillipson, R. 1998. Globalizing English: Are Linguistic Human Rights an Alternative to Linguistic Imperialism?. *Language Sciences* 20(1): 101–112.

Rassool, N. 1998. Postmodernity, Cultural Pluralism and the Nation-State: Problems of Language Rights, Human Rights, Identity and Power. *Language Sciences* 20(1): 89–99.

Rattansi, A. 1992. Changing the Subject? Racism, Culture and Education. In: J. Donald and A. Rattansi, eds., *"Race," Culture and Difference* (11–48) London: Sage.

Said, E. 1978. *Orientalism*. London: Routledge and Kegan Paul.

Samoff, J. 1992. The Intellectual/Financial Complex of Foreign Aid. *Review of African Political Economy* 53: 60–87.

Slack, D. 1996. The Theory and Method of Articulation in Cultural Studies. In: D. Morley and K. Chen, eds., *Stuart Hall: Critical Dialogues in Cultural Studies* (112–130) London: Routledge.

Shohat, E. 1992. Notes on the Postcolonial. *Social Text* 31/32: 103–132.

Spivak, G. C. 1988. Can the Subaltern Speak. In: C. Nelson and L. Grossberg, eds., *Marxism and the Interpretation of Culture* (271–313) Basingstoke: McMillan Education.

Stone, M. 1984. The Education of the Black Child in Britain. In: R. James and R. Jeffcoate, eds., *The School in the Multicultural Society* (45–57). London: Harper and Row.

Taylor, N. ed. 1993. *Inventing Knowledge: Contests in Curriculum Construction*. Cape Town: Maskew Miller Longman.

Tikly, L. 1995a. Levelling the Playing Fields Whilst moving the Goal Posts: Changing Discourses on Race in South African Education Policy. In: C. Criticos, R. Deacon and C. Hemson, eds., *Education Reshaping the Boundaries: Proceedings of the Twentieth Kenton Conference Held in Scotburgh Natal in October 1993* (11–28). Durban: School of Education, University of Natal.

Tikly, L. 1995b. The Racial Interpretations of the Democratic Movement. In: G. Kruss and H. Jacklin, eds., *Realising Change: Education Policy Research, Kenton, 1994* (67–80). Cape Town: Juta.

Tikly, L. 1997. Changing South African Schools?: An Analysis and Critique of Post-Election Government Policy. *Journal of Education Policy* 12(3), Spring 1997: 177–188.

Tollefson, J. ed. 1995. *Power and Inequality in Language Education*. Cambridge: University of Cambridge Press.

Watson, K. ed. 1982. *Education in the Third World*. London: Croom Helm.

Watson, K. ed. 1984. *Dependence and Interdependence in Education*. London: Croom Helm.

Wetherell, M. and Potter, J. 1992. *Mapping the Language of Racism*. Hemel Hempstead: Harvester Weatsheaf.

Williams, P. and Chrisman, L. eds. 1994. *Colonial Discourse and Postcolonial Theory*. Hemel Hempstead: Harvester Wheatsheaf.

Young, R. 1992. Colonialism and Humanism. In: J. Donald and A. Rattansi, eds., *"Race," Culture and Difference* (243–251). London: Sage.

The author

Leon Tikly attended state schools in North London before working as a science teacher in a London comprehensive and subsequently at a school for South African refugees in Tanzania. Prior to his present position as a lecturer in education policy and management at the University of Bristol, Leon worked as a research officer at the Education Policy Unit, University of the Witwatersrand, and as a lecturer in international education at Birmingham University.

Contact address: Dr Leon Tikly, Graduate School of Education, University of Bristol, 35 Berkeley Square, Bristol BS8 1JA, UK. E-mail: Leon.Tikly@bristol.ac.uk.